"Trust is the primary currency that enables the charitable sector to exist. Ken Phillips reminds us of the need for charities to demonstrate trustworthiness. This is perhaps more critical now than ever before. We are experiencing historically low numbers of people donating to charities. If this is to change, charity leaders would do well to consider the themes in this book."
— **H. Art Taylor,** President & Chief Executive Officer, BBB Wise Giving Alliance

"Based on decades of practical, hands-on success with international charities, Ken Phillips sets forth in this book detailed prescriptions for nonprofit organizations to build greater trust from donors, increased impact for beneficiaries, expanded achievement of mission, and achieve more fundraising success."
— **Renowned fundraising consultant Roger M. Craver,** Editor, *The Agitator*, U.S.A.

"Trust in people, purpose, and performance is fundamental to establish and maintain relationships between donors and NGOs, and is therefore a primary currency for all nonprofits. Ken's book, enlivened with personal stories and case studies, will help you build trust and enhance your impact."
— **James Magowan,** Coordinating Director, European Community Foundation Initiative, E.U.

"Today trust and impact are the corner stones of fundraising and without them the whole fundraising house will tumble. Indeed, I cannot recommend this book too highly as it deals explicitly and brilliantly with both these key issues."
— **John Baguley,** Owner, International Fundraising Consultancy (IFC), U.K.

"The importance of trust, impact, learning, and accountability of NGOs cannot be overstated. In this edition of his civil society series, Ken Phillips shares knowledge, reflection, and tools from his half-century of professional experience, underlining the role of values, ethics, learning, and the vital role of evaluation for continuous improvement and impact to enhance organizations' achievements and increase donor support. He shares case studies and practical experience from his decades-long career, reminding how account-ability through leadership, transparency, and communication are core in these efforts. A readable resource for practitioners at all levels of organizations."
— **Abby Maxman,** President and CEO, Oxfam America

"I'm impressed with the topics Ken Phillips is addressing. Certainly, there is need to improve the performance and impact of NGOs, both the smaller ones and the big ones."
— **Jim Rugh,** Founder of RealWorld Evaluation, former Head of Design, Monitoring, and Evaluation for Accountability and Learning for CARE International, U.S.A.

"Ken, you are an unwavering advocate of ethics in every organization – including government. I am grateful for your leadership in the Rhode Island Constitutional Convention Ethics Committee. As revealed here, your vision shaped what became the most powerful Ethics Commission in the country."
— **Phil West,** former Executive Director, Common Cause Rhode Island

"It is essential that NGOs have the capabilities and operational policies to document and communicate that they work in an ethical manner and deliver the results they promise. Ken Phillips take the mystery out of these complex expectations for NGOs and provides a step-by-step guide to increase organizational success with increased funding and a more effective organization."

– **Rebecca Morley,** Principal, Rebecca Morley Consulting, former director, Health Impact Project, Pew Charitable Trusts, and former executive director, National Center for Healthy Housing

Trust, Impact, and Fundraising for Nonprofits

Distilling decades of leadership expertise into an effective framework, this is a practical guidebook for nonprofits around the globe, with practical recommendations for the urgently needed steps to make this a better world. Charities in the United States and NGOs globally need to overcome two glaring and persistent weaknesses in the eyes of potential donors: trustworthiness and effectiveness. After examining possible causes for these deficits, fundraising and organizational development guru Ken Phillips guides readers through the process that leads to greater trust and respect by donors, better results for beneficiaries, significantly increased funding, and better and bigger programs. Alongside helpful worksheets, he presents seven steps to make sure ethics are meaningful, eight disciplines to ensure programs achieve good results, and a communications approach to demonstrate responsibility and accountability, all interwoven with inspiring case studies from his own international experience and other organizations' stories.

Staff and volunteers at registered nonprofits around the world, as well as any individual or group raising funds more informally, will value this guide to empower organizations to win trust, raise more funds, and achieve greater program impact.

Author, strategist, and mentor **Kenneth H. Phillips** – called a Master of Fundraising and Organizational Development – is internationally renowned for his expertise in strategy, teamwork, and leadership for nonprofit organizations and community associations.

Trust, Impact, and Fundraising for Nonprofits

How Meaningful Ethics and Strategic Evaluation Can Multiply Your Revenue and Expand Your Program

Kenneth H. Phillips

Routledge
Taylor & Francis Group

NEW YORK AND LONDON

Designed cover image: © Nick Zelinger

First published 2023
by Routledge
605 Third Avenue, New York, NY 10158

and by Routledge
4 Park Square, Milton Park, Abingdon, Oxon, OX14 4RN

Routledge is an imprint of the Taylor & Francis Group, an informa business

Library of Congress Cataloging-in-Publication Data
Names: Phillips, Kenneth H., author.
Title: Trust, impact, and fundraising for nonprofits : how meaningful ethics and strategic evaluation can multiply your revenue and expand your program / Kenneth H. Phillips.
Description: New York, NY : Routledge, 2023. |
Includes bibliographical references and index.
Identifiers: LCCN 2022041999 (print) | LCCN 2022042000 (ebook) |
ISBN 9781032370798 (hbk) | ISBN 9781032370781 (pbk) | ISBN 9781003335207 (ebk)
Subjects: LCSH: Nonprofit organizations. | Nonprofit organizations--Moral and ethical aspects. | Nonprofit organizations--Finance.
Classification: LCC HD62.6 .P52 2023 (print) | LCC HD62.6 (ebook) |
DDC 658.1/148--dc23/eng/20221104
LC record available at https://lccn.loc.gov/2022041999
LC ebook record available at https://lccn.loc.gov/2022042000

ISBN: 978-1-032-37079-8 (hbk)
ISBN: 978-1-032-37078-1 (pbk)
ISBN: 978-1-003-33520-7 (ebk)

DOI: 10.4324/9781003335207

Typeset in Baskerville
by MPS Limited, Dehradun

Dedicated to those who initiate learning for ethics and evaluation

This book is dedicated to all the individuals and groups who make a difference in ethics and evaluation – the members of InterAction, the voters of Rhode Island, and the leaders of so many non-governmental organizations (NGOs) for making so much progress in meaningful ethics, strategic impact evaluation, and stakeholder accountability and to all those non-governmental advocacy organizations and community groups around the world who are working to make government, business, and nonprofits more responsible and more accountable.

The best performing NGOs base all their work on eight key components of their vision, mission, values, culture, goals, strategies, impact, and trust.

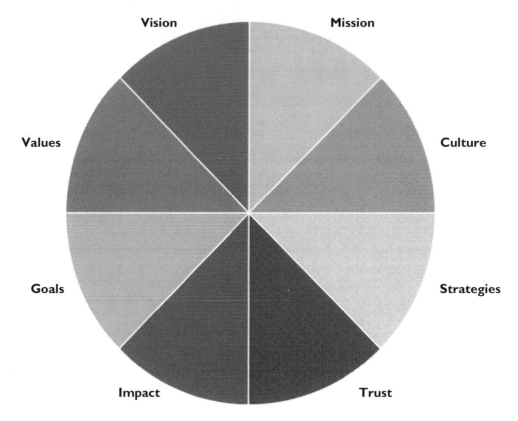

Figure 0a.1 The eight elements of strategic planning. Image by the author.

Contents

Contributors

Aravinda Karunaratne is a management consultant and researcher. He earned a Doctorate in Public Administration from the University of Georgia, a Master of Science in Applied Economics from Singapore Management University, and a Bachelor of Civil Engineering from Nanyang Technological University. He is a passionate AIESEC alumnus. USA

Haru Nishigaki, research assistant and project manager at Global Development Lab UCLA, is a dual citizen who speaks three languages (Chinese, English, and Japanese) and has multi-faceted perspectives with a focus on development economics and international development. USA

Sawyer Phillips is an artist and musician who is currently living nomadically. He is interested in spending time outdoors, dancing, and improvisational music. On any given day you might find Sawyer cultivating mushrooms, banging nails, or drawing pictures of pre-human hominids. He hopes that one day we live in a world without borders. USA

Wills Phillips is an artist interested in the relationship between art and environment. Wills became involved in activism in high school and later lived at Twin Oaks Community where they dug their hands into the dirt and gained life perspective. Wills looks forward to a future filled with art, social engagement, and community striving for equity. USA

Patrice Rhoades-Baum, a business writer, editor, and communicator, writes on-target content for company websites and marketing collateral. As a professional editor, she teams with business leaders to ensure their book's content is clear and compelling. Patrice's career experience includes twenty-five years in high-tech corporate marketing. USA

Nick Zelinger, a multi-award-winning book designer with over 30 years' experience at NZ Graphics in publishing, is the cover designer for the author's Civil Society Series. USA

Foreword

"We have to devise means of making known the facts in such a way as to touch the imagination of the world."
—Eglantyne Jebb, Founder, Save the Children

Nonprofit organizations, whether they be small, local community enterprises or large-scale international NGOs, rely on a steady stream of philanthropic contributions to sustain and expand their work. When asked, most people express a general desire to leave the world a little better than they found it – supporting nonprofits that share their values and goals would seem a natural way of doing so. Yet, charitable giving in the United States has been stuck at a paltry 2% of disposable income for decades.

Why? Trust. Or rather, a lack thereof. "Does the money really get to the people who need it" is a much-heard refrain, even among loyal supporters of non-profit organizations. As Dan Pallota identified a decade ago, the nonprofit sector is caught in a "circular mess" of lowering overhead because of fear of public opinion, spending less on investments that would improve their work and shortchanging growth and scale. Ultimately this leads to underwhelming results, therefore confirming public opinion that we can't make a difference.

At the same time, philanthropy in the United States is projected to see the largest wealth transfer in history, driven by a Baby Boomer generation thinking actively about how to pass on their wealth and younger donors demanding a much more active and engaged role in their giving. And donors have access to information (and disinformation) 24/7 at their fingertips.

I think these two facts present us with a huge opportunity.

Those of us in nonprofit leadership roles understand just how difficult it is to build a foundation of trust in a public primed to question where their contributions are going, how they are used, and what actually reaches the programs we claim to support. Glossy marketing materials and celebrity spokespeople can only carry us so far. The real work is less glamorous.

Most nonprofits are structurally underfunded and have little flexibility to turn on a dime. Notwithstanding sophisticated project planning and management skills, our plans are frequently upset by real life and failure to achieve our goals and objectives. We may have to keep communication lines open to and have relationships with individuals and groups that are knowingly suppressing human rights or worse. Some of our colleagues pay the highest price, often by just being in the wrong place at the wrong time.

I'm listing these challenges, not because I think we are victims of circumstance. On the contrary, there is no bigger privilege than to work in this sector, trying, in some small way, to figure out how humanity can win the day. But leaders in the nonprofit sector have to step up their efforts to earn trust and to measure and report on their impact.

At Save the Children US, where author Ken Phillips served as chief development officer back in the 1970s and where I'm privileged to serve as president and CEO today, creating this culture demands rigorous attention to monitoring and evaluation expectations, regulatory compliance, and accountability to an independent board and audit process. To further underscore our commitment to cultivating this environment, in 2021 we rolled out a new Code of Ethics and Business Conduct which all staff, consultants, and board members must affirm in writing. We hold regular discussion sessions looking at where we didn't deliver on our promises or had near-misses, with the aim to further create a learning organization, rather than one solely focused on compliance.

Save the Children US. is part of a global network that dates back more than 100 years, and it has evolved constantly since its founding. During Ken's tenure, he was part of an early movement that professionalized our fundraising and marketing activities and raised awareness of the importance of thorough reporting to supporters on how funds are used. We now have to take that transparency further still and be bolder about where our interventions have had real impact and where they have been less successful. But for most nonprofits, this more radical transparency carries almost existential risk. It's much easier to stick with measures such as total reach numbers or overhead ratios, which are ultimately fairly meaningless, but don't get you in trouble. I think we can and should do better, in the following ways:

1   Focus our areas of impact and resist impact creep. No more than four to five big impact goals.
2   Robust evaluations for all interventions, ideally done by independent parties and published widely.
3   Radical transparency: About our impact and about our operational delivery (including fraud or safeguarding incidents, overhead costs and the like).
4   Establish, uphold, and make public a trust statement in your communications and on your website, such as a Code of Ethics.
5   Seek out sophisticated philanthropic sources to fund more experimental interventions, where more risk is understood and accepted, and where a 'failing fast" culture is embraced.

The world is falling behind in its ambition to deliver dignity and prosperity for all. The progress on Sustainable Development Goals in a world reeling from a pandemic, climate change, and conflict has all but ground to a halt. Now is the time for leaders and trustees in the nonprofit sector to meet the moment, but we will have to accept that this moment asks of us different leadership. It asks of us to count what really counts, to open ourselves up to robust questioning and criticism of all stakeholders, not least the communities we are aiming to support, and help our supporters understand and trust not just in our missions, but in *how* we are delivering and inspiring change, how we are learning from our successes *and our failures*, and how we can and should take risks to bring our successful interventions to scale.

Trust, Impact, and Fundraising for Nonprofits: How ethics and evaluation can multiply your revenue and expand your program is a practical guide that can help any nonprofit enhance its impact by developing and implementing a meaningful monitoring and evaluation program (or strengthening an existing one). It also highlights just how important it is to communicate with donors about the measurable effect their support is providing. It provides thought-provoking case studies into how these principles are being put into action at organizations large and small – and how you can adapt their approaches to support your goals.

Janti Soeripto
President & CEO
Save the Children US

Preface

Why write a book on trust and impact for nonprofits? They are the biggest challenges for NGOs.

All my life has been guided by my father who always said, "Whatever you do, do it well" and by my mother who always said, "Whatever you do, do something good." My last name Phillips has the same roots as philanthropy or "goodwill to fellow members of the human race *especially*: active effort to promote human welfare."[1] It seems that my career and this book were destined.

When I completed my two years as president of AIESEC-United States, the international youth-led organization working for peace and international understanding, I had job offers from a large international bank and the Institute of International Education and naturally chose a career in international development. Since then, I have learned so much from my practical experience (Save the Children, Plan International, Red Cross, and NGOs in many countries). The goal was always helping them make a better world.

I have seen that nearly every organization – small and large – needs to do a better job of demonstrating their trustworthy behavior and their program impact. These two topics – trust and impact – are essential, because the public is skeptical about charities, especially their ethics and their results. When this happens, people call them "just fundraising organizations."

My first career was actually doing things as president, fundraiser, manager, executive director, board chair, and team leader. My second career was teaching as consultant, lecturer, trainer, advisor, and mentor. Some years ago, I began writing what I had learned in six decades from all my experience and work with NGOs, and this is now my third career to share through books to a broader audience.

Curious, I explored the origins of my first name Ken and discovered that "*ken* nowadays almost always implies a range of perception, understanding, or knowledge."[2] Colleagues say I was destined to publish the perceptions, understandings, and knowledge I learned in those 60 years. My three previous books are on leadership and fundraising, strategic planning and culture, and proven strategies for fundraising.[3]

As a leader, staff member, or volunteer for a nonprofit or community organization, you know it is important to raise more money to expand your program. Your very purpose, your vision and mission, demand you do that. I wrote this book to help you succeed in doing exactly that.

This is a "how to" book based on actual experience, the successes and failures I had, extensive field research, and thousands of interviews with NGO leaders and donors about what makes an NGO trusted and respected and what makes it fail.

Pressing problems are obvious to all of us at local, national, and global levels. The world needs NGOs to get better. I believe so many more people can step up wherever they live, work, and travel to help NGOs and informal groups make a better world. I hope reading this book will inspire and enable you to do so.

Kenneth H. Phillips

Acknowledgments

I am so pleased that I received valuable inputs and updates for many of the case studies in this book, especially from the following expert practitioners and nonprofit leaders:

Lorie Broomhall, Senior MERL Advisor, Plan International USA; Heather Dolphin, Deputy Director, MEAL, Catholic Relief Services; Linda Fogarty, Head of MERL Team, International Youth Foundation; Kitty Holt, Director, Ethics & Compliance, Plan International USA; Amy Coates Madsen, Director, Standards for Excellence Institute, Maryland Nonprofits; John Marion, Executive Director, Common Cause Rhode Island;

Frank Mohrhauer, Director of National Society Policy and Knowledge Development, International Federation of Red Cross and Red Crescent Societies; Erin Morse, Senior Program Officer for Monitoring, Evaluation, and Learning, Children International; Lyubov Palyvoda, Founder and President, Counterpart Creative Center; Lauren Pisani, Advisor, Research, Evidence and Learning, Save the Children US;

Kate Schecter, CEO of World Neighbors; Zsuzsa Szikszay, Community Impact Leader at the United Way of Hungary; H. Philip West, Jr., author of *Secrets & Scandals, Reforming Rhode Island 1986-2006*; Bennett Weiner, Executive Vice President & COO, Better Business Bureau Wise Giving Alliance; research associates Haru Nishigaki and Aravinda Karunaratne; artists Sawyer Phillips and Wills Phillips; and

Sasakawa Peace Foundation for its initiation and funding of my research on International NGO Evaluation Methodologies for Capacity Building which provided a basis for parts of this book.[4]

I am so grateful for the encouragement and tolerance of my wife Rebecca and other members of my family in my work and my writing.

Notes

1 "philanthropy," *Merriam-Webster Dictionary*, accessed July 1, 2022, https://www.merriam-webster.com/dictionary/philanthropy.
2 "ken," *Merriam-Webster Dictionary*, accessed July 1, 2022, https://www.merriam-webster.com/dictionary/ken.
3 Ken Phillips, *Make a Better World: A practical guide to leadership for fundraising success* (NGO Futures LLC, 2020), *Strategic Planning and Culture for Nonprofits: Clear and doable steps to create motivating plans and the supporting culture you need for success*, (NGO Futures LLC, 2021), and *25 Proven Strategies for Fundraising Success: How to win the love and support of donors* (NGO Futures LLC, 2021).
4 I acknowledge Sasakawa Peace Foundation as the initiator and funder of my research on *Considering International NGO's Evaluation*, published in Japanese by the Sasakawa Peace Foundation, Tokyo, 2001. https://www.spf.org/en/

About the Author

Author, strategist, and mentor **Ken Phillips** – called a Master of Fundraising and Organizational Development – is internationally renowned for his expertise in strategy, teamwork, and leadership for nonprofit organizations and community associations.

Backed by six decades of experience with nonprofits like Save the Children, Plan International, the Red Cross Movement, Catholic Relief Services, Help Age International, CARE International, and International Youth Foundation and based on extensive field research in numerous countries with thousands of structured interviews on NGO performance, Ken Phillips is the author of *Make a Better World* (through leadership and fundraising), *Strategic Planning and Culture for Nonprofits*, and *25 Proven Strategies for Fundraising Success*.

This fourth book on *Trust, Impact, and Fundraising for Nonprofits* provides roadmaps for nonprofits to become more trusted, more respected, and more accountable and thereby raise more funds and expand effective programs to help more people and the planet.

Charitable giving in the United States has been stuck for decades at only 2% of disposable income! Why? Research reveals that people do not trust charities enough. Their concerns boil down to three questions: "Can I trust you? What is your impact? Another fundraising letter?"

In lively text and with clear examples, the author guides readers through a process to develop *meaningful ethics* to earn trust and *strategic evaluation* to achieve impact. You will learn seven steps to ensure ethics are meaningful, eight disciplines to ensure programs achieve real impact, and a proven approach to *communicate more effectively*. As a consequence, your organization will raise more funding and expand your programs to make a better world.

Figure 00a.2 NGO Futures logo, Design by Nick Zelinger.

Figure 00a.3 Make a Better World in a circle of people working. Design by Nick Zelinger.

Look for these paperback books and e-books in Ken Phillips' *Civil Society Series*

Figure 00a.4a Image of the cover of the first book in the author's Civil Society Series. Design by Nick Zelinger.

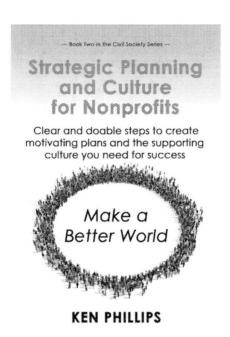

Figure 00a.4b Image of the cover of the second book in the author's Civil Society Series. Design by Nick Zelinger.

Figure 00a.4c Image of the cover of the third book in the author's Civil Society Series. Design by Nick Zelinger.

Figure 00a.5a Image of the cover of the Spanish translation of the first book in the Civil Society Series. Translation by Rosa de Morales and Ali Espinoza Vargas. Design by Nick Zelinger.

Figure 00a.5b Image of the cover of the Spanish translation of the second book in the Civil Society Series. Translation by Florencia Santillán. Design by Nick Zelinger.

Figure 00a.5c Image of the cover of the Spanish translation of the third book in the Civil Society Series. Translation by Carlos Enrique Diaz Medina. Design by Nick Zelinger.

Figure 00a.5d Image of the cover of the French translation of the first book in the Civil Society Series. Translation by Léa Duperray. Design by Nick Zelinger.

Figure 00a.5e Image of the cover of the Romanian translation of the first book in the Civil Society Series. Translation by Sara Neagu. Design by Nick Zelinger.

Figure 00a.5f Image of the cover of the Ukrainian translation of the first book in the Civil Society Series. Translation by O. Nikolska. Design by Nick Zelinger.

Figure 00a.6 The author with his three books. Photograph by Rebecca Phillips.

The Civil Society Series (3 book series) Kindle Edition (amazon.com) – paperbacks and e-books in English

la Serie Sociedad Civil (3 book series) Kindle Edition (amazon.com) – e-books in Spanish translation

Construire Un Monde Meilleur: Un guide pratique du leadership et d'une collecte de fonds réussie – e-book in French translation

Bibliography

1 "ken." *Merriam-Webster Dictionary*. Accessed July 1, 2022. https://www.merriam-webster.com/dictionary/ken.

2 "philanthropy" . *Merriam-Webster Dictionary*. Accessed July 1, 2022. https://www.merriam-webster.com/dictionary/philanthropy.

3 Phillips, Ken. *Make a Better World: A Practical Guide to Leadership for Fundraising Success*. NGO Futures LLC, 2020.

4 Phillips, Ken. *Strategic Planning and Culture for Nonprofits: Clear and Doable Steps to Create Motivating Plans and the Supporting Culture You Need for Success*. NGO Futures LLC, 2021.

5 Phillips, Ken. *25 Proven Strategies for Fundraising Success: How to Win the Love and Support of Donors*. NGO Futures LLC, 2021.

6 Phillips, Ken. *Considering International NGO's Evaluation*, published in Japanese by the Sasakawa Peace Foundation, Tokyo, 2001. https://www.spf.org/en/.

Introduction

The importance of the charitable sector and its two biggest challenges

Civil society is an essential sector in society. Government cannot do everything. Business has its own focus. Healthcare workers and educators are essential, media has an important role, and essential workers keep us all going. But only civil society organizations collectively have as their overriding purpose the welfare and improvement for people in need and for the planet. For those of us who work in the civil society sector, our role is to provide support and services, inform and educate the public, advocate for improvements, and engage others as donors and volunteers – all to make this a better world.

Civil society has always existed, and civil society leaders were the first caregivers and the original social entrepreneurs. Family, of course, cares for family, but civil society extends caring and helping to broader segments of society. I have seen that these organizations are very often better than government and business in providing programs and services and innovating new approaches to help people and planet. When civil society organizations work as they should, they innovate better ways to make a better world, and they often motivate government to scale up their programs and business to be better as well.

The World Economic Forum states: "When mobilized, civil society – sometimes called the 'third sector' (after government and commerce) – has the power to influence the actions of elected policy-makers and businesses. ... It is hard to quantify just how big the sector is globally. However, one study says that NGOs across 40 countries represent $2.2 trillion in operating expenditures. That figure is larger than the gross domestic product of all but six countries ... [and the sector] employs around 54 million full-time equivalent workers and has a global volunteer workforce of over 350 million."[1]

The World Bank Group defines civil society as "the wide array of non-governmental and not for profit organizations that have a presence in public life, express the interests and values of their members and others, based on ethical, cultural, political, scientific, religious, or philanthropic considerations." It enumerates civil society as "a wide array of organizations: community groups, non-governmental organizations [NGOs], labor unions, indigenous groups, charitable organizations, faith-based organizations, professional associations, and foundations."[2]

Brookings Institution, a nonprofit public policy organization, calls civil society "an essential ingredient for development and national cohesion. In a country blessed with peace and stability, civil society fills the space untouched by government and the private sector. In a fragile and conflict-ridden country, it plays an even more important role of providing services normally the responsibility of the state and business and can lay the foundation for reconciliation."[3]

In its section on non-governmental organizations, *Britannica* affirms that "Although NGOs vary considerably in size, organization, and approach, they share the basic belief that principled individuals working together can do much to solve human and environmental problems through grassroots organizing, the creative use of information, and sophisticated political strategies.

DOI: 10.4324/9781003335207-1

NGOs have played central roles in global campaigns against slavery, the trade in ivory, whaling, violence against women, apartheid in South Africa, and the proliferation of nuclear weapons."[4]

Key point: My definition of civil society is what all of us do day to day, individually and collectively, to help others. This includes participation in non-governmental organizations, community associations, faith groups, informal groups, and social and professional organizations dedicated to caring and helping, as well as individuals who create a volunteer group or a funding effort to help others.

In this book, I refer to all the groups, formal and informal, working in civil society as non-governmental organizations (NGOs), charities, nonprofits, or organizations, because they all are organized and work to make a better world, not to make a profit. Whether they work on a large scale or by focusing on one small part of our world, together they are truly the indispensable ingredient in making society civil.

The business model for NGOs is more complicated that for most business and governments. NGOs have two completely different elements – their donors in the public and their beneficiaries in society. The NGO has to satisfy both parts (Figure 1).

My background is not academic and my writing is not based on the research of others. Instead, my writing is based on 60 years of working as a fundraiser, leader, and consultant with hundreds of NGOs, both small and large, while volunteering for a wide variety of global and community-based organizations. I received an excellent classical education, learned so much from the world's great literature, conducted many economic and development studies, and have been immersed in the nonprofit world my entire career starting in 1961.

Through 60 years of leading and managing NGOs in the U.S. and training and consulting with NGOs in numerous countries, I have had many thousands of interviews, discussions, and meetings with board members, staff and volunteers, donors and non-donors, and authorities and evaluation agencies about what it takes for an NGO to succeed and grow. Based on this research of a lifetime, my guiding slogan is "Working Together for a Better World through Strategy, Teamwork, and Leadership" and the key themes in my *Civil Society Series* are:

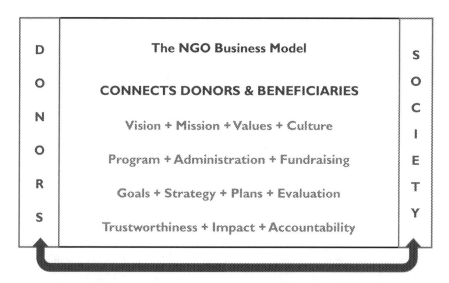

Figure 1 The NGO business model with the two key stakeholder groups of donors and beneficiaries. Image by the author.

1   How to step up to leadership and understand the fundamentals of fundraising
2   How to plan strategically with clear goals, strong values, and energizing culture
3   How to get the right strategies for success in fundraising and growth
4   How to earn the trust and respect of others through ethics and evaluation
5   How to get governance, management, and teams working together
6   How to motivate everyone to step up wherever they are to make a difference

Key point: In all my writing, my objective is to enable nonprofit organizations and caring individuals to get better in their thinking, planning, and managing to make a difference. They must be trusted for their behavior and respected for their results. As a result, they will have greater appeal to involve more donors and volunteers, and they will achieve so much more.

To succeed in that requires a good strategic plan. And that must include the following eight components – vision, mission, values, culture, goals, strategies, impact, and trust[5] (Figure 2).

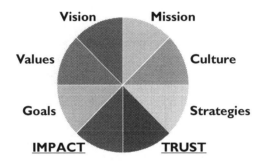

Figure 2 A strategic plan includes vision, mission, values, culture, goals, strategies, impact, and trust. Image by the author.

The two biggest challenges – Ethics and evaluation

Ethics and evaluation have always been a priority for me. My mom always told me as a youth, "Whatever you do, do something good." And my dad always told me, "Whatever you do, do it well." These two values inevitably led me to a career with nonprofits. My first career was working with five leading nonprofits to "do something good and do it well" and my second career was consulting and teaching others how to "do something good and do it well." Now my focus is writing and sharing more widely what I have learned in a lifetime of experience, research, and getting results in the civil society sector.

Civil society organizations are at risk in many countries as I write this book. NGOs are dismissed or even under attack for various reasons such as aiding those subject to discrimination or oppression, advocating for freedom or justice, opposing divisive decisions or regressive actions, or just bringing truth to people. They are also limited because many people – or perhaps most people – are not convinced of the trustworthiness and effectiveness of charities or don't see the problems beyond their own immediate surroundings.

The purpose of this book is to address the trustworthiness and impact of nonprofits. I have seen enough to know that trust comes from ethical behavior, and impact comes from strategic evaluation. The best NGOs already perform well in these areas – trust/ethics and impact/ evaluation – and, as a result, are increasing their revenues and expanding their programs. These best NGOs are getting bigger, because in the public's eyes they are better.

The challenge for smaller and mid-size organizations, and some older large ones that are not getting better and bigger, is to address ethics and evaluation as a priority. Why would anyone give their financial support or volunteer their time to an organization if they question its ethics and don't trust it – or if they don't see evaluations that show lasting impact?

As reported in the December 2020 issue of *NonProfit Times*, we know from the Internal Revenue Service (IRS) that in the U.S., "the vast majority of nonprofits raise $1 million or less each year."[6] Globally, the vast majority of all nonprofits are small. Imagine if they all could become completely trusted and highly respected how much more they could achieve!

I included value to society and value to donors as two "must have" strategies and image and trust as two essential strategies about who you are in my book 25 Proven Strategies for Fundraising Success[7] which have informed me in writing this book.

What is the question?

When Bennett Weiner, Executive Vice President & COO of the Better Business Bureau Wise Giving Alliance, invited me to speak at a meeting of the leading charity evaluation agencies from 25 countries, he asked me what *big idea* they should address during this meeting. My immediate response was, "Trust – or rather the lack of trust – in charities."

Donors want to know, first of all, whether they can trust and respect a nonprofit. You earn trust from *meaningful ethics* and accountability, and you earn respect from *strategic evaluation* and reporting that show real and lasting impact.

Key point: To get people to donate or volunteer, an organization must be trusted for its behavior and respected for its results.

To be credible, behavior and results are measured, assessed, and verified, and then they are communicated. It is not enough (and can lead to mistrust) to claim good behavior and good results without measurement, assessment, and verification. Demonstrating *good behavior*, getting *good results*, and being *accountable* to stakeholders are *the* three critical issues you must master in order to increase your fundraising success and expand your program impact. If you master all three, you will also become a model for other organizations, leading to overall increase in public trust.

To succeed, an essential role for everyone in an organization is to ensure that their activities and efforts, their values and culture, their policies and strategies, and their plans and assessments are all dedicated to earning trust and respect and to fulfilling their obligations to their six essential stakeholder groups:

1   Program participants and beneficiaries
2   Current and prospective donors
3   Staff and volunteers
4   Authorities
5   Partners
6   The public at large

It is important that every leader, staff member, and volunteer in the organization actively supports the six essential stakeholder groups. In particular, fundraisers have to step up. Gayle Gifford, a former colleague at Foster Parents Plan, and I delivered a presentation to the 2021 Conference of the Association of Fundraising Professionals (AFP ICON) on "How to lead your organization to get the internal support you need for fundraising success."[8] We opened with the challenges that fundraisers face today and what we hear from them. These challenges are significant and strategic. While much of the literature focuses on implementation of fundraising, my focus is at the strategic level of making an organization attractive to donors, that is, trusted for its ethical behavior and respected for its program impact. See What Fundraisers Tell Us and Fundraisers Today (Figure 3 and 4).

Fundraisers Tell Us

1. I don't get support from within the organization
2. We don't have a strong fundraising strategy
3. Our executive director has other priorities
4. The finance director says to work harder
5. The program director says it's not his job
6. Our culture doesn't value fundraising
7. Staff don't want to be donor driven
8. The board doesn't help enough
9. We don't prioritize being attractive to donors

© NGO Futures LLC 2021

Figure 3 Nine common complaints from fundraisers. Infographic by the author.

Fundraisers Today

Surveys and our experience of 90+ years tells us:
1. Charitable giving seems stuck at 2% of GNP
2. 51% of fundraisers want to leave their job
3. 50% of fundraisers lack strong strategic plans
4. 76% of AFP members cited sexual harassment
5. High turnover of fundraisers is a problem
6. Fundraisers at big NGOs work in a different world
7. Fundraisers for midsize NGOs face big problems

© NGO Futures LLC 2021

Figure 4 Seven important challenges in fundraising. Infographic by the author.

Key point: In order to succeed, fundraisers have a unique responsibility to work inside their organization to ensure it is attractive to donors. Why would a potential donor contribute to any organization that is not attractive in how it behaves, what it achieves, and what it reports?

Trust and impact are the answers

The Better Business Bureau Wise Giving Alliance's 2021 survey asked donors across six age groups about the most important aspects in their giving. The findings presented in the *Donor Trust Special Report on Charity Impact* indicate the top priorities: "Charity trust was most frequently selected as a very important aspect in the giving process for every generation" and "Charity impact was the second most popular choice"[9] among five of the six age groups.

Other less frequently chosen choices were spending ratios, instinct or gut feelings, stories about the charity's work, and the donor's relationship with the charity. The *Donor Trust Special Report on Charity Impact* noted, "Charity trust was most frequently selected as a very important aspect in the giving process among all giving levels $51 and above. Among donors who gave $1,000 and above, charity impact came behind charity trust and financial ratios, but is an important consideration."

I have been working on the two key issues addressed in this book – trust and impact – for years and know from thousands of interviews with NGO workers and their donors that trust and impact are the two most important criteria for fundraising success. PART I of this book addresses ethics, transparency, and accountability, which build donor and volunteer trust in an organization. PART II addresses monitoring, evaluation, learning, and capacity building, which build donor and volunteer respect for the organization's lasting impact. I was thrilled to see recent BBB Wise Giving Alliance research validating my longstanding convictions.

Key point: *Trust* comes from *meaningful ethics that show correct behavior.* **Respect** comes from *strategic evaluation that shows lasting impact.* **Accountability** comes from *full reporting* to key constituents what you have done in the two most critical areas of responsibility: trust and impact.

Trust and respect are fragile. Nonprofits have special obligations to beneficiaries for what they have been promised, to donors in return for the funding they have given, to authorities in return for the special status they have been granted, and to local communities in recognition of their exemption from property and sales taxes. There are clear actions every nonprofit can take to demonstrate their trustworthiness, effectiveness, and accountability:

1   Fulfill their obligations to beneficiaries, donors, authorities, and the public.
2   Draft and adhere to a code of ethics for their own good behavior.
3   Create internal policies, plans, and culture to assure trustworthiness.
4   Prioritize effective monitoring, evaluation, and learning to get better results.
5   Report clearly and responsibly to stakeholders about ethics and evaluation.
6   Promote ethics and evaluation to other NGOs and through their associations.

To improve confidence in an organization, I present in this book what a nonprofit must do for meaningful ethics, what it must do for strategic evaluation, and what it must do for effective communication. Without good behavior and good results, an organization is untrustworthy and lacks impact. Without good communication, key stakeholders (beneficiaries, donors, authorities, and the public) will not know whether they can trust or respect an organization. The two critical issues of ethical behavior and impactful results – combined with clear and consistent communication – are essential responsibilities of board members, executives, fundraisers, finance and program staff, and everyone else including volunteers. That's the way to attract and keep donors! And to achieve ever-greater impact!

This book on ethics and evaluation (and communication) builds on the themes in my previous books of leadership opportunities and fundraising fundamentals, strategic planning with strong values and energizing culture, and proven strategies for fundraising. My next book after this one continues to build on these topics by addressing the importance of governance, management, and teams working well together.

Important steps for trust and impact certainly include having an active, effective, and responsible board of directors. Trust comes from integrity and good behavior, strong values and an inspiring culture, and excellent communication and responsiveness to stakeholders. Lasting impact comes from an inspiring vision and motivating mission, excellent planning, effective strategies, learning, and great implementation. Underlying all of these is the importance of encouraging leadership initiatives at all levels of the organization, which will enable successful management, extraordinary programs, and unprecedented fundraising results.

This book flows from my own experience of leadership in developing ethical standards and evaluation methods, conducting thousands of interviews and consultations, conducting research for various clients around the world, and consulting for the Sasakawa Peace Foundation on how leading NGOs evaluate themselves. In addition, the book draws on my numerous presentations and training sessions on these topics to client organizations as well as university lectures and philanthropy discussions in many countries and conferences of national fundraising associations, board members and staff leaders of Red Cross National Societies, InterAction and CIVICUS members, the Better Business Bureau Wise Giving Alliance, and the International Committee on Fundraising Organizations.

Let's be perfectly clear …

Donors want to know whether they can trust and respect your organization. If they do not trust or respect your organization, they will not consider you worthy of support. It is quite simple: To get them to consider donating or volunteering, you must be seen as *trustworthy* and *impactful*. The world – both people and planet – urgently need you to do this. See the figure on Trust and Impact for Success (Figure 5).

Key point: Only when organizations are trusted for their good behavior and respected for their lasting impact will they receive the support they need to carry out the work they were created to do. They earn trust through ethical behavior and gain respect by achieving real results, then communicating these qualities to be accountable.

In a July 2022 report from Michael Stone, President of the IFRC Alumni Association (International Federation of Red Cross and Red Crescent Societies), Penny Lawrence, Chair of Refugee Action, challenges the big International NGOs to upgrade their commitment to achieve and demonstrate better behavior and improved trustworthiness.[10]

"Many large international non-government organizations (INGOs) are big well-known brands. However, there is little evidence of strategic thinking about the future. We are living in a time of extraordinary disruptive change, including digital transformation, changing societal norms and engagement expectations, in the context of political upheaval and challenge."

"There has been a decline in trust in large humanitarian organizations. Contributing to this has been: 1. A complacency, believing that the argument for aid has been won. 2. Fund raising backlash, with repeated mailshots to individuals. 3. Scandals involving sexual abuse. 4. Proximity to Government with loss of independence."

"Generally, INGOs are slow to respond, prone to the dangers of complacency, and do not realize how much they need to change to respond to rapidly moving circumstances. Their size and structures often restrict agility. They are usually too internally focused, dominated by contract funding, reporting requirements and compliance procedures."

"If change does not happen, INGOs will fail in their ambitious goal of reducing global poverty in our changing world. INGOs will need to re-invent themselves. *'There is no bigger risk than just staying where we are.'* The ability to respond to changing needs of the humanitarian world will be the key to their future success."

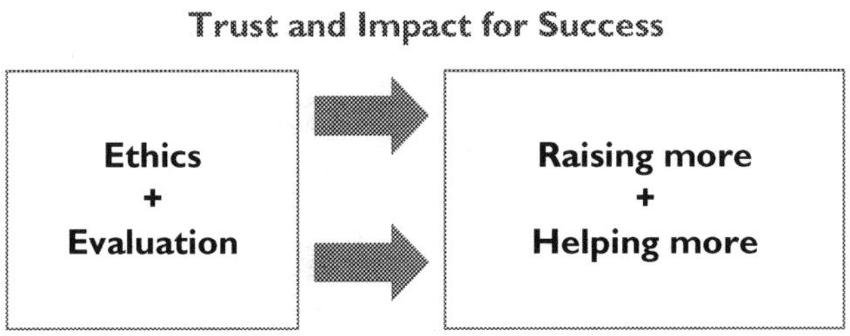

Trust and Impact for Success

Ethics + Evaluation	→	Raising more + Helping more

Figure 5 Ethics and evaluation lead to raising more funds and helping more. Image by the author.

➡️ If this is true for these big INGOs, then probably most other NGOs need to be responding to the same challenge to achieve and demonstrate better behavior and improved trustworthiness.

Notes

1 Adam Jezard, "Who and what is 'civil society'?," *World Economic Forum*, April 18, 2018, accessed June 25, 2022, https://www.weforum.org/agenda/2018/04/what-is-civil-society/
2 "Civil Society," *The World Bank*, February 28, 2022, accessed June 25, 2022, https://www.worldbank.org/en/about/partners/civil-society/overview
3 George Ingram, "Civil Society: An Essential Ingredient of Development," *Brookings'Up Front'*, April 6, 2022, accessed June 25, 2022, https://www.brookings.edu/blog/up-front/2020/04/06/civil-society-an-essential-ingredient-of-development/
4 Margaret P. Karns, "Nongovernmental Organization," *Britannica*, accessed June 25, 2022, https://www.britannica.com/topic/nongovernmental-organization
5 You can see the detailed study in my book *Strategic Planning and Culture for Nonprofits: Clear and doable steps to create motivating plans and the supporting culture you need for success:* Ken Phillips, *Strategic Planning and Culture for Nonprofits: Clear and doable steps to create motivating plans and the supporting culture you need for success* (NGO Futures LLC, 2021).
6 The NonProfit Times, "New Data Shows Small NPO Fundraising Hammered," *The NonProfit Times*, December 8, 2020, accessed June 25, 2022, https://www.thenonprofittimes.com/report/new-data-shows-small-npo-fundraising-hammered/
7 Ken Phillips, *25 Proven Strategies for Fundraising Success: How to win the love and support of donors* (NGO Futures LLC, 2021), 101–112, 121–132.
8 Conference of the Association of Fundraising Professionals (AFP ICON) (2021).
9 Better Business Bureau, "BBB Wise Giving Alliance releases Donor Trust Report," *Better Business Bureau*, November 15, 2021, accessed June 25, 2022, https://www.bbb.org/article/news-releases/26158-bbb-wise-giving-alliance-releases-donor-trust-report
10 "Alumni Association," *IFRC*, accessed July 1, 2022, https://www.ifrc.org/alumni-association

Bibliography

1 Better Business Bureau. "BBB Wise Giving Alliance releases Donor Trust Report." *Better Business Bureau*, November 15, 2021. Accessed June 25, 2022. https://www.bbb.org/article/news-releases/26158-bbb-wise-giving-alliance-releases-donor-trust-report
2 Conference of the Association of Fundraising Professionals (AFP ICON). 2021.
3 "Alumni Association." *IFRC*. Accessed July 1, 2022. https://www.ifrc.org/alumni-association
4 Ingram, George. "Civil Society: An Essential Ingredient of Development." *Brookings'Up Front'*, April 6, 2022. Accessed June 25, 2022. https://www.brookings.edu/blog/up-front/2020/04/06/civil-society-an-essential-ingredient-of-development/
5 Jezard, Adam. "Who and what is 'civil society'?" *World Economic Forum*, April 18, 2018. Accessed June 25, 2022. https://www.weforum.org/agenda/2018/04/what-is-civil-society/
6 Karns, Margaret P. "Nongovernmental Organization." *Britannica*. Accessed June 25, 2022. https://www.britannica.com/topic/nongovernmental-organization
7 Phillips, Ken. *25 Proven Strategies for Fundraising Success: How to win the love and support of donors.* NGO Futures LLC, 2021.
8 Phillips, Ken. *Strategic Planning and Culture for Nonprofits: Clear and doable steps to create motivating plans and the supporting culture you need for success.* NGO Futures LLC, 2021.
9 The NonProfit Times. "New Data Shows Small NPO Fundraising Hammered." *The NonProfit Times*, December 8, 2020. Accessed June 25, 2022. https://www.thenonprofittimes.com/report/new-data-shows-small-npo-fundraising-hammered/
10 "Civil Society." *The World Bank*, February 28, 2022. Accessed June 25, 2022. https://www.worldbank.org/en/about/partners/civil-society/overview

Part I

Meaningful ethics for trust

The following statements were made by actual nonprofit leaders. Which statement best describes your organization's attitude toward ethics, accountability, trust, and respect?

- "Our donors know us already, so we don't have to worry about ethics and results. Our executive director takes care of all this."
- "We have learned so much from our accountability reviews and our program evaluations. We know we must have a strong code of ethics and careful monitoring and evaluation, so we can demonstrate our learning and effectiveness. Everyone is involved to make sure donors can trust and respect what we do."

Nonprofit ethics and building trust

After working with nonprofits for 60 years, I am ever more firmly convinced of their value and benefit to society. The needs in the world are so pressing and in so many ways unmet that we need responsible, effective, and efficient civil society organizations. The programs and services of most NGOs are good, many are excellent, and the professional improvements in NGOs in recent decades have been remarkable. Governments are unable or unwilling to meet all the needs in society, and corporations have their own priorities. So why can't NGOs fill the gaps?

Nonprofits, community associations, and informal groups do not have anywhere near enough resources to meet the demands for their programs and services. I have wrestled for years to understand why the shortfall in funding is so large. Reasons that I have heard from donors are:

- "We don't have enough money to give to all the appeals we get."
- "There are so many NGOs; I don't know which ones to trust."
- "We are already doing enough. It's overwhelming."
- "I read that NGOs don't get results, and they waste money."
- "All I ever get are requests for more money."
- "It's not my responsibility to help everyone."
- "We don't have enough tax incentives to give more."
- "People are more selfish now."
- And the latest one: "I heard that billionaires say they can't give away their money fast enough. Their grants will make a lot more difference than donations from me."

NGOs must focus on what they can control, that is, first of all on their own activities – their behavior, their results, their learning, and their accountability. Then, second, they must

DOI: 10.4324/9781003335207-2

encourage other NGOs and NGO associations to make similar improvements. The rising level of income and wealth in most countries over recent decades indicates that there could be significantly increased support if organizations seriously address the issues of behavior, results, and accountability. The best organizations, as stated above, are already doing this well, and they are accordingly growing bigger and achieving more.

Key point: The image of other NGOs affects the success of any individual NGO, so it is worthwhile to dedicate serious attention to improve the reality and image of the entire sector. I have worked for this again and again in individual organizations, NGO associations, and global federations. You can do it as well.

To be awesome!

I recently read new research on *awe* and the effect of *experiencing awe* on attitudes toward the world, appreciation of people, and even on generosity. The researchers had one group of participants look at a beautiful scene from nature and a control group look at an ugly building. Then they gave everyone an amount of money for their own use but suggested they might want to share some of it with the poor folks on the street nearby. The finding was that those people who had experienced the awe of nature were substantially more generous. My takeaway is that experiencing something *awesome* inspires people to greater appreciation and greater generosity.

My own story about awareness of awe happened when I was on an assignment in Kyiv, Ukraine, just before the COVID-19 pandemic invaded the world. I saw – actually experienced – three extraordinary ballets, some of the very best ballet I've seen in my lifetime. I was totally in awe of the dancers, their movements, the music, the drama, the emotion, and the flow of feeling from the audience itself. I looked around at the people there, and I felt a powerful sense of group appreciation and affection. We were joyful, together, and connected in awe from our shared experience. Then at the intermission, the person sitting next to me said there was more – all the emotion from the people behind us flowing through us as well. See the photograph of ballet dancers (Figure 1).

In this book, I want to help you convey to your public a lot more awe for what your nonprofit does and more affection for the people involved and the cause they serve. In my career as fundraiser, leader, and consultant, I have worked hard to be able to demonstrate to donors the ethics, effectiveness, and accountability of that particular nonprofit. I wanted people to *see the organization as awesome* in what it does to make this a better world. For many years I have held as a key fundraising principle the importance of enabling your donors' dreams to come true. That is an awesome experience. It is the sixth principle of fundraising in my first book, *Make a Better World*.

As I write this, most of the United States is emerging from the pandemic and two years of isolation with limited interaction with other people and too many virtual Zoom calls. Talk show hosts discuss how to return to a normal world and how to get over years of depressing news, infection rates, hospitalizations, death tolls, and lack of connection with others. Yes, we gained a higher appreciation of healthcare personnel and essential workers, and many people demonstrated their caring for others through donations and other support, but there was an overwhelming lack of awe in our lives. Instead: Sad. Lonely. Isolated. Boring. Stir-crazy. Depressed.

My conclusion is that there is something needed – something special – in our connection with other human beings. When I asked friends and colleagues what makes them happy, the answers were friends, family gatherings, group activities, close connections, meaningful communion, cheering on a sports team with others, sharing a musical performance with others, togetherness on vacation, working in a team, and, yes, being in love.

Figure 1 Watching ballet dancers perform is an awesome experience. Photo by Michael Afonso on Unsplash – Photo by Pixabay https://www.pexels.comphotoactive-adult-artist-ballerina-358010.

When I think of connecting with others, one of my own awesome experiences was restoring a historic house in great disrepair in Providence, Rhode Island. Living with me and my son, who led the process, were several of his friends, all working to update everything in the house. We started in November with no electricity except a line coming in from a neighbor's house, no plumbing (thank heaven for friendly neighbors!), and no heat until we repaired the chimney flue and installed a wood stove. Every night, about five to ten of us would gather around the stove, talking, sharing, eating, and laughing. Even complaining was fun!

I was not the father figure, the place was often a mess, and scrounging up the next meal was uncertain. But eventually someone would say, "Let's clean this place up. Come on. Get up and help!" Or someone would say, "I'm going out and will bring back pizza. Everyone give me a few bucks." It was an incredibly happy time in my life living, as I look back on it, in a commune of sorts with wonderful, energetic, young people. Of course, I paid them a reasonable wage for their work, and every two weeks or so I'd take us all out to an enjoyable meal at a favorite local restaurant. Why was I happy? We were all working together to achieve something important and, in this case, beautiful: a restored 1895 house in the Historic Armory District in Providence. It was *awesome*! (Figure 2).

Years before, I was privileged to attend a Hopi ceremony in a small kiva in Old Oraibi, a Hopi village in Arizona, where I saw the dancers in one group after another perform in increasingly rhythmic forms. They appeared to be closely connected. The next day, my friend and colleague at Save the Children, who had invited me to his home and to the ceremony, told me that he had started off in the first dances feeling a bit alone but soon came to feel unified with the other dancers as an integral part of the group and finally feeling part of something even larger, connected, and integrated in something wonderful, of all time, truly awesome.

Figure 2 The awesome progress of an 1895 house in Providence before and after restoration. Photographs by Tania Phillips.

At my 60th reunion of my high school graduation, one of my classmates said, "We learned teamwork from each other and that we had to protect each other." We rarely won our basketball games (I was a low-scoring guard) and almost never won our football games (I was the quarterback), but we had something more important, which was working together, helping each other, and supporting each other. When I look back on those experiences, I know they were really important in my life and quite awesome, and they guided me to my life's work with NGOs.

When I completed my term as elected president of AIESEC-United States (the international youth organization), I had job offers in banking and international development. I didn't expect to experience any awe from a career in banking, but I did expect to experience awe from the work I could do in international development. I chose a position with the Institute of International Education. My instinct was right; I can truthfully say I have experienced awe on many occasions in my travels around the world, meeting a wide variety of people, and working to accomplish amazing things in their cities, towns, and villages.

Recently, the feedback I received from former colleagues at NGOs where I had worked has been so gratifying, because there was a lot of teamwork, mentoring, and supporting each other as we worked together to achieve something important to make the world better for others. The mentoring of young people that I do these days gives me a similar sense of teamwork and gratification. I learn much from them, because it is, after all, their world in the future, and what they think, fear, and desire is important for me to know. Mentoring is teamwork, and it is joyful to experience the sharing we do.

I have heard businesspeople criticize nonprofits for how they let everyone talk in a meeting (with some order presumably). My corporate friends consider all this "extraneous" talk to be highly ineffective and a waste of valuable time. However, surveys regularly indicate that workers in nonprofits have higher satisfaction levels in their work than do people in other sectors. It is my conviction that the higher level of involvement of everyone in an organization – including active participation in meetings – ends up giving them greater connection with others, creates greater satisfaction in their work, and empowers them to achieve greater results. This is awesome!

Adam Grant, the organizational psychologist at The Wharton School at the University of Pennsylvania, wrote in a July 2021 *New York Times* opinion piece about *A Specific Kind of Joy We've Been Missing*.[1] He opens with an example of 15,000 people at an event at Madison Square Garden in New York City and how "the audience erupted in the closest thing I've seen to rapture in a solid year and a half." He goes on to say that "emotions are inherently social" and that "Peak happiness lies mostly in collective activity. … We find our greatest bliss in moments of collective effervescence." In the article, he cites David Émile Durkheim, one of the founding fathers of sociology, who used the phrase *collective effervescence* "to describe the sense of energy and harmony people feel when they come together in a group around a shared purpose."

Durkheim's biography in *The Internet Encyclopedia of Philosophy* provides the foundations of his thinking: "Collective effervescence refers to moments in societal life when the group of individuals that makes up a society comes together in order to perform a religious ritual. During these moments, the group comes together and communicates in the same thought and participates in the same action, which serves to unify a group of individuals. When individuals come into close contact with one another and when they are assembled in such a fashion, a certain 'electricity' is created and released, leading participants to a high degree of collective emotional excitement or delirium. This impersonal, extra-individual force, which is a core element of religion, transports the individuals into a new, ideal realm, lifts them up outside of themselves, and makes them feel as if they are in contact with an extraordinary energy"[2] (Figure 3).

"Yes! Wonderful! Joy! Awesome!"

Figure 3 People experiencing awesome music. Artwork by Sawyer Phillips.

These descriptions remind me of the cheering crowds in a football stadium, the exuberant fans at a rock concert, or working in an NGO with donors, volunteers, and each other. In my own experience over the years, many donors and volunteers have thanked me for what we have given them by working together. My slogan "Working Together for a Better World through Strategy, Teamwork, and Leadership" points toward something awesome. This is how NGOs operate: strategy makes daily work, communication, and appreciation effective; teamwork is the relationship with donors, partners, and each other; and leadership is what donors – and you – are doing together to make a better world.

Teamwork is exhilarating!

What I want to convey here is that it's your teamwork with donors that makes a nonprofit successful. It also takes your leadership within the organization to make sure it is attractive to donors and, of course, to have strategies for effective fundraising, programs, and communication. Imagine what donors experience when they feel connected with you and their beneficiaries – actually working together for a better world. Imagine if they come into this relationship because they trust your organization and because they see from your communication that you are achieving impact in so many ways, and their relationship grows closer through the shared experience of making a better world. Yes, those relationships, the fundraising, and the results can be awesome.

For this to work, however, you need to take the steps outlined in the next chapters to earn the trust of donors and to demonstrate the effectiveness of what you achieve, which is the impact donors want to see. Consider what is in the next chapters about why people fail to have a high level of trust or respect for NGOs and decide what you will do about that.

In my hierarchy of human values, helping and caring for others and the planet ranks far above taking care of yourself and your family. Imagine if large numbers of individuals who shared your vision for a better world also trusted and respected your nonprofit. It would be so easy to find ways to bring them together with you in a joyous relationship that truly would be awesome for them and for you and for your beneficiaries.

Adam Grant's article continues to highlight "the sense of energy and harmony people feel when they come together in a group around a shared purpose [… and] the deep fun of creating together and solving problems together."[3] Anyone working in a nonprofit with a good leader-manager and a good strategic plan will know exactly what I'm talking about – the joy of working for a trustworthy, impactful organization.

Key point: I always found it awesome to connect with donors and volunteers. Evidence abounds about the joy of giving, sharing, and working together! Teamwork makes that happen.

The challenge is to find ways to create and share *joy* (Adam Grant's term), *collective effervescence* (David Émile Durkheim's term), or *awesome experience* (my term) with your donors. And earn their trust and respect. The next chapters will show you exactly how to do that (Figure 4).

In my last visit to my eye doctor, the technician Katie gave me the standard instructions as she took photographs of my retina: "Lean into the camera. Hold still. Look at the star in the center. Don't move. OK blink." After each of the four photographs, she told me how I did. She said, "Perfect." At the end of the session, I told her that I had never heard I was perfect four times in a row. She smiled with great joy that I appreciated what she said, especially when I concluded with: "And you were awesome!" What a perfect example of how sharing appreciation with another person is, in fact, awesome!

Your donors need to hear more about all you do and your appreciation more often. They are looking for ways to create and share joy, experience collective effervescence, and participate in an awesome experience. Keep reading to discover how to do this!

Enable Donors to Have
Their Dreams Come True

1. Find donors who share your concerns.
2. Get to know them better.
3. Know more about what they dream of doing.
4. Enable them to achieve their dreams.
5. Exceed their expectations.

Figure 4 Five steps to enable donors to have their dreams come true. Infographic by the author with art by Wills Phillips.

Notes

1 Adam Grant, "There's a Specific Kind of Joy We've Been Missing," *The New York Times*, July 10, 2021, accessed June 30, 2022, https://www.nytimes.com/2021/07/10/opinion/sunday/covid-group-emotions-happiness.html.
2 Paul Carls, "Émile Durkheim (1858–1917), "*Internet Encyclopedia of Philosophy*, accessed June 30, 2022, https://iep.utm.edu/emile-durkheim/
3 Adam Grant, ibid.

Bibliography

1 Carls, Paul. "Émile Durkheim (1858–1917)." *Internet Encyclopedia of Philosophy*. Accessed June 30, 2022. https://iep.utm.edu/emile-durkheim/
2 Grant, Adam. "There's a Specific Kind of Joy We've Been Missing." *The New York Times*, July 10, 2021. Accessed June 30, 2022. https://www.nytimes.com/2021/07/10/opinion/sunday/covid-group-emotions-happiness.html

Chapter 1

Funding in the charitable sector –
Large but underperforming

The United States is often cited as a leading global example of success thanks to about 1.8 million registered nonprofit organizations,[1] numerous conferences for nonprofit workers, state-of-the-art fundraising strategies, multimillion dollar donations, amazing news articles about donors, and contributions growing nearly every year. The nonprofit sector in the United States is huge. "Of the nonprofit organizations registered with the IRS, 501(c)(3) public charities accounted for just over three-quarters of revenue and expenses for the nonprofit sector as a whole ($2.04 trillion and $1.94 trillion, respectively) and just under two-thirds of the nonprofit sector's total assets ($3.79 trillion)."[2]

I use the phrase *total social value of civil society* to encompass expenditures of registered nonprofits, the large but unreported expenditures by informal groups, friends helping friends, and the value of donated time by volunteers and beneficiaries in both registered and informal groups. That is the total social value of the charitable sector, and it is certainly much higher than the figures cited above. According to the U.S. Bureau of Labor Statistics: "Nonprofits account for 12.3 million jobs, 10.2% of private sector employment, in 2016."[3] That's larger than state and local government, finance and insurance, manufacturing of durable goods, wholesale trade, retail trade, and many other sectors. It is probably much larger now years later.

As I look at the economic and employment significance of the nonprofit sector in the United States, I do wonder why it is so underreported in the media. Year in and year out, nonprofits are a significant contributor to employment as well as to the public good. "The solutions to many of the greatest challenges of our time – from climate change to cancer – lie in the nonprofit sector. We also know that we need an effective nonprofit sector now more than ever." So says Prosper Strategies,[4] a nonprofit consulting firm committed to building "a more effective and impactful social sector."

As a 2019 article in *Forbes Magazine* reports, "It's no surprise to anyone that nonprofits play a vital role in solving major social problems. But despite being catalytic agents that promote change, nonprofits have not always been recognized as major players in our economy. Now, creating more than just social impact, nonprofits have risen to become the third-largest employers in the U.S. economy." The *Forbes* article is titled "The Nonprofit Sector Is Growing: Why Nonprofits Should Act Now To Leverage Their Position."[5]

I agree it is time for nonprofits to step up! The main themes of this book are that nonprofits need to get so much better in what they do, how they do it, and what they communicate to their constituents. That will truly make a better world!

The U.S. charity sector is large but underperforming

Donations reached a new all-time high of $484.9 billion in 2021. However, this is actually a small decline from the year before in inflation-adjusted terms.[6] Warning: You may not like what follows!

DOI: 10.4324/9781003335207-3

Drawing on a wide range of data about trends in donations, the Urban Institute reaches several key conclusions: "As one concern, several recent studies of individual donors have shown that participation rates in charitable giving among low- and middle-income donors in the United States is declining, suggesting that although donations have generally been increasing, nonprofits appear to be relying more on wealthier donors … . Moreover, rates of volunteering—an important resource for many nonprofit organizations, especially smaller ones with few or no paid staff …—have also declined over the past two decades."[7] (6)

Compared to the affluence of the United States and the unmet needs domestically and globally, the charity sector *could* – and I say *should* – be raising so much more in donations and volunteering and accomplishing so much more! In fact, the reality seems to be going in the opposite direction. Just a few years ago (2017), *The Chronicle of Philanthropy* reported the disturbing news by Drew Lindsay that "Fewer Americans Find Room in Their Budgets for Charity," and Paul Clolery reported in *NonProfit Times* that "Roughly 40% of Americans have no 'philanthropic footprint' and can't be counted on for a meaningful relationship with charitable organizations."[8]

More recent clarion calls have been issued by Patrick M. Rooney in "The Growth in Total Household Giving Is Camouflaging a Decline in Giving by Small and Medium Donors: What Can We Do About It?" in the *Nonprofit Quarterly*, August 27, 2019, and Shena Ashley in "Why the Decline in Individual Donors Should Matter to Institutional Philanthropy – and What to Do about It" in the *Nonprofit Quarterly*, December 3, 2019.[9]

The situation appears even more serious as time goes by. In a December 2019 *Nonprofit Quarterly* article titled "Where Have All the Donors Gone? The Continued Decline of the Small Donor and the Growth of Megadonors" Mr. Rooney concludes that "the share of Americans giving at all to 501(c)(3)s continues to erode."[10] Rooney is professor of economics and director of the Indiana University Lilly School of Philanthropy. In this article, he cites the share of households giving at 66.2% in 2000, falling to 61.1% in 2010, and continuing to decline to 53.9% in 2016. Others have documented further declines to 50% or less.

Membership in centers of religion is down, inequality continues to rise, millennials may not be responding to fundraising requests, donor fatigue may be more prevalent, and the COVID-19 pandemic disrupted everything. According to "The Giving Environment: Understanding Pre-Pandemic Trends in Charitable Giving: Data on Declining US Donor Participation" by the Indiana University Lilly Family School of Philanthropy, "In 2018, 49.6% of American households donated to charity, according to the PPS data, down from 66.2% of American households of American donating in 2000 when the PPS began tracking … . The share of American households that donate to charity has been steadily declining since the Great Recession. This trend can be seen across multiple datasets."[11] (5, 7)

In a June 6, 2022 podcast on "Perspectives on Philanthropy | Giving USA 2022 and Today's Philanthropic Landscape" presented by CCS Fundraising, panelists cited a decline in the household giving rate to 50%.[12]

➡️ *These are not trends any industry would like to see.*

The figures cited may actually exaggerate actual behavior. As an author with extensive research in donor behavior and a master's degree in economics, I believe that many opinion-based polls may often overstate reality when they ask people about their donations. Research that essentially asks "Are you a good person?" will always get high affirmative responses. It's the same thing when people are asked "Have you donated money to charity this past year?" Unsubstantiated opinion research can dramatically overstate behavior reality. The results of such opinion-based polls are more like a focus group, which may provide insights or suggest trends, but we need to be cautious of opinion polls that may not reflect actual behavior.

⟹ *Sadly, the charity sector has not been growing its share of the total market.*

Total donations of $484.9 billion could grow to $969.8 billion

Imagine if you can that people really trusted the ethics and performance of nonprofits and simply doubled their donations!

Table 1.1 Potential increase by doubling donations from individuals, bequests, corporations, and foundations. Data from Giving USA

	2021 donations		Possible donations
Individuals	$326.9 billion	if doubled to	$653.8 billion
New bequests	46.0 billion	if doubled to	92.0 billion
Corporations	21.1 billion	if doubled to	42.2 billion
Foundations	90.9 billion	if doubled to	181.8 billion
	$484.9 billion		**$969.8 billion**

Why not think like this? The richest economy in the world can support this doubling in donations. Proven strategies exist to achieve it! Nonprofits that understand what donors want, that let leadership flourish at all levels, that have excellent plans and great implementation, and that are trusted and have real impact are significantly growing their level of donations year after year.

Individuals could step up to higher levels of giving if they believed more in their charities. Wealthy individuals could give far greater amounts to charity each year and in their wills if they truly believed in the American way of helping. Corporations would donate far more if they cared about their employees, their communities, and the environment (as they say they do). And the managers of large foundations and donor advised funds with millions or billions of dollars in investments could certainly decide to make a greater impact sooner rather than later.

In that 2019 article,[13] Rooney observes that "big donors are playing an even bigger role than in earlier years." As an example of actual giving, he includes a chart of total donations from the top 50 donors between 2000 and 2018. The average annual total amount donated was $7.4 billion per donor for 2000 to 2005 and $8.4 billion for 2007 to 2018. Updated data show the average annual total amount donated from the top 50 donors in 2019 climbed to $15.8 and, in 2020, rose to $24.7 billion and in 2021 to $27.7 billion.[14] This sounds like generous giving amounts but, to put this in perspective, Amazon founder Jeff Bezos gave or rather pledged $10 billion to his foundation in 2020 while he ended 2020 with a $75 billion *increase* in wealth. These donation totals are a lot of money, but I believe they are nowhere near enough or even a fair share.

Here are other reasons for concern. In its October 2019 issue, *Forbes* reported, "For the first time in American history, the 400 wealthiest people paid a lower tax rate than any other group," according to a new study by economists Emmanuel Saez and Gabriel Zucman at the University of California, Berkeley."[15] Todd C. Frankel and Douglas MacMillanhe reported in the *Washington Post* on June 8, 2021: "IRS records show wealthiest Americans, including Bezos and

Musk, paid little in income taxes as share of wealth."[16] Other reports described that not only have the wealthy increased their wealth dramatically and been levied the lowest tax rate in 50 years, but they have become very adept in avoiding taxes.

Steve Dubb reported in the *NonProfit Quarterly*[17] on November 10, 2021, that: "According to testimony earlier this year to Congress by Charles Rettig, the Internal Revenue Service (IRS) commissioner, the wealthy in the United States evade an estimated $1 trillion in taxes a year or, to do the complicated math, $10 trillion over 10 years. Recall that the entire Biden bill, if passed as originally submitted, would have cost $3.5 trillion [over ten years]."

The reason for concern is extreme: The rich and super-rich are donating only a modicum of their income or their wealth. Nonprofits have not yet been able to inspire them as a group to contribute commensurate to their means or to compensate for what their appropriate tax payments would have accomplished for society.

There was some good news in 2021: Airbnb's co-founder and CEO Brian Chesky provides a model for others, pledging "to give away his entire 2020 award" to philanthropic causes.[18] Tour manager Rick Steves challenged his followers to donate to Bread for the World and promised to match their donations – as of December 15, 2021, they gave $450,000, which he matched with his own $450,000.[19]

Will others increase their giving commensurately? It depends on many factors including one factor that every nonprofit can control:

➨ *BUILDING TRUST is essential for your nonprofit and for the sector.*

Nonprofits need to look inward

Rather than expecting that a rising stock market will lift your fundraising results, I believe every nonprofit needs to do better in its own work to warrant increased support from donors. A key tenet in my training and consulting is to pay little attention to external factors you cannot control such as the economy. Instead, focus on what you can change through better leadership, thorough planning, and new strategies for trustworthiness in all you do, effectiveness in your programs, and accountability in your communications.

To paraphrase U.S. President John F. Kennedy,[20] I say to all fundraisers, leaders, staff, and volunteers of nonprofits: "Ask not what the economy can do for you. Ask what you can do for society, for your donors, and for the image of nonprofits." Read the following as just one alarming example to see why I say to look inside your own organization.

Based on data from 2,500 nonprofits, the 2021 *Fundraising Effectiveness Survey*,[21] conducted by the AFP Foundation for Philanthropy, found significant problems in donor retention, with an overall donor retention rate of only 43.6%. This reflects an extremely small retention rate of only 19.3% for new donors and a discouraging retention rate of only 59.6% for repeat donors, figures that I find alarming. When more than 80% of new donors and 40% of repeat donors drop out, what does this say about their experience with the organization? The report aptly notes that "retention is still an issue across the sector." Successful businesses do not have such low retention numbers.

Donor retention is a longstanding challenge and – as Stacy Mihaly, a former colleague and advertising expert, told me – this has to do in large part with "many nonprofits pulling out all the stops to acquire donors but falling flat when it comes to stewarding them, engaging them, and moving them beyond a 'transactional' relationship" ("You give us some money, and we will keep asking you for more and never tell you what we did with the money you gave us"). This is not acceptable, and it certainly is not awesome.

When we were expanding our marketing effort at Foster Parents Plan (now called Plan International USA), we examined the different retention rates as well as acquisition costs, first donations, renewal donations, and estimated lifetime value of new donors that came to us from different messages and different media (for example, TV ads versus direct mail). When we found that the lower acquisition costs in TV were followed by higher dropout rates, we adjusted our marketing strategies and budgets to account for the differences. Over eight years, this helped us increase our donors from 10,000 to 30,000 and our income from $10 million to $30 million ($62.5 million in 2022 currency). In your nonprofit, you may find that marketing results from social media have similar high responses but weak lifetime value, or you may have cracked the code as we did in Foster Parents Plan.

Key point: A rising stock market and growing economy may help lift donation levels, but the real growth will come only when nonprofits look inward to raise their own attractiveness to donors through meaningful ethics to be trusted and long-term impact to be respected.

Let's look again at what you can learn from the Better Business Bureau's 2021 *Donor Trust Special Report on Charity Impact*[22] initially cited in the Introduction. According to this report, trust and impact are the two most important issues for donors. This book is dedicated to those two most likely reasons for low retention rates and slow growth of the NGO sector: low levels of trust and insufficient confidence in impact. People will not trust if you fail to demonstrate good behavior, and they will not respect you if you fail to demonstrate good impact.

The Lilly Family School of Philanthropy's July 2021 report *The Giving Environment: Understanding Pre-Pandemic Trends in Charitable Giving. Data on Declining US Donor Participation*[23] found that "The percentage of American households that donate to charity fell to 49.6% in 2018 for the first time since the Philanthropy Panel Study begin tracking charitable giving." (7) The report also concluded that "trends in trust can be compared to changes in giving participation rates." (21)

The Independent Sector's 2022 report *Trust in Civil Society: Understanding the factors driving trust in nonprofits and philanthropy on trust*"[24] should be required reading for everyone working for non-profits. The report "revealed that 56% of Americans said they trust nonprofits, down a statistically significant 3-points from the 2020 benchmark study (59%)" and that "Public trust is the currency of the nonprofit sector. The public's belief that nonprofits will 'do the right thing' is one of the central reasons the sector exists." (5, 4) This 2022 report continues:

- "Consistent with past waves, integrity and purpose contribute most to trust for both nonprofits and philanthropy. Distrusters in both sectors point to perceived mismanagement of funds and instances of corruption and scandals. Neutral trusters say financial transparency and proof of impact is necessary for them to see an organization as trustworthy. Public figure endorsements, communicating clear organizational mission and values, and demonstrating results remain the top drivers of trust for nonprofits and philanthropy." (6)
- 81% reported "I need to know a great deal about an organization before I choose to support it." (12)
- 78% reported "Nonprofits must earn my trust before I support them." (12)
- "Signals of Nonprofit Trustworthiness: (Asked of Respondents Reporting Neutral Trust)

  - Financial transparency
  - Demonstrable results using donations
  - Transparency about political affiliations/ideology
  - More information about the organization generally." (17)

- "The frequency of people's engagement with nonprofits as donors, volunteers, advocates, and constituents positively impacts their level of trust in the broader sector. Trust also is a prerequisite for many people to engage nonprofits, creating a self-reinforcing cycle that appears to be weakening. This report indicates the public wants solutions for complex societal issues, but increasingly shuns institutions. More than half believe giving directly to individuals and causes can make a bigger impact than working through a nonprofit organization. Viewing this finding alongside other research showing a decline in the number of donors and volunteers over the past two decades indicates it may be time for the sector to change course in order to restore trust, giving, and volunteerism. Now is the time to break from the status quo and try new strategies to reverse downward trends across these interdependent variables." (30)

> ➤ *If they care about their future, individual nonprofits and the entire charity sector must address trustworthiness as an urgent priority.*

Over many decades, I have seen giving totals go up but never up to the levels that would be expected in the richest country in the world. Even if individuals and corporations doubled their support of charities, the total giving would, surprisingly, still be nowhere near the 10% tithing people often talk about or reflect the generosity we often see attributed to social and corporate leaders.

So what is money really worth?

Value of money to the donor and to charity – How to increase total social value to society

Let's look at money and donations in a new way, which could increase understanding of what really matters to donors at various levels of income and to society.

What is the *value of money*? It's relative. Consider how life-changing a $10,000 lottery win would be for a family with a $25,000 annual income. What would it take for a middle income or wealthy family to have the same level of life-changing importance? Or for the very richest families?

To a family with $25,000 annual income, a gift or lottery win of $10,000 (40% of income) is an amazingly large and a meaningful amount, because it could be used for important essentials and basics of life. For example, the family could use this windfall to pay college tuition or purchase a reliable vehicle to get to work. To a family with a $100,000 annual income, $10,000 is a notable amount and would be very nice to get, for example, to help with a down payment on a house. To those with a $500,000 annual income, $10,000 is fairly insignificant (2% of income) and would not make a big difference in their lives. For those with large annual incomes and even larger net worth (wealth), a $10,000 windfall means essentially nothing.

Clearly, the richer you are, the less significance a particular sum of money has. To have the same *value* for different families, you have to look at their income level, how much they need that money for essentials, and how they would use that amount of money. To widen your perspective on the value of money, consider the following chart based on annual income:

1   For a family with a $25,000 annual income, $10,000 is a life-changing amount.
2   For a family with a $100,000 annual income, $50,000 could be a life-changing amount.
3   For a family with a $500,000 annual income, $500,000 might be a life-changing amount.
4   For a family with an income of $2 million a year, what could be life-changing? More millions. But would that really change their lives?

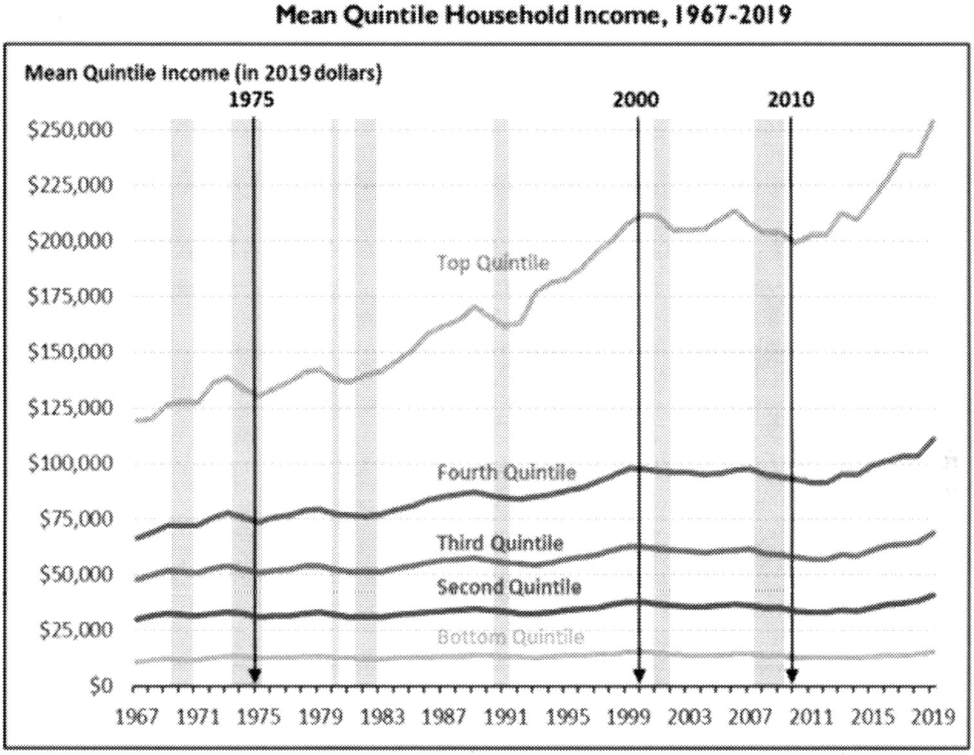

Mean Quintile Household Income, 1967-2019

Figure 1.1 A chart of household income showing dramatic increases for the richest Americans.

Moreover, it is clear that the richer you are, the richer you get. The Mean Quintile Household Income chart in Figure 1.1 shows the increase in U.S. household income for five income groups – with a dramatically greater increase for the wealthiest households in the top quintile. Figure created by the Congressional Research Service (CRS) based on data from U.S. Census Bureau, Current Population Survey (CPS), Annual Social and Economic Supplements (ASEC).

We can also look at these figures to see how much it means (or matters) for a family to donate. Giving $10,000 to charity every year is a significant stretching amount for a family with $100,000 income. To get that same degree of significance or stretch, I believe, the $500,000 family and the $1 million family need to give not just five times or ten times more, but many multiples more. As you go up those quintiles of income, the more wealth, the less sacrifice. What would people really miss by giving more? At the highest level, just about nothing. As Mother Teresa said, "Give until it hurts."[25]

To put this into perspective, a colleague working for an NGO recently wrote to me that "I give more than 10% of my income to church and charity and it's not to feel good; it's because we strongly believe in what we are doing and know that we are very fortunate and that others can benefit from our sacrifice more than we can benefit from it."

If everyone gave that 10% of their income to charity and based on the personal income of $21,056 billion in 2021, the total U.S. donations to charity would have been $2,106 billion, more than four times the actual giving.[26] It is pertinent to note that the American stock market, even with recent declines, has grown at about 10% each year, as documented in chapter 2.

What about the value of money for the recipient charity and society?

If nonprofits can encourage donors to give based on their ability to give – considering their income and wealth and the value of their contributions to society – then the total value to society will be enormously increased. It "costs" the donors increasingly less to give more, the richer they are, and the benefits to society dramatically increase with the larger donations.

The truly amazing reality is that when funds are received, all dollars have the same value. So $1,000 is important and $100,000 is 100 times more important, since every amount enables the recipient organization to do that much more. Let me say it again: Donations at increasing amounts have increasing benefits to society but have decreasing significance for donors as they go up the wealth scale. Their larger donations would increase the total social benefit dramatically. Society benefits so much more than the donors sacrifice. See the image on *Optimizing Total Social Value* (Figure 1.2).

To optimize total social value, then, society should expect that the richer you are the more you give as a percentage of annual income or, better yet, of overall wealth. Remember, larger donations of money have less significance (or sacrifice) for the donor but greater significance for society. I call it *Optimizing Total Social Value* as you go up the scale of affluence.

As a leader or fundraiser in a nonprofit, you must continually think about the value of money as it relates to your organization and to your various donor groups. Find a way to share this idea diplomatically with your upper-income donors: Giving a certain amount (perhaps $10,000, $100,000, or more) is a relatively small sacrifice or commitment to wealthy donors while providing a much greater benefit worth far more to others who are in need of the basics of life, an

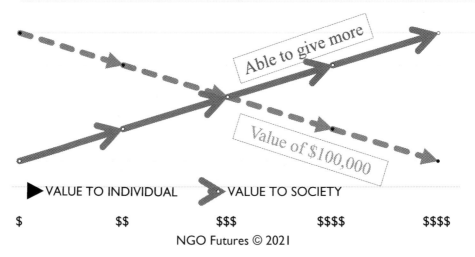

Figure 1.2 Optimizing Total Social Value showing the richer you are, the less each $100.00 means. Image by the author.

Hierarchy of Human Values

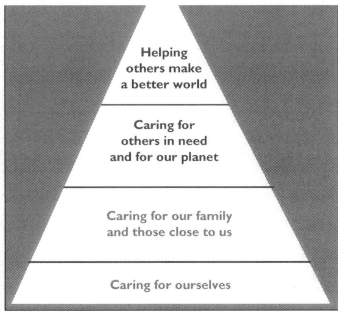

Ken's Hierarchy of
Human Values based
on caring and helping
(after Maslow)

**Based on all my years
interacting with
people, groups,
organizations,
governments, and
companies, what are
the real values for
humanity?**

**It is all about caring!
Being civil-ized!**

Figure 1.3 A hierarchy of human values, based on Maslow, showing the high value of caring and helping.
Image by the author.

education for a better future, a safe place to live, or so many other needs in society. You will make it an *awesome* experience for the beneficiaries, and that will be *awesome* for the donors who makes it happen.

Key point: While there is decreasing value of a particular sum of money the richer you are, there is increasing value for the larger amounts of money you can give for the benefit of society.

On the scale of human values, caring for others in need and for the planet and especially helping others make a better world are higher than caring for ourselves, our family, and others close to us. This is what generosity and charity are all about (Figure 1.3).

Questions for implementation

1   Are you satisfied with the rate of growth in your fundraising results?
2   What are your retention rates for new and repeat donors and what have you done to improve them?
3   Do you survey your donors and what do you learn from those who do not renew support?
4   How can you use the "value of money" discretely and effectively in fundraising?

Notes

1 Lewis Faulk et al., "Nonprofit Trends and Impacts 2021," *Urban Institute*, October 2021, 1, accessed July 16, 2022, https://www.urban.org/research/publication/nonprofit-trends-and-impacts-2021

2 NCCS Team, "The Nonprofit Sector in Brief," June 18, 2020, 1, accessed June 26, 2022, https://nccs.urban.org/project/nonprofit-sector-brief

3 US Bureau of Labor Statistics, "Nonprofits account for 12.3 million jobs, 10.2 percent of private sector employment, in 2016," *The Economics Daily*, August 31, 2018, 1, accessed June 25, 2022, https://www.bls.gov/opub/ted/2018/nonprofits-account-for-12-3-million-jobs-10-2-percent-of-private-sector-employment-in-2016.htm

4 Alyssa Conrardy, "2020 Nonprofit Stats: A Few Things That Might Surprise You About the Nonprofit Sector," January 27, 2020, 1, accessed June 25, 2022, https://prosper-strategies.com/2020-nonprofit-stats/

5 Sarah Hamilton, "The Nonprofit Sector Is Growing: Why Nonprofits Should Act Now To Leverage Their Position," *Forbes*, October 2, 2019, 1, accessed June 25, 2022, https://www.forbes.com/sites/forbescoachescouncil/2019/10/02/the-nonprofit-sector-is-growing-why-nonprofits-should-act-now-to-leverage-their-position/?sh=66ff6e477b52

6 Emily Haynes and Drew Lindsay, "2021s Surprisingly Strong Giving … and the Dark Clouds over 2022," *The Chronicle of Philanthropy*, June 21, 2022, 1, accessed June 25, 2022, https://www.philanthropy.com/article/2021s-surprisingly-strong-giving

7 Faulk et al., "Nonprofit Trends and Impacts 2021," 6.

8 Drew Lindsay, "Fewer Americans Find Room in Their Budgets for Charity, Chronicle Data Shows," *The Chronicle of Philanthropy*, October 3, 2017, accessed June 25, 2022, https://www.philanthropy.com/article/fewer-americans-find-room-in-their-budgets-for-charity-chronicle-data-shows/

9 Patrick M. Rooney, "The Growth in Total Household Giving Is Camouflaging a Decline in Giving by Small and Medium Donors: What Can We Do about It?," *Nonprofit Quarterly*, December 4, 2019, accessed June 25, 2022, https://nonprofitquarterly.org/total-household-growth-decline-small-medium-donors/

10 Patrick M. Rooney, "Where Have All the Donors Gone? The Continued Decline of the Small Donor and the Growth of Megadonors," *Nonprofit Quarterly*, December 4, 2019, accessed June 25, 2022, https://nonprofitquarterly.org/where-have-all-the-donors-gone-the-continued-decline-of-the-small-donor-and-the-growth-of-megadonors/

11 Indiana University Lilly Family School of Philanthropy, "The Giving Environment: Understanding Pre-Pandemic Trends in Charitable Giving," July 2021, accessed June 26, 2022, https://scholarworks.iupui.edu/bitstream/handle/1805/26290/giving-environment210727.pdf

12 CCS Fundraising, "Perspectives on Philanthropy: Giving USA 2022 Release Webinar: Online video clip. *YouTube*," November 23, 2015, accessed June 26, 2022, https://www.youtube.com/watch?v=PDp3ukuU4i4

13 Patrick M. Rooney, "Where Have All the Donors Gone? The Continued Decline of the Small Donor and the Growth of Megadonors."

14 Maria Di Mento, "The Philanthropy 50," *The Chronicle of Philanthropy*, February 8, 2022, accessed June 26, 2022, https://www.philanthropy.com/article/the-philanthropy-50/#id=browse2021

15 Jack Kelly, "For The First Time In History, U.S. Billionaires Paid A Lower Tax Rate Than The Working Class: What Should We Do About It?," *Forbes*, October 11, 2019, accessed June 26, 2022, https://www.forbes.com/sites/jackkelly/2019/10/11/for-the-first-time-in-history-us-billionaires-paid-a-lower-tax-rates-than-the-working-class-what-we-should-do-about-it/?sh=7da2a2d41fce

16 Todd C. Frankel and Douglas MacMillan, "IRS records show wealthiest Americans, including Bezos and Musk, paid little in income taxes as share of wealth, report says," *The Washington Post*, June 8, 2021, accessed June 26, 2022, https://www.washingtonpost.com/business/2021/06/08/wealthy-irs-taxes/

17 Steve Dubb, "The Rich Also Cry: As Congress Skimps, the Wealthy Squirrel Away Assets," *Nonprofit Quarterly*, November 10, 2021, 3, accessed June 25, 2022, https://nonprofitquarterly.org/the-rich-also-cry-as-congress-skimps-the-wealthy-squirrel-away-assets/

18 "Some Rewards Are Given Away" in "C.E.O.s Cash In, Increasing Gap With Workers" featuring Airbnb's CEO Brian Chesky," *The New York Times*, June 13, 2021,

19 Rick Steves in a December 15, 2021 email communication to his followers.

20 "And so, my fellow Americans: ask not what your country can do for you—ask what you can do for your country.": "Ask Not What Your Country Can Do For You," *ushistory.org*, accessed July 1, 2022, https://www.ushistory.org/documents/ask-not.htm

21 Association of Fundraising Professionals, "Fundraising Effectiveness Project: Giving Increases Significantly in 2020, Even as Donor Retention Rates Shrink," March 15, 2020, accessed June 26,

2022, https://afpglobal.org/fundraising-effectiveness-project-giving-increases-significantly-2020-even-donor-retention-rates

22 Better Business Bureau Wise Giving Alliance, "BBB Wise Giving Alliance releases Donor Trust Report," *Better Business Bureau*, November 15, 2021, accessed June 25, 2022, https://www.bbb.org/article/news-releases/26158-bbb-wise-giving-alliance-releases-donor-trust-report

23 Indiana University Lilly Family School of Philanthropy, "The Giving Environment: Understanding Pre-Pandemic Trends in Charitable Giving," 21.

24 Independent Sector, "Trust in Civil Society—Understanding the Factors Driving Trust in Nonprofits and Philanthropy," May 2022, 4, 6, 12, 17, accessed June 27, 2022, https://independentsector.org/trust

25 "'Give Until It Hurts': The Christian Wisdom of Mother Teresa in 9 Quotes," *Christian Today*, September 5, 2017, accessed July 1, 2022, https://www.christiantoday.com/article/give-until-it-hurts-the-christian-wisdom-of-mother-teresa-in-9-quotes/113084.htm

26 "Personal income in the United States from 1991 to 2021," *Statista*, accessed June 26, 2022, https://www.statista.com/statistics/216756/us-personal-income/

Bibliography

1 Association of Fundraising Professionals. "Fundraising Effectiveness Project: Giving Increases Significantly in 2020, Even as Donor Retention Rates Shrink," March 15, 2020. Accessed June 26, 2022. https://afpglobal.org/fundraising-effectiveness-project-giving-increases-significantly-2020-even-donor-retention-rates

2 Better Business Bureau Wise Giving Alliance. "BBB Wise Giving Alliance releases Donor Trust Report." *Better Business Bureau*, November 15, 2021. Accessed June 25, 2022. https://www.bbb.org/article/news-releases/26158-bbb-wise-giving-alliance-releases-donor-trust-report

3 Conrardy, Alyssa. "2020 Nonprofit Stats: A Few Things That Might Surprise You About the Nonprofit Sector," January 27, 2020. Accessed June 25, 2022. https://prosper-strategies.com/2020-nonprofit-stats/

4 CCS Fundraising. "Perspectives on Philanthropy: Giving USA 2022 Release Webinar: Online video clip. *YouTube*," November 23, 2015. Accessed June 26, 2022. https://www.youtube.com/watch?v=PDp3ukuU4i4

5 Dubb, Steve. "The Rich Also Cry: As Congress Skimps, the Wealthy Squirrel Away Assets." *Nonprofit Quarterly*, November 10, 2021. Accessed June 25, 2022. https://nonprofitquarterly.org/the-rich-also-cry-as-congress-skimps-the-wealthy-squirrel-away-assets/

6 "'Give until It hurts': The Christian wisdom of Mother Teresa in 9 quotes." *Christian Today*, September 5, 2017. Accessed July 1, 2022. https://www.christiantoday.com/article/give-until-it-hurts-the-christian-wisdom-of-mother-teresa-in-9-quotes/113084.htm

7 Faulk, Lewis, Mirae Kim, Teresa Derrick-Mills, Elizabeth Boris, Laura Tomasko, Nora Hakizimana, Tianyu Chen, Minjung Kim, and Layla Nath. "Nonprofit Trends and Impacts 2021." *Urban Institute*, October 2021. Accessed July 16, 2022. https://www.urban.org/research/publication/nonprofit-trends-and-impacts-2021

8 Frankel, Todd C., and Douglas MacMillan. "IRS records show wealthiest Americans, including Bezos and Musk, paid little in income taxes as share of wealth, report says." *The Washington Post*, June 8, 2021. Accessed June 26, 2022. https://www.washingtonpost.com/business/2021/06/08/wealthy-irs-taxes/

9 Hamilton, Sarah. "The Nonprofit Sector Is Growing: Why Nonprofits Should Act Now To Leverage Their Position." *Forbes*, October 2, 2019. Accessed June 25, 2022. https://www.forbes.com/sites/forbescoachescouncil/2019/10/02/the-nonprofit-sector-is-growing-why-nonprofits-should-act-now-to-leverage-their-position/?sh=66ff6e477b52

10 Haynes, Emily, and Drew Lindsay. "2021's surprisingly strong giving … and the dark clouds over 2022." *The Chronicle of Philanthropy*, June 21, 2022. Accessed June 25, 2022. https://www.philanthropy.com/article/2021s-surprisingly-strong-giving

11 Independent Sector. "Trust in Civil Society—Understanding the Factors Driving Trust in Nonprofits and Philanthropy," May 2022. Accessed June 27, 2022. https://independentsector.org/trust

12 Indiana University Lilly Family School of Philanthropy. "The Giving Environment: Understanding Pre-Pandemic Trends in Charitable Giving," July 2021. Accessed June 26, 2022. https://scholarworks.iupui.edu/bitstream/handle/1805/26290/giving-environment210727.pdf

13 Kelly, Jack. "For The First Time In History, U.S. Billionaires Paid A Lower Tax Rate Than The Working Class: What Should We Do About It?" *Forbes*, October 11, 2019. Accessed June 26, 2022. https://www.forbes.com/sites/jackkelly/2019/10/11/for-the-first-time-in-history-us-billionaires-paid-a-lower-tax-rates-than-the-working-class-what-we-should-do-about-it/?sh=7da2a2d41fce

14 Lindsay, Drew. "Fewer Americans Find Room in Their Budgets for Charity, Chronicle Data Shows." *The Chronicle of Philanthropy*, October 3, 2017. Accessed June 25, 2022. https://www.philanthropy.com/article/fewer-americans-find-room-in-their-budgets-for-charity-chronicle-data-shows/

15 Mento, Maria Di. "The Philanthropy 50." *The Chronicle of Philanthropy*, February 8, 2022. Accessed June 26, 2022. https://www.philanthropy.com/article/the-philanthropy-50/#id=browse2021

16 NCCS Team. "The Nonprofit Sector in Brief," June 18, 2020. Accessed June 26, 2022. https://nccs.urban.org/project/nonprofit-sector-brief

17 Rooney, Patrick M. "The Growth in Total Household Giving Is Camouflaging a Decline in Giving by Small and Medium Donors: What Can We Do About It?" *Nonprofit Quarterly*, December 4, 2019. Accessed June 25, 2022. https://nonprofitquarterly.org/total-household-growth-decline-small-medium-donors/

18 Rooney, Patrick M. "Where Have All the Donors Gone? The Continued Decline of the Small Donor and the Growth of Megadonors." *Nonprofit Quarterly*, December 4, 2019. Accessed June 25, 2022. https://nonprofitquarterly.org/where-have-all-the-donors-gone-the-continued-decline-of-the-small-donor-and-the-growth-of-megadonors/

19 "Personal income in the United States from 1991 to 2021." *Statista*. Accessed June 26, 2022. https://www.statista.com/statistics/216756/us-personal-income/

20 "Some Rewards Are Given Away" in "C.E.O.s Cash In, Increasing Gap With Workers" featuring Airbnb's CEO Brian Chesky." *The New York Times*, June 13, 2021.

21 Steves, Rick. December 15, 2021 email communication to his followers.

22 US Bureau of Labor Statistics. "Nonprofits account for 12.3 million jobs, 10.2 percent of private sector employment, in 2016." *The Economics Daily*, August 31, 2018. Accessed June 25, 2022. https://www.bls.gov/opub/ted/2018/nonprofits-account-for-12-3-million-jobs-10-2-percent-of-private-sector-employment-in-2016.htm

23 US History. "Ask Not What Your Country Can Do For You." *ushistory.org*. Accessed July 1, 2022. https://www.ushistory.org/documents/ask-not.htm

Chapter 2

Possible causes for the underperformance of funding

Why Is Giving Not Larger?

Hypothesis 1: People don't have enough money
Hypothesis 2: The needs are already being met
Hypothesis 3: Tax benefits don't provide enough incentive for donations
Hypothesis 4: Charity and generosity have decreased these days – People just don't care
Hypothesis 5: Nonprofits don't have enough trust, impact, or non-fundraising communication

Figure 2.1 Five hypotheses why people are not giving more. Sidebar by the author.

Even if your nonprofit's fundraising has been growing at 5% or 10% a year, that's not enough. I know from experience that it's possible to raise much more money and continuously grow your program, year after year. As a result, those substantially increased funds would empower your organization to have significantly more impact. The world needs more NGOs to do that!

Let's look at possible reasons for the underperformance of funding for nonprofits. I have heard the following as justifications for continuously low giving levels – lack of enough money, lack of unmet needs, lack of adequate tax benefits, lack of generosity and caring, and lack of impact, trustworthiness, and communication by charities. The following paragraphs examine each of these possible reasons for the underperformance of funding.

Hypothesis 1: People don't have enough money

There is an old saying that even in famine there is food, the only problem is its distribution. Strange, but it's really about sharing. The same can be said for money: there is plenty of money, the only problem is its distribution. More to the point here, the higher your income or net worth, the more you have available after basic needs to help others.

Both the American economy and the stock mark have grown significantly (Figure 2.2).

"Figure 2.2 depicts the United States' annual per capita personal income over 1959–2021 in current and constant (2012) dollars. Constant dollar measurements remove the effects of inflation. They allow for comparison of changes in the real purchasing power of the United States over time.

"When measured in current dollars, the United States' per capita personal income increased **2,738.2%**, from **$2,260** in 1959 to **$64,143** in 2021. When measured in constant 2012 dollars to adjust for inflation, it advanced **297.1%**, from **$13,971** in 1959 to **$55,477** in 2021."[1]

DOI: 10.4324/9781003335207-4

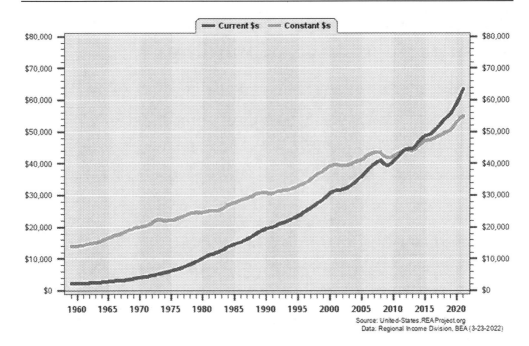

Figure 2.2 U.S. GDP per capita by year showing large increases over the past 62 years. Calculations by the United States Regional Analysis Project.

The U.S. stock market has grown significantly over time.

• "The stock market has returned an average of 10% per year over the past 50 years."[2]
• For 2012 to 2021, 14.8% average annual return or 12.4% adjusted for inflation
• For 1992 to 2021, 9.9% average annual return or 7.3% adjusted for inflation

However, data from the United States indicate that overall giving is stuck at a low percentage of disposable income (around 2%), that the wealthy give relatively less than the less affluent (as a portion of income), and that corporate giving has declined from past decades as a share of pre-tax profits – all of this happening as taxes have been reduced and tax-avoidance has increased. Surprising, is it?

Regarding donations by individuals, tithing in major religions is generally 10% of income. However, according to *Giving USA*, the figures for the rate of giving are far below that 10% standard. Here is the update for 1980, 2000, 2010, 2015, and 2020, with the normal rate of giving stuck at about 2% of disposable personal income over the course of four decades. (Disposable personal income is the amount that an individual or household has left to spend or save after income taxes have been deducted.)

Individual giving as percent of disposable income

Table 2.1 Individual giving as percent of disposable income. Data from *Giving USA*[3]

Year	1980	2000	2010	2015	2020	Norm
Annual level of giving	2.0%	2.3%	1.8%	1.9%	1.9%	**2.0%**

Suzanne Perry wrote in the *The Chronicle of Philanthropy* back in 2013 about "The Stubborn 2% Giving Rate: Even as more fundraisers seek donations, Americans don't dig deeper."[4]

This continues the pattern I first saw in 1975 in a report from the Commission on Private Philanthropy and Public Needs, known as the Filer Commission.[5] Based on its extensive research, the Commission concluded: "The voluntary sector is a large and vital part of American society, more important today than ever" (9). However, it also reported "a disturbing finding is that the purchasing power of giving did not keep pace with the growth of the economy through the expansive years of the 1960s and early 1970s and that in recent years it has fallen off absolutely when discounted for inflation" (15).

A 2000 study by the Council of Economic Advisers examined the difference in giving as a percentage of income and as a percentage of wealth and found that *giving actually declines* when looking at giving *as a portion of net worth (wealth)*: "The share of net worth contributed to charities actually falls as net worth increases. Among those with positive net worth, families in the 20 to 40% range of the wealth distribution gave 1% of their wealth to charitable organizations, while the wealthiest gave just 0.4%."[6]

These figures may change year to year, but the conclusion is quite clear. Even though billionaires collectively saw their wealth increase by $1.2 trillion in 2020, their increase in donations did not keep pace. This is sad, but I am not surprised. People in villages I have visited in Africa, Asia, Eastern Europe, and Latin America are more generous and take better care of their neighbors, relative to their ability to help.

Some news is that the Giving Pledge, initiated by Bill and Melinda Gates and Warren Buffet in 2010, to give at least half of their net worth to charity has a growing number of subscribers (231 at the end of 2021). Newspapers and magazines regularly carry articles praising the rich for their large gifts. For example, this article appeared in a 2015 issue of *Business Insider* magazine: "9 Billionaires Who Plan to Give Away the Majority of Their Fortunes."[7] The reality check in 2021 is that, according to the Institute for Policy Studies, "Of the 62 living U.S. Pledgers who were billionaires in 2010, their combined wealth has increased from $376 billion in 2010 to $734 billion as of July 18, 2020, an increase of 95%, in 2020 dollars."[8]

What about corporations? We see similar behavior in giving by American corporations over recent years even as their value rose to new heights. Statistics from *Giving USA* show a decline from 0.9% to 0.8% in corporate giving as a percentage of pretax profits, a significant decline when you consider the millions of dollars at stake. As summarized in the following table, corporate giving declined in the 15 years between 2005 and 2020. While that may not seem like a worrisome change – it is actually quite worrisome. Consider how many millions of dollars in donations this represents. Consider how much positive impact those monies would have made for people and planet. And consider this: What if the downward trend continues?

Corporate giving as a percentage of corporate pretax profits

Table 2.2 Corporate giving as a percentage of corporate pretax profits. Data from Giving USA[9]

2005	2015	2020
0.90%	0.80%	0.80%

Money is important to me

Figure 2.3 Images of money. Artwork by Sawyer Phillips.

The relative decrease in corporate giving ratios has occurred even as corporations got richer. Some experts claim corporate giving follows the stock market, but data from Giving USA actually show corporate donations increasing minimally while stock market value has soared higher over recent decades. How do we explain the fact that the richer companies get, the less they give?

This is not to diminish the great work that many affluent people and community-minded corporations are doing every day. They are the heroes in our struggle for justice, caring, and helping. I just wish there would be more.

Per capita income and the stock market have both increased significantly in the United States over many decades. But the level of giving has been stagnant at about 2% of disposable income, and corporate giving has not increased even as stock values and profits have increased (Figure 2.3).

➡ *Conclusion: It is not lack of money that prevents giving from increasing dramatically. There is lots of money, and the better off people get, there's so much more they could do to make a better world. Simple!*

Hypothesis 2: The needs are already being met

I sometimes hear people say that all the needs are already being met by current programs, and that government actually spends too much. The hypothesis that needs are being met can be discarded quite quickly just by looking at the commitment and challenge in the United Nations' Sustainable Development Goals,[10] which were adopted unanimously by world leaders in September 2015.

The Sustainable Development Goals

1 No poverty
2 Zero hunger
3 Good health and wellbeing
4 Quality education
5 Gender equality

6 Clean water and sanitation
7 Affordable and clean energy
8 Decent work and economic growth
9 Industry, innovation, and infrastructure
10 Reduced inequalities
11 Sustainable cities and communities
12 Responsible consumption and production
13 Climate action
14 Life below water
15 Life on land
16 Peace, justice, and strong institutions
17 Partnerships for the goals

Key point: That the nations of the world have all joined together to set these goals reflects their recognition of the huge needs yet to be met and an opportunity for everyone to step up.

Natural disasters (hurricanes, tornadoes, typhoons, earthquakes, tsunamis, rising sea levels, floods, fires, droughts, and famines) along with man-made disasters (regional wars, civil conflicts, gang wars, terrorism, mass shootings, and family violence) are producing *vast unmet needs*. Progress on the Sustainable Development Goals has certainly taken a hit from the COVID-19 pandemic and the Russian invasion of Ukraine with impacts on so many issues around the world. The needs are great! And these needs are *not* being met (Figure 2.4)!

➤ *The conclusion here is clear: The hypothesis that there is not enough need in the world to justify substantially increased donations is simply not viable.*

Figure 2.4 Graphic of the Sustainable Development Goals. Source UNorg.

Hypothesis 3: Tax benefits don't provide enough incentive for donations

A third hypothesis is that tax benefits are insufficient to provide adequate incentive for charitable donations.

The Historical Highest Marginal Income Tax Rates[11] tell a very important story about giving in America. The rates for the most affluent have been 37% in 2018–2022, 50% in 1982–1986, 70% in 1971–1980, and 91% in 1954–1963. The trend has been clear for 60 years, which means that the most affluent Americans have benefitted from increasingly favorable tax rates over six decades. In 1952–1953, the rate was 92%!

At higher income levels, moreover, there are numerous ways to reduce reported income, which are not available to lower and middle income taxpayers. If all actual income levels were included in the giving data, in all likelihood, the giving ratios would plunge dramatically as income rises. Currently, wealthy American citizens can write off major deductions for investment costs, carried interest, hidden bank accounts, unreported income, expense accounts, depreciation, special trusts, and a host of other tax benefits, which most of us don't even know about.

According to their essay in the *New York Review of Books* titled "The Undermining of American Charity," Lewis B. Cullman and Ray Madoff state that the tax benefit for mega-donors in the United States is huge. "For someone taxed in the highest bracket (39.6%), a $100 donation produces almost $40 in tax savings … [and] a gift of $100 of property can save the taxpayer close to $60 in combined income and capital gains taxes. … The ability to get this enhanced charitable deduction for donations of complex assets [e.g., commercial and residential real estate, art, private business interests, and even mineral rights, yachts, and taxidermy collections] is particularly valuable for taxpayers who have invested in hedge funds and other business interests that are not publicly traded … if a donor invested $100,000 in a hedge fund, and it grew to be worth $2 million, the donor would get … a $2 million deduction if it were given to a DAF [donor-advised fund]."[12] (Cullman gave away over 90% of his wealth to charitable causes. Madoff is a professor of law at Boston College and the director of a think tank on philanthropy at Boston College Law School.)

Taxes here actually pose a greater burden on lower income segments of the population. "The Institute on Taxation and Economic Policy found that the lowest-earning fifth paid 11.4% of their income in state and local taxes. These include sales, property, and income tax. Most of the highest-earning fifth paid from 8% to 8.9%, and the highest-earning 1% paid only 7.4% of their income."[13]

Over the past seven decades, tax legislation have been of increasing benefit to wealthy taxpayers. It has also been well documented over the past years and decades that there is growing inequity of income and capital with the rich (top 10%, top 1%) getting richer and the superrich (top 0.1%) getting far richer and far faster than ever before. New tax legislation approved in August 2022 will improve this but not significantly.

Of course, the tax burden on people in the middle and lower income categories could be reduced through more progressive (fair) tax policies, as many economists and commissions have advocated for decades. The landmark Filer Commission,[14] for example, included these recommendations in 1975: "That all taxpayers who take the standard deduction should also be permitted to deduct charitable contributions as an additional, itemized deduction." and "That families with incomes below $15,000 a year be allowed to deduct twice the amount of their giving, and those with incomes between $15,000 and $30,000 be allowed to deduct 150 per cent of what they contribute" (20–21). I believe there is strong and growing public support for this.

This brief review and the preceding chapter show that tax benefits of charitable donations are significantly more beneficial to people with higher incomes and more assets. Certainly, there are not enough tax benefits for the vast number of people in the United States and maybe other countries, and NGOs should be seriously lobbying about this. But that's a topic for another book.

➡️ *The conclusion is clear: the hypothesis that there are not sufficient tax benefits for donations for those most able to give to justify substantially increased donations is not viable.*

➡️ *However, increased tax benefits for donations for the majority of taxpayers are certainly needed and would provide needed incentives for most taxpayers to increase donations.*

About Paying Taxes[15]

- **Plato**: "When there is an income tax, the just man will pay more and the unjust less on the same amount of income" (90).
- **Arthur Vanderbilt**: "Taxes are the lifeblood of government and no taxpayer should be permitted to escape the payment of his just share of the burden of contributing thereto" (15).
- **Franklin Roosevelt**: "Taxation according to income is the most effective instrument yet devised to obtain just contribution from those best able to bear it and to avoid placing onerous burdens upon the mass of our people" (41).
- **Warren Buffett**: "I think that people at the high end – people like myself – should be paying a lot more in taxes. We have it better than we've ever had it" (121).
- **Ken Phillips:** "Paying taxes is a responsibility of those who have benefitted so much from the enabling culture, laws, infrastructure, and freedom."

Hypothesis 4: Charity and generosity have decreased these days – People just don't care

Much of the history of generosity was built on the major religions of the world, which value charity and generally indicate a tithing of 10% for charity. My first book, *Make a Better World*, includes a chapter on the historic tradition of fundraising in religious teachings. My second book, *Strategic Planning and Culture for Nonprofits*, emphasizes the importance of having strong values for organizational success. My third book, *25 Proven Strategies for Fundraising Success*, develops these ideas further and indicates that successful fundraising by religious and even secular organizations is often based on traditional religious concepts of charity, morality, and compassion along with the obligation to help others who are less fortunate.

In the 1960s, the conflict between capitalism and communism was on everyone's mind. I was then a student leader in AIESEC at Princeton University and, later, at the University of Michigan, and then as the elected national president of AIESEC-US, an international youth organization dedicated to peace and international understanding. I was meeting frequently with corporate executives (Bank of New York, Ford, General Motors, Mobil Oil, New Jersey Power, Olivetti, Richardson-Merrell, Time Life, etc.), deans of business schools, and government officials about world issues, seeking their personal and financial support. I found them *genuinely* interested in promoting international understanding and national development and seeking to demonstrate that capitalism was *not* the evil portrayed in communist writings. It is now clear to me that the threat from communism as an alternate system to capitalism acted as a powerful pressure on corporate, business school, and government leaders to behave in a way to prove that capitalism and democracy were, in fact, more beneficial to people. I look back on the 1960s as a decade of progress to make the world better in civil rights, disability rights, economic progress, and anti-poverty programs and the end of colonialism and spread of democracy in the world. What happened?

The Upswing[16] by Robert D. Putnam and Shaylyn Romney Garrett presents an "I-we-I" curve operating in American history. The "I" represents those times when people are selfish and the "we" is about those times of high social cooperation when people care about others and want to help those less fortunate and do something about discrimination and economic inequality. The best "we" time, they argue, was in the mid-20th century (1940s to 1970s), but it has been increasingly "I" since then.

The most recent three or four decades have been marked by stagnation in incomes for most families, loss of well-paying blue-collar work, increase in the gig economy with limited benefits, rising inequity, anger at what is happening, hate-based social media, and a divisive political environment. And now, as I write this, the COVID-19 pandemic and work from home, new pressures on families, closings of public places, and discontent with traditional work conditions are changing how people want to work and, I believe, how they see their place in society with an increased focus on self rather than on relationships with others.

Usually, donations in response to disasters rise dramatically, even phenomenally, and the COVID-19 pandemic was the greatest disaster in the United States since the Great Depression or the Civil War. "The Giving USA report says donations in 2021 were 4% higher than the record-setting $466 billion contributed in 2020. But they were down 0.7% when adjusted for inflation."[17] What is going on?

External pressures have certainly led more people to focus on the "I". However, there are significant movements in segments of the population that are more about the "We". Even though issues like racism, violence, and abuse are pervasive, they are now receiving more attention. More people are caring.

The recent examples people of color being brutalized by police, and killed by them, are so far beyond justified behavior that much of society is crying out for reform. Public opinion is clear that such abuse and violence must stop!

The September 2021 testimony by Simone Biles, McKayla Maroney, Maggie Nichols, and Aly Raisman at a U.S. Senate hearing about the sexual abuse they suffered in their gymnastics training and how the FBI ignored and then lied about their earlier statements was extraordinary. I was in tears about what these young women said and so angry that they were not heard and the abuse continued."[18] Being abused is a crisis, and being discounted by the FBI is unforgiveable. Viewers were outraged because they cared!

Overwhelmingly, I know that people are caring individuals who have dreams for things to be better. Instinctively, people want to help others. Long ago, I learned in my marketing for Save the Children and Foster Parents Plan that you have to bring the human element to the attention of the potential donor. People respond to need when they see it and feel it. Television brought the unforgivable abuse of young gymnasts and the willful murder of African-Americans into the homes of the American people and there was outrage and caring by millions. The murder of school children, most recently in Uvalde, Texas, which was the 27th such school shooting in the United States in 2022 was yet another horrific example of human tragedy.[19] The public was moved, and finally the politicians responded with new gun legislation. Good but not enough!

In a recent *Boston Globe* article, Robert Putnam adds his voice for moderation as he writes about abortion and gun control: "The polling also shows that Americans' views, far from becoming more extreme, have become more moderate. In fact, this trend toward moderation is even more marked among younger Americans."[20]

A college student I am mentoring recently told me that the younger generation is now seeking to have a meaningful impact in what they do. From her perspective, involving young people in solving big issues is the big opportunity. I agree.

When I was presenting a lecture on leadership and planning to students in Chisinau, Moldova, for example, I asked how many of them wanted to go into business. About two-thirds of the students responded, but most of them emphasized it should be small businesses where "We can have an impact." One-third responded that they wanted to work for NGOs where they felt their impact would be greater. We are, I believe, entering a new era of caring and helping, comparable to the 1960s, because we are hearing so much more about things that need to be changed. And we also learned from the COVID-19 pandemic to appreciate dedicated health workers and essential workers.

What charities and fundraising are all about is *other* people and *other situations*. Charity is helping others and is a core tenet or belief of the world's great religions. Fundraising is showing people how they can help others. At Save the Children, the charity appeal that worked best was not an abstract situation but the individual situation of another human being. "You can help save Maria Lopez or you can turn the page" was a highly successful fundraising appeal we placed in national magazines, because it focused on one representative individual, *Maria*, who needed help and one person, *you*, who could help. Another successful appeal we used was, "You can help save a child for the price of a cup of coffee every day." Both of these ads brought another part of the world right to the reader's attention in a very personal and appealing way. People respond when they see the humanity of a person in need.

Today, those who do not give or who give little may be too busy or too unaware or too lonely or too angry. But compassion and caring and the will to help others are *an inherent and innate part of being human*, sometimes just below the surface; these qualities only need to be nurtured and developed to reawaken. It works when you focus on the problem and the solution, the humanity involved, and the opportunity and responsibility to get things done. When people know this, feel connected, and understand how they can help, their charity and generosity will rise to the surface. Fundraisers for nonprofits can help people understand and benefit from ths reality.

In a January 23, 2022, article in the *New York Times* about shared sacrifice, Max Fisher wrote: "Since our origin as a species, societies have functioned on an implicit pact: each of us is better off if we all contribute to the common good, even if it means giving some things up … . In the nomadic tribes where our communal instincts evolved over hundreds of thousands of years, this was a matter of life and death. Without trust and cooperation, the group would perish."[21]

Here is an example of how people's compassion, caring, and the will to help others are ready to awaken. Just a few decades ago, Americans overwhelmingly opposed gay relationships, but when they learned that a good friend or close relative was gay, they came to see that the relationships were about love, and the people they knew and loved just wanted to be happy with the person they loved. With this growing awareness, acceptance of civil unions and then gay marriage soon followed.

Much research has confirmed that helping others is important for the helpers, too. Two examples

- Douglas Heingartner shared that "A new meta-analysis in the journal *Psychological Bulletin* shows that helping others also improves *your own* health and happiness. It adds to the growing scientific literature showing that helping others also helps yourself, in more ways than you might expect" in a review titled "Helping others also helps yourself: these new studies explain why. Helping others also improves your own physical and mental health. We explain why that is, and show you how easy it is to get started!"[22]

- In its self-help site, Acts of Kindness explained "People who care for others' well-being through acts of altruism, volunteering, or formation of communal relationships seem to be happier and less depressed. This seems to be especially true in older individuals."[23]

However, other research is troubling. Two examples:

- Zurich Insurance Group reported to the World Economic Forum in 2019 that the "Decline in Human Empathy Creates Global Risks in the 'Age of Anger.' Our interconnected world has never had more lonely, angry people." The report continued: "As today's economy grows more interconnected, a new global phenomenon has emerged: the growing number of people who feel disconnected and isolated ... . The result of this blurring has been an increase in loneliness, rising polarization and a corresponding decline in empathy."[24]
- Judith Hall and Mark Leary reported in Scientific American in September 2020 that "The U.S. Has an Empathy Deficit." The article elaborated: "America is a country in deep pain. The coronavirus pandemic, racial injustice, economic insecurity, political polarization, misinformation and general daily uncertainty dominate our lives to the point that many people are barely able to cope. And life wasn't exactly a cakewalk before 2020. Out of all the fears, stresses and indignities our citizens are living with, there emerges a kind of primal insecurity that undermines every aspect of life right now. It's no wonder that anxiety, depression and other psychological problems are on the rise."[25]

The *Scientific America* article added: "On top of that, everyone is confronted with people who seem indifferent." And "Remind yourself that almost everyone is at the end of their rope these days."

I welcome these last two statements as *a clear challenge to NGOs* to find ways to communicate to current and prospective donors that caring and helping other people and the planet are proven ways to move forward, to cope better, and, in fact, to be helped by helping and caring for others. These are human acts of compassion that will cure or ameliorate the 'deep pain' so many feel, for both donors and beneficiaries.

Let's give people (and corporations) the credit that lack of compassion, caring, and the will to help others is not the real factor in their low levels of giving, but that the real reasons are their lack of exposure, lack of awareness, lack of feeling connected, lack of trust, and lack of information about what they can do to make a better world – and how they will benefit from living in that better world – with greater satisfaction for themselves from doing the right things and doing them well. This will improve social harmony and facilitate progress for the benefit of everyone. It is only together that we will get through these hard times. Love breeds love.

Finally, I want to assert that we can all be social entrepreneurs and fundraisers! As an employee or volunteer in your workplace or school, the neighborhood where you live, the community where you meet, and even with your own family, you can help people see how they can help others. The challenge is to bring the reality of life for others who are in need into the consciousness of those who can help, so people see the vital role they can play and actually make dreams come true. It is truly awesome when people help and care for others. They will be happier for it (Figure 2.5).

> ➡ *The hypothesis that there is not enough charity or generosity in the world is not true. They are there, and these qualities just need to be awakened.*

> ➡ *It is an opportunity for caring and helping organizations to respond and help people as donors and volunteers to help others and feel better for doing that.*

Love, teamwork, and partnership are important to me

Figure 2.5 Images of love, teamwork, and friendship. Artwork by Sawyer Phillips (center) and Wills Phillips (left and right).

Hypothesis 5: Nonprofits don't have enough trust, impact, or non-fundraising communication

In many cultures, people do not trust their governments, people they don't know, or (not surprisingly) charities that are always asking for money. In spite of generally good performance by NGOs around the world, there have been failures in charity ethics and results that taint the whole sector. One of the most frequent complaints about charities is that "they are always asking for more money."

NGOs need to look internally to understand that three factors – lack of trustworthiness, lack of demonstrated impact, and lack of communication that does not ask for money – are really the most significant causes for lack of donor response.

Worse, as noted previously, scandal in the charity sector taints the entire sector. Examples of scandals exist in all countries. Here are just a few from the United States:

- The chief of the New York State Attorney General's Charities Bureau reported in 2015 that fraud and embezzlement are often done by "trusted" people within an organization. Related-party transactions are fraught with conflicts of interest. Audits by unrelated parties are needed to review internal controls and financial reporting. Strong and clear standards to prevent conflicts of interest are necessary. Charities need strong internal systems of checks and balances, a culture of accountability, and a regular flow of new board members. A whistleblowing process is a best practice to prevent as well as uncover bad practices.[26]
- A 2016 article in the *New York Times* reported many cases of embezzlement by insiders in the 14,000 youth sports organizations in the United States, which have 30 million participants and revenues of $9 billion. The article's author, Bill Pennington, wrote: "Yet watchdogs of the nonprofit industry note that youth sports organizations rarely put in place routine checks and balances, such as having multiple people in charge of the money, opening the door to fraud."[27]
- The November 23, 2021, *New York Times* article "She Ran a Bronx Homeless Shelter. Here's What She Spent Millions On." by Andy Newman describes extensive mismanagement and outright larceny by Ethel Denise Perry, executive director of Millennium Care, a nonprofit 100-room homeless shelter in New York City. She failed to file required financial reports and had no board of directors.[28]
- CharityWatch, an American charity watchdog, created what it calls its Hall of Shame Members: Father Bruce Ritter (Covenant House); William Aramony (United Way of America);

John Bennett, Jr. (Foundation for New Era Philanthropy); Lorraine Hale (Hale House); Roger Chapin (Help Hospitalized Veterans and Coalition to Salute America's Heroes); Larry Jones (Feed the Children); John Donald Cody (United States Navy Veterans Association); Greg Mortenson (Central Asia Institute); the Wingo Family (Angel Food Ministries); Somaly Mam (Somaly Mam Foundation); James Reynolds, Sr. (Cancer Fund of America); Zvi Shor (National Children's Leukemia Foundation); Kim Williams (Healing Arts Initiative); Brian Mullaney (WonderWork); and Lola Jean Amorin (The Arc in Hawaii)."[29]

- As reported by *The Chronicle of Philanthropy*, a 2016 British Parliament report warns charities to get their own regulations and enforcement in order or face new government regulations. The report was a response to scandals about high-pressure fundraising tactics and inadequate oversight by charity boards concerning solicitations.[30]

Trust is a fragile commodity, and whenever there is a charity scandal, trust in NGOs in general is damaged. The questions I hear often are about charity scandals or mismanagement, ineffectiveness or lack of results, and inefficiency or excessive overhead costs. Sometimes these are valid concerns, but often these remarks are cynical and off the mark, maybe just excuses for not donating. The behavior, performance, and accountability by charities need to be above reproach. Unfortunately, the occasional news coverage of bad examples is long remembered. Cynicism and skepticism created by scandals become easy reasons for rejecting charity appeals.

➡ *We may not want to remember these and other scandals but the public certainly does remember.*

What I have seen in the NGO sector over the decades leads me to the following conclusion: Scandals will occur but they should always be used to provide insight into preventive action to ensure against future bad behavior and scandals. When I was at Save the Children, for example, we faced a scandal about the advertising messages used by our organization and five other national NGOs. Rather than fight the allegations, I arranged to meet with representatives of the other organizations and, working together, we created a new code of advertising ethics, which all six organizations promptly adopted. The subsequent and positive news coverage immediately changed to respect for what we did! This was learning and improving.

Repeatedly over recent decades, surveys of public opinion in the United States have included mixed reviews for charities. Of course, charities and regulation agencies need to assure that top salaries are appropriate, overhead is not excessive, fundraising is honest, governance is good, and all the other things that the best charities do all the time. There will be no increase in the level of giving until more people believe that charities are, at their core, trustworthy and achieving long-term impact.

As an example of the problem of trust, I was talking with a small group of wealthy visitors at a museum in Mexico. As soon as I mentioned that I worked for NGOs, their very first comments were about how the president of a particular international NGO was "overpaid." I was stunned, because everyone there was very wealthy and their focus was on how much the CEO of a major NGO was paid (far less, I'm sure, than any of them). Nothing was said about the needs of children around the world and the good work of the organization.

Polls over the years reach the same conclusion. In a 1993 Gallup opinion poll of the American public, 81% of the respondents were very or somewhat concerned about how charities spend their money, 67% felt charities did not provide enough information, and 74% felt charities needed more mandatory regulations.[31]

A survey conducted in 2001 by the Better Business Bureau Wise Giving Alliance when I was a member of their Standards Review confirmed "What donors want to know" with ratings of "very important" as follows: "How much of the charity's spending goes toward charitable programs as opposed to fundraising or administrative costs > 79%, Whether the charity makes an annual report on their activities and finance available to the public > 75%, Whether the charity's advertising and promotion clearly and specifically describe who they are and what they do > 73%, and How successful the charity's programs have been in achieving their purpose or mission > 70%."[32] Although most charities now provide an annual report, the concerns about efficient spending, comprehensive information, and program impact remain as relevant concerns in the 2020s.

A 2015 issue of *The Chronicle of Philanthropy* opinion poll conducted by Princeton Survey Research Associates, for example, reported some good news for charities but with a heavy dose of concerns. Suzanne Perry reported that "Almost two-thirds of Americans have a great deal or a fair amount of confidence in charities."[33] This sounded like good news until I read the detailed finding that only "Fifteen percent of those surveyed said they had a 'great deal' of confidence in charitable organizations over all." The two-thirds figure includes the other respondents who had only "a fair amount" of confidence in charities …, "And 35% said they had little or no confidence in charities." Wow! That is troubling!

Is 15% of people with a great deal of confidence good news? According to Paul Light, a professor of public service at New York University and organizer of the research, "If charitable organizations become identified as just another set of mediocre organizations – a mediocre destination for taxes, funding, and cash – you've got a big problem."

Because charitable giving is about money, I was particularly disturbed to read in this same research that 13% (I add – *only* 13%) said charities do a "very good" job "in spending money wisely." This suggests a serious problem of trust if you are thinking about money. The other noteworthy finding was: "When asked about factors that influence their giving decisions, 68% of those who responded to the *Chronicle* poll said it was very important that a charity have evidence its programs are effective—the highest score of all factors listed."

The conclusion is clear that the public believes there are serious problems in the nonprofit sector. When collective trust has been violated, it is very difficult to restore. Nonprofits should know that once a person feels betrayed in their charitable behavior, the betrayal is not easily forgiven. After such a failure, every nonprofit faces a steep path to demonstrate its ethical behavior. The leadership of nonprofits should be focused on avoiding such calamities. In interpreting conclusions about donor attitudes, I believe it is wise to be skeptical of what may well be overly positive findings as they can lead to complacency about meeting the real concerns and simply deciding more fundraising appeals are the answer.

> *The takeaway from this research is the continuing importance for donors of trust and impact. This has been a wakeup call for all too long! And it continues.*

The Independent Sector, the membership organization of nonprofits, foundations, and corporate giving programs, reported in its *Trust in Civil Society – 2021 Key Findings*[34] that:

- "Institutional trust is declining – and nonprofits and philanthropy are not immune to this trend."
- "Sizable majorities say trust is a necessary factor for them to support nonprofit organizations."
- "While trust in the sector is declining overall, the good news is that those who are familiar with nonprofits and philanthropy are more likely to trust them."
- "Statistical modeling shows the top factors contributing to people's trust lie in individual nonprofits' ability to demonstrate purpose and integrity."

The Independent Sector's 2022 *Trust in Civil Society: Understanding the factors driving trust in nonprofits and philanthropy* expands on the previous year's report, leading with the important statement that "Public trust is the currency of the nonprofit sector."[35] The report continues:

- "Integrity and Purpose remain critical to building and maintaining trust. Consistent with past waves, integrity and purpose contribute most to trust for both nonprofits and philanthropy. Distrusters in both sectors point to perceived mismanagement of funds and instances of corruption and scandals. Neutral trusters say financial transparency and proof of impact is necessary for them to see an organization as trustworthy. Public figure endorsements, communicating clear organizational mission and values, and demonstrating results remain the top drivers of trust for nonprofits and philanthropy."
- "Roughly 6 in 10 Americans report donating to a nonprofit at least once in the past year and more than half have advocated for a cause." But does this include the token handout to a homeless person on the street?
- "Many Americans believe giving directly to causes or individuals makes a bigger impact than giving through a nonprofit organization." But is this a rationalization not to donate to established organizations?
- "Trust is a necessary condition for public engagement with nonprofit organizations."

   ◦ "81% agree: I need to know a great deal about an organization before I choose to support it."
   ◦ "78% agree: Nonprofits must earn my trust before I support them."

- "Trusters in nonprofits and philanthropy focus on humanitarianism and past achievements, while distrusters point to greed, past scandals, and perceived self-serving motives."
- "Neutral trusters want to see financial transparency and a proven record of results before they trust nonprofit and philanthropic organizations."
- "Familiarity is a key factor predicting trust in nonprofits and philanthropy. Those familiar with nonprofits and philanthropy were 39 points and 36 points, respectively, more likely to trust each sector compared to those unfamiliar."
- "Frequent Constituent Engagement May Breed Trust. While trust in the sector is steady or slightly declining, the good news is that those who are familiar with nonprofits and philanthropy are more likely to trust them. People with high trust in nonprofits report personal experience and strong ties to nonprofits."

These findings by the Independent Sector provide so much evidence that nonprofits must attend to their evident failings to earn trust for their integrity (ethics), respect for their results (impact), and better understanding (communications). These are not new issues as they have been identified and reported over many past decades, as documented in this and the previous chapter.

Key point: Questionable ethics, unproven results, and communications that only ask for money are major reasons for the low support for charities.

When I was leading a taskforce to get a large group of American NGOs to adopt a strong code of ethics, I conducted a confidential survey of all 140 executive directors asking where our sector of NGOs was vulnerable to criticism and where their own NGO was vulnerable. The results: virtually every executive believed that others in the group were quite vulnerable but that their own NGO was not vulnerable at all. They gave themselves high ratings but the other executives did not. This was an eye-opener for everyone and led to the realization that as a group they had to take meaningful steps to achieve a better reputation. My conclusion for all NGOs then and now: Wake up to reality! We are responsible!

In 1970, the cartoonist Walt Kelly created the Pogo poster for the first Earth Day with the caption "We Have Met the Enemy and He Is Us."[36] Pogo was a wildly popular cartoon figure in those days and his message then was that we should look in the mirror and see that we are the ones responsible for pollution. Now, I submit it refers to the failure in the NGO community to remedy the public concerns about trust and impact.

Personally, I know from 60 years of experience that charity performance is not as bad as the polls suggest. I know performance is highly commendable given all the obstacles. Nevertheless, nonprofits need to look at themselves both individually and collectively to make changes to become more trusted and more respected. The public perception of bad behavior and poor results becomes a reality and barrier that every nonprofit can – and should – work to overcome!

The real questions for NGOs are:

- What are your donors' hopes and dreams for people and the planet?
- How do you help those in need and how can you prove lasting impact?
- How can your organization be more accountable to gain the public trust?

NGOs often think they are in competition with each other for funds. Yes, that's true, but NGOs are *really* in competition with all other and much larger uses of money – dinners at fancy restaurants, expensive clothes, second homes, exclusive vacations, private clubs, personal airplanes, huge yachts, and more investments. When overall giving is just 2% of disposable income, this is an indicator of failure by the charitable sector to earn trust and to demonstrate its worth to those who could give much more at all levels of income.

Certainly, governments are often corrupt, but we still have to pay our taxes. Corporations can put profits before people and planet, but we still buy their products and services. The finance industry may cause recessions, but people still put money in banks and stocks. FIFA was corrupt, but fans still go to football (soccer) games. On the other hand, when people get appeals for support, they don't *have* to make donations. This is the critical difference. Charities *have* to earn the trust of donors and *have* to prove they are effective, because they are asking for money to help someone else, so the tangible benefits are for the beneficiaries of the programs – not for the donors who rely on promises.

The reported increase in giving directly, rather than through established nonprofits, may be seen by some as a threat to those established nonprofits, but I see it as a challenge and therefore an opportunity for nonprofits to step up their game in three specific ways: 1) Take the needed actions to achieve trustworthy behavior, significant program impact, and informative communications, 2) Encourage your constituents to be more personally involved through more visiting, volunteering, promoting, and advocating, and not just asking for money, and 3) Accept your responsibility to help improve the image of NGOs in general and especially for the specific sector of your activities.

What's it take? Leadership. In my first book, I quoted Harvard Professor Rosabeth Moss Kanter who wrote "Persistence is the number one success factor for leadership." Then I added "YOU have complete control over the level of your persistence."[37] (Figure 2.6)

➡ *While the first four hypotheses in this chapter above are not true (not enough money, needs are being met, inadequate tax benefits for those most able to donate, lack of caring), it is clear that this last hypothesis is true: Nonprofits don't have enough trust, demonstrated impact, or informative communication that doesn't plea for money.*

➡ *The good news is, you can change that! Throughout this book, you will learn more about developing and communicating trust and impact, so your nonprofit can flourish as a trusted organization, have better impact, raise more support, and make a better world.*

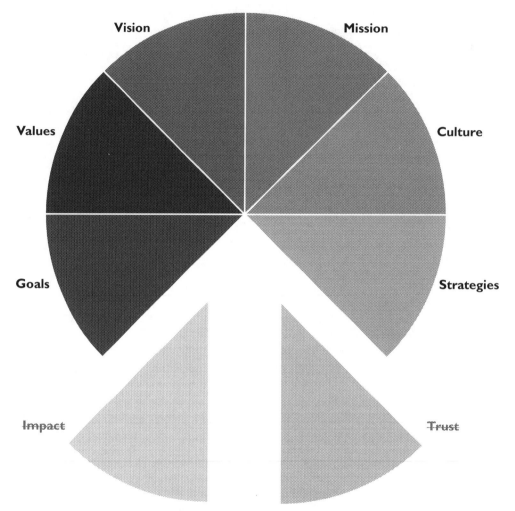

Poor trust and poor impact sabotage your vision, mission, values, goals, and strategies.

Figure 2.6 Elements of strategic planning with trust and impact missing. Image by the author.

Questions for implementation

1   What do your public opinion polls and donor surveys reveal about your trustworthiness?

2   How do you respond in your work and communication to each of the hypotheses above?

3   How do you enable donor dreams to come true?

4   How do you demonstrate trust and accountability on your website?

Notes

1 "United States Per Capita Personal Income, 1959-2021 Current vs. Constant Dollars," March 2022, 3.
2 Mike Price, "Average Stock Market Return," *The Motley Fool*, February 1, 2022, accessed June 25, 2022, https://www.fool.com/investing/how-to-invest/stocks/average-stock-market-return/.
3 "What is Giving USA?," accessed June 25, 2022, https://givingusa.org/about/.
4 Suzanne Perry, "The Stubborn 2% Giving Rate," *The Chronicle of Philanthropy*, June 17, 2013, accessed June 26, 2022, https://www.philanthropy.com/article/the-stubborn-2-giving-rate/.
5 Commission on Private Philanthropy and Public Needs, "Giving in America—Toward a Stronger Voluntary Sector," 1975, 9, 15, accessed June 26, 2022, https://archives.iupui.edu/bitstream/handle/2450/889/giving.pdf.
6 "Philanthropy in the American Economy—A report by the Council of Economic Advisers," accessed June 26, 2022, https://clintonwhitehouse4.archives.gov/media/pdf/philanthropy.pdf.
7 Melissa Stanger, "9 Billionaires Who Plan to Give Away the Majority of Their Fortunes," *Insider*, October 15, 2015, accessed June 26, 2022, https://www.businessinsider.com/billionaires-giving-away-their-money-2015-10.
8 Chuck Collins and Helen Flannery, "REPORT: Gilded Giving 2020: How Wealth Inequality Distorts Philanthropy and Imperils Democracy," *Inequality.org*, July 28, 2020, accessed June 26, 2022, https://inequality.org/great-divide/gilded-giving-2020/.
9 "What is Giving USA?."
10 "What are the Sustainable Development Goals?," accessed June 26, 2022, https://www.undp.org/sustainable-development-goals.
11 "Historical Highest Marginal Income Tax Rates 1913–2022," accessed June 26, 2022, https://www.taxpolicycenter.org/statistics/historical-highest-marginal-income-tax-rates.
12 Lewis Cullman, "New York Review of Books: "The Undermining of American Charity"," June 22, 2016, accessed June 26, 2022, https://www.prnewswire.com/news-releases/new-york-review-of-books-the-undermining-of-american-charity-300288196.html.
13 Kimberly Amadeo, "Regressive Tax With Examples—How Regressive Taxes Increase Your Costs," *The Balance*, May 17, 2022, accessed June 26, 2022, https://www.thebalance.com/regressive-tax-definition-history-effective-rate-4155620.
14 Commission on Private Philanthropy and Public Needs, "Giving in America—Toward a Stronger Voluntary Sector." 20–21.
15 Geoffrey James, "130 Inspirational Quotes About Taxes," *Inc.*, April 13, 2016, accessed July 2, 2022, https://www.inc.com/geoffrey-james/130-inspirational-quotes-about-taxes.html.
16 Robert D. Putnam and Shaylyn Romney Garrett, *The Upswing: How Americans Came Together a Century Ago and How We Can Do It Again.* (Simon & Schuster, 2020).
17 Thalia Beaty and Glenn Gamboa, "US Charitable Giving Hit Record in 2021 But Inflation Looms," *CHRON*, June 21, 2022, accessed June 27, 2022, https://www.chron.com/news/article/US-charitable-giving-hit-record-in-2021-but-17254938.php.
18 Juliet Macur, "Biles and Her Teammates Rip the F.B.I. for Botching Nassar Abuse Case," *The New York Times*, September 15, 2021, accessed June 27, 2022, https://www.nytimes.com/2021/09/15/sports/olympics/fbi-hearing-larry-nassar-biles-maroney.html.
19 Jaclyn Diaz, "27 School Shootings Have Taken Place So Far This Year," *NPR*, May 25, 2022, accessed June 27, 2022, https://www.npr.org/2022/05/24/1101050970/2022-school-shootings-so-far.
20 Robert D. Putnam, "On abortion and gun control, it's the politicians who are polarized," The Boston Globe, July 6, 2022, accessed July 7, 2022. https://www.bostonglobe.com/2022/07/06/opinion/abortion-gun-control-its-politicians-who-are-polarized/
21 Max Fisher, "Why Boris Johnson May Finally Have Gone Too Far," *The New York Times*, January 22, 2022, accessed June 27, 2022, https://www.nytimes.com/2022/01/22/world/europe/coronavirus-boris-johnson-novak-djokovic-hypocrisy.html.
22 Douglas Heingartner, "Helping Others Also Helps Yourself: These New Studies Explain Why," *Psych News Daily*, May 27, 2021, accessed June 27, 2022, https://www.psychnewsdaily.com/new-study-shows-that-helping-others-also-helps-yourself/.
23 "Acts of Kindness," *Pursuit of Happiness*, accessed July 2, 2022, https://www.pursuit-of-happiness.org/science-of-happiness/caring/.
24 "Decline in Human Empathy Creates Global Risks in the 'Age of Anger'," *Zurich*, April 8, 2019, accessed July 2, 2022, https://www.zurich.com/en/knowledge/topics/global-risks/decline-human-empathy-creates-global-risks-age-of-anger.

25 Judith Hall, "The U. S Has an Empathy Deficit," *Scientific American*, September 17, 2020, accessed July 2, 2022, https://www.scientificamerican.com/article/the-us-has-an-empathy-deficit/.

26 Frank G. Runyeon, "Attorney General's Charity Chief: Fraud Is "Surprisingly Common"," *New York Nonprofit Media*, August 6, 2015, accessed June 27, 2022, https://www.nynmedia.com/news/attorney-general-s-charity-chief-fraud-is-surprisingly-common.

27 Bill Pennington, "The Trusted Grown-Ups Who Steal Millions From Youth Sports," *The New York Times*, July 7, 2016, accessed June 27, 2022, https://www.nytimes.com/2016/07/10/sports/youth-sports-embezzlement-by-adults.html.

28 Andy Newman, "She Ran a Bronx Homeless Shelter. Here's What She Spent Millions On.," *The New York Times*, November 23, 2021, accessed June 27, 2022, https://www.nytimes.com/2021/11/23/nyregion/ethel-denise-perry-millennium-care-fraud.html.

29 "CharityWatch Hall of Shame: The Personalities Behind Charity Scandals," *CharityWatch*, August 24, 2018, accessed June 27, 2022, https://www.charitywatch.org/charity-donating-articles/charitywatch-hall-of-shame.

30 "Parliament Members Warn British Charities This Is 'Last Chance' to Self-Regulate," *The Chronicle of Philanthropy*, January 25, 2016, accessed June 27, 2022, https://www.philanthropy.com/article/parliament-members-warn-british-charities-this-is-last-chance-to-self-regulate/.

31 George Gallup Jr., ed., *The 1993 Gallup Poll: Public Opinion* (Rowman & Littlefield, 1994).

32 Princeton Survey Research Associates, *BBB Wise Giving Alliance Donor Expectations Survey*, Washington, 2001.

33 Suzanne Perry, "Poll Rates Public Confidence in Charities, Their Programs, and Spending," *The Chronicle of Philanthropy*, October 5, 2015, accessed June 27, 2022, https://www.philanthropy.com/article/poll-rates-public-confidence-in-charities-their-programs-and-spending/.

34 Independent Sector, "Trust in Civil Society—Understanding the Factors Driving Trust in Nonprofits and Philanthropy," July 2021, accessed June 27, 2022, https://independentsector.org/wp-content/uploads/2021/08/trust-report-2021-8421.pdf.

35 Independent Sector, "Trust in Civil Society—Understanding the Factors Driving Trust in Nonprofits and Philanthropy," May 2022, 4, 6, 9, 11, 12, 16, 17, 19, 31, accessed June 27, 2022, https://independentsector.org/trust.

36 ""We Have Met the Enemy and He Is Us [*Pogo* comic illustrations by Walt Kelly]"," *Tales from the Vault—40 Years / 40 Stories*, 2017, accessed June 27, 2022, https://library.osu.edu/site/40stories/2020/01/05/we-have-met-the-enemy/.

37 Ken Phillips, *Make a Better World: A practical guide to leadership for fundraising success* (NGO Futures LLC, 2020), 214.

Bibliography

1 Amadeo, Kimberly. "Regressive Tax With Examples—How Regressive Taxes In- crease Your Costs." *The Balance*, May 17, 2022. Accessed June 26, 2022. https://www.thebalance.com/regressive-tax-definition-history-effective-rate-4155620.

2 Beaty, Thalia, and Glenn Gamboa. "US Charitable Giving Hit Record in 2021 But Inflation Looms." *CHRON*, June 21, 2022. Accessed June 27, 2022. https://www.chron.com/news/article/US-charitable-giving-hit-record-in-2021-but-17254938.php.

3 "CharityWatch Hall of Shame: The Personalities Behind Charity Scandals." *CharityWatch*, August 24, 2018. Accessed June 27, 2022. https://www.charitywatch.org/charity-donating-articles/charitywatch-hall-of-shame.

4 Collins, Chuck, and Helen Flannery. "REPORT: Gilded Giving 2020: How Wealth Inequality Distorts Philanthropy and Imperils Democracy." *Inequality.org*, July 28, 2020. Accessed June 26, 2022. https://inequality.org/great-divide/gilded-giving-2020/.

5 Commission on Private Philanthropy and Public Needs. "Giving in America—Toward a Stronger Voluntary Sector," 1975. Also known as the Filer Commission. Accessed June 26, 2022. https://archives.iupui.edu/bitstream/handle/2450/889/giving.pdf.

6 Cullman, Lewis. "New York Review of Books: "The Undermining of American Charity"," June 22, 2016. Accessed June 26, 2022. https://www.prnewswire.com/news-releases/new-york-review-of-books-the-undermining-of-american-charity-300288196.html.

7 Diaz, Jaclyn. "27 School Shootings Have Taken Place So Far This Year." *NPR*, May 25, 2022. Accessed June 27, 2022. https://www.npr.org/2022/05/24/1101050970/2022-school-shootings-so-far.

8 Fisher, Max. "Why Boris Johnson May Finally Have Gone Too Far." *The New York Times*, January 22, 2022. Accessed June 27, 2022. https://www.nytimes.com/2022/01/22/world/europe/coronavirus-boris-johnson-novak-djokovic-hypocrisy.html.

9 Gallup, George Jr., ed. *The 1993 Gallup Poll: Public Opinion*. Rowman & Littlefield, 1994.

10 Hall, Judith. "The U. S Has an Empathy Deficit." *Scientific American*, September 17, 2020. Accessed July 2, 2022. https://www.scientificamerican.com/article/the-us-has-an-empathy-deficit/.

11 Heingartner, Douglas. "Helping Others Also Helps Yourself: These New Studies Explain Why." *Psych News Daily*, May 27, 2021. Accessed June 27, 2022. https://www.psychnewsdaily.com/new-study-shows-that-helping-others-also-helps-yourself/.

12 "Historical Highest Marginal Income Tax Rates 1913 –2022." Accessed June 26, 2022. https://www.taxpolicycenter.org/statistics/historical-highest-marginal-income-tax-rates.

13 Independent Sector. "Trust in Civil Society—Understanding the Factors Driving Trust in Non- profits and Philanthropy," July 2021. Accessed June 27, 2022. https://independentsector.org/wp-content/uploads/2021/08/trust-report-2021–8421.pdf.

14 Independent Sector. "Trust in Civil Society—Understanding the Factors Driving Trust in Non- profits and Philanthropy," May 2022. Accessed June 27, 2022. https://independentsector.org/trust.

15 James, Geoffrey. "130 Inspirational Quotes About Taxes." *Inc.*, April 13, 2016. Accessed July 2, 2022. https://www.inc.com/geoffrey-james/130-inspirational-quotes-about-taxes.html.

16 Kelly, Walt. ""We Have Met the Enemy and He Is Us [*Pogo* comic illustrations by Walt Kelly]"." *Tales from the Vault—40 Years / 40 Stories*, 2017. Accessed June 27, 2022. https://library.osu.edu/site/40stories/2020/01/05/we-have-met-the-enemy/.

17 Macur, Juliet. "Biles and Her Teammates Rip the F.B.I. for Botching Nassar Abuse Case." *The New York Times*, September 15, 2021. Accessed June 27, 2022. https://www.nytimes.com/2021/09/15/sports/olympics/fbi-hearing-larry-nassar-biles-maroney.html.

18 Newman, Andy. "She Ran a Bronx Homeless Shelter. Here's What She Spent Millions On." *The New York Times*, November 23, 2021. Accessed June 27, 2022. https://www.nytimes.com/2021/11/23/nyregion/ethel-denise-perry-millennium-care-fraud.html.

19 Pennington, Bill. "The Trusted Grown-Ups Who Steal Millions From Youth Sports." *The New York Times*, July 7, 2016. Accessed June 27, 2022. https://www.nytimes.com/2016/07/10/sports/youth-sports-embezzlement-by-adults.html.

20 Perry, Suzanne. "Poll Rates Public Confidence in Charities, Their Programs, and Spending." *The Chronicle of Philanthropy*, October 5, 2015. Accessed June 27, 2022. https://www.philanthropy.com/article/poll-rates-public-confidence-in-charities-their-programs-and-spending/.

21 Perry, Suzanne. "The Stubborn 2% Giving Rate." *The Chronicle of Philanthropy*, June 17, 2013. Accessed June 26, 2022. https://www.philanthropy.com/article/the-stubborn-2-giving-rate/.

22 "Philanthropy in the American Economy—A report by the Council of Economic Advisers." Accessed June 26, 2022. https://clintonwhitehouse4.archives.gov/media/pdf/philanthropy.pdf.

23 Phillips, Ken. *Make a Better World: A practical guide to leadership for fundraising success*. NGO Futures LLC, 2020.

24 Price, Mike. "Average Stock Market Return." *The Motley Fool*, February 1, 2022. Accessed June 25, 2022. https://www.fool.com/investing/how-to-invest/stocks/average-stock-market-return/.

25 Princeton Survey Research Associates. *BBB Wise Giving Alliance Donor Expectations Survey*. Washington, 2001.

26 "Acts of Kindness." *Pursuit of Happiness*. Accessed July 2, 2022. https://www.pursuit-of-happiness.org/science-of-happiness/caring/.

27 Putnam, Robert D., and Shaylyn Romney Garrett. *The Upswing: How Americans Came Together a Century Ago and How We Can Do It Again*. Simon & Schuster, 2020.

28 Putnam, Robert D. "On abortion and gun control, it's the politicians who are polarized." *The Boston Globe*, July 6, 2022. Accessed July 7, 2022. https://www.bostonglobe.com/2022/07/06/opinion/abortion-gun-control-its-politicians-who-are-polarized/.

29 Runyeon, Frank G. "Attorney General's Charity Chief: Fraud Is "Surprisingly Common"." *New York Nonprofit Media*, August 6, 2015. Accessed June 27, 2022. https://www.nynmedia.com/news/attorney-general-s-charity-chief-fraud-is-surprisingly-common.

30 Stanger, Melissa. "9 Billionaires Who Plan to Give Away the Majority of Their Fortunes." *Insider*, October 15, 2015. Accessed June 26, 2022. https://www.businessinsider.com/billionaires-giving-away-their-money-2015-10.

31 "Parliament Members Warn British Charities This Is 'Last Chance' to Self- Regulate." *The Chronicle of Philanthropy*, January 25, 2016. Accessed June 27, 2022. https://www.philanthropy.com/article/parliament-members-warn-british-charities-this-is-last-chance-to-self-regulate/.

32 "United States Per Capita Personal Income, 1959-2021 Current vs. Constant Dollars," March 2022.

33 "What Are the Sustainable Development Goals?" Accessed June 26, 2022. https://www.undp.org/sustainable-development-goals.

34 "What is Giving USA?" Accessed June 25, 2022. https://givingusa.org/about/.

35 "Decline in Human Empathy Creates Global Risks in the 'Age of Anger'." *Zurich*, April 8, 2019. Accessed July 2, 2022. https://www.zurich.com/en/knowledge/topics/global-risks/decline-human-empathy-creates-global-risks-age-of-anger.

Chapter 3

Decrease in public trust in NGOs and the importance of speaking up

Individual donors account for three-fourths of all donations to U.S. nonprofits. Consequently, gaining trust and confidence from individuals is essential for NGOs to run their projects. I am pleased to include here the excellent research findings and analysis by my research assistant Haru Nishigaki. Her research provided much of the basis for this chapter starting with findings from the 2020–2022 Edelman Trust Barometers and four mechanisms to gain trust. Her conclusion about non-fundraising communication is especially important.

Key point: To be trusted, your code of ethics must be *meaningful*, not just words or intentions. Essential components are to create and define your core values and ethical principles in a code of ethics and then establish and implement the requisite monitoring, assessing, enforcing, and sanctioning to give the code meaning and credibility. When this is communicated, it shows donors that your nonprofit can be trusted for its good behavior.

The bad news: The 2021 Edelman Trust Barometer report shows declining trust in NGOs in many countries and lower levels of trust especially in richer ones. Refer to the bar chart: "Trust in NGOs decreases in 11 of 27 countries."[1] Note that the 2022 Edelman Trust Barometer report finds that trust in NGOs grew globally in the past year but declined in six of the twelve larger developed countries including the United States, where trust fell 5% points to 45. These twelve richer countries have trust levels between 40 and 58, while trust levels in less affluent countries range from 59 to 78 (on a scale of 0 to 100), not including Russia at 28%[2] (Figure 3.1).

This is a critical problem for nonprofits, because they need the trust and voluntary support from the public that business and government do not need. NGOs ask for donations from one group (individuals, foundations, companies, and partners) to help others (program beneficiaries or participants). This business model is fundamental to how every NGO works, and it requires a great deal of trust and confidence on the part of donors.[3]

A very disturbing finding in the 2022 Edelman Trust Barometer report is that people are "More convinced we're being lied to by societal leaders" with approximately two-thirds of respondents saying that journalists and reporters, government leaders, and business leaders are "purposely trying to mislead people by saying things they know are false or gross exaggerations."[4]

A spokesperson for Edelman said trust in institutions is based on two things: *competence* to get the job done, and even more important by far is *ethics*, the desire and ability to do the right thing. This conclusion parallels the recent Better Business Bureau Wise Giving 2021[5] survey finding that trust and impact are the two largest concerns of potential donors.

The 2020 Edelman Trust Barometer Spring Update multi-country surveys also find that most people believe NGOs are *not* getting things done and are *not* doing well. In a chart titled Urgent Call for NGOs to Get Things Done, the same report shows most respondents claim that NGOs have not performed well – that only "38% say NGOs are doing well on taking care of people

DOI: 10.4324/9781003335207-5

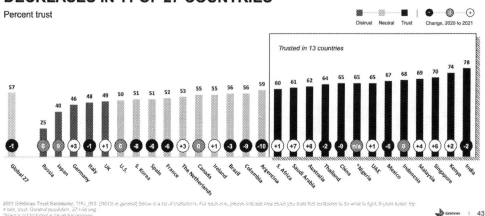

Figure 3.1 Trust in NGOs decreases in 11 of 27 countries. Bar chart from the 2021 Edelman Trust Barometer.

who are suffering," 41% on "raising money for pandemic relief efforts," and 43% on "co-ordinating local relief efforts." Refer to the "Urgent call for NGOs to get things done" image[6] (Figure 3.2).

Clearly, when NGOs are failing to earn sufficient trust and respect, they must work harder to gain trust and confidence. This book specifically addresses that "urgent call" for NGOs to get things done and do them well – Part I is on meaningful ethics for trustworthiness, and Part II addresses strategic evaluation for effectiveness and impact.

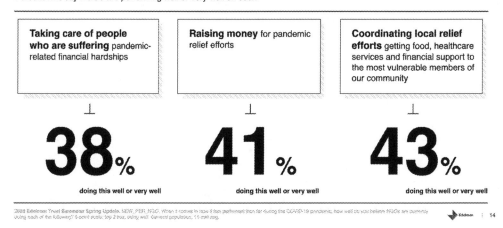

Figure 3.2 Urgent call for NGOs to get things done. Image from the 2020 Edelman Trust Barometer Spring Update.

Some good news ...

The 2022 Edelman Trust Barometer report finds that "NGOs and business must act as stabilizing forces" compared to media and government, because the current "Cycle of distrust threatens societal stability" and "Government [is] not seen as able to solve societal problems." Compared to government and media, only business and NGOs are seen by a majority to have a strength as institutions to "Take a leadership role – Coordinate cross-institutional efforts to solve society problems" and to "Get results – Successfully execute plans and strategies that yield results."

Another positive finding for NGOs is that they are seen as both the most unifying and least dividing force in society. Also significant is that both "Business and NGOs are seen as competent and effective drivers of positive change" with NGOs receiving the highest score for effectiveness, vision, and fairness.[7]

As shown in the "NGOs and business must act as stabilizing forces" chart, the 2022 Edelman Trust Barometer data find that both NGOs and business are the only institutions seen as both competent and ethical. NGOs receive the highest ethical rating and a positive competence rating, while business is seen as more competent but less ethical than NGOs. Government is seen as far less ethical and far less competent than both NGOs and business (Figure 3.3).

It is significant that NGOs are perceived to be so much more competent and so much more ethical than government. This is why NGOs should take advantage of their non-governmental status and their vision, mission, and values for a better world to step up to secure increased government grants. Performing better than government when it comes to helping people was one of the critical strategies I put forth in my book, *25 Proven Strategies for Fundraising Success*.[8]

However, being perceived as more ethical than business and government is *not* a high bar and, as demonstrated earlier in this book, this is not enough to be well trusted. Trust has to be earned.

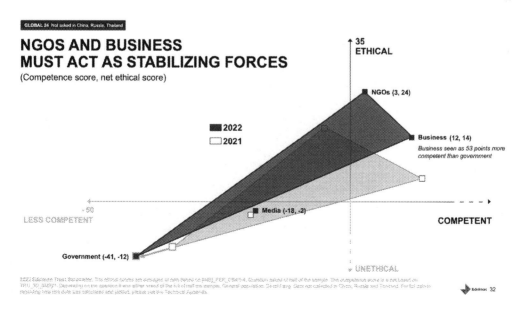

Figure 3.3 NGOs and business must act as stabilizing forces. Chart from the 2022 Edelman Trust Barometer.

The 2022 Edelman Trust Barometer confirms that "Information quality [is] now most powerful trust builder across institutions" and "Restoring trust is key to societal stability." The report elaborates with important conclusions that reflect much of what this book advocates:

- "Demonstrate tangible progress – Restore belief in society's ability to build a better future: show the system works."
- "Leadership must focus on long-term thinking – Solutions over divisiveness; long-term thinking over short-term thinking."
- "Every institution must provide trustworthy information – Clear, consistent, fact-based information is critical to breaking the cycle of distrust."

The 2021 Edelman Trust Barometer Spring Update: A World in Trauma concluded that "Institutions [are] failing to address existential challenges. Institutions are not doing well on … their pandemic response [and] their climate change solutions."[9] An even more challenging statement is in the 2022 Edelman Trust Barometer that "NGOs and business [are] pressured to take on societal problems beyond their abilities."[10] What does this all mean? NGOs have to step up, they have to get better and they have to earn public trust for their ethics and public respect for their impact. The public expects more.

Trust is essential. My own experience in managing fundraising is that when there is a disaster, the media provides intense coverage with heart-rending stories about individuals that make people aware and ready to respond – and they turn to *trusted* nonprofits. Then the fundraising (for trusted organizations) is very successful, because people understand the need and want to respond to help. The relationship between communication and response became clear during the COVID-19 pandemic. With non-stop media coverage, everyone became aware of essential workers, dedicated medical staff, vulnerable seniors, and underserved communities, and a common theme was "we can get through this together." Contributions to help people affected increased in 2020–2021.

Earn trust through six qualities

Based on repeated research findings over recent decades on the trust level in NGOs, it is apparent NGOs as a group need to work harder to gain trust from the public. How can an NGO show donors that it adheres to the high level of ethical standards to be worthy of donations of money and time?

According to "The Essential Importance of Trust: How to Build It or Restore It," an article in *Forbes*: "Trust is hard to define, but we do know when it's lost. When that happens, we withdraw our energy and level of engagement."[11] The article then poses Six Building Blocks of Trust:

1   Reliability and Dependability
2   Transparency
3   Competency
4   Sincerity, Authenticity and Congruency
5   Fairness
6   Openness and Vulnerability

"On the positive side, trust makes people feel eager to be part of a relationship or group, with a shared purpose and a willingness to depend on each other." However, in the article's concluding paragraph, we read that "The dynamics of trust are delicate in important relationships, and the loss of trust can be costly – not only psychologically, but also financially and in terms or work and livelihood. What's helpful to remember is that trust is an ongoing exchange between people and is not static. Trust can be earned. It can be lost. And it can be regained."

It is clear from everything I read and hear that most NGOs must communicate better with the general public and their donors to demonstrate their organization is reliable, transparent, competent, authentic, fair, and open, which I translate in nonprofit termi- nology to be transparent and trustworthy, competent and achieving impact, consistent and reliable, honest and not overpromising, and actively communicating. At the conclusion of her work with me, my research colleague Haru Nishigaki gave her first conclusion that "Transparency plays a most critical role in gaining trust from the public for NGOs. The transparency must include informing the public about the core values and ethical principles the organization follows."

When Nishigaki contacted six big international NGOs, sadly, she was unable to get clear and prompt responses from most of them. This suggests that when potential donors reach out to NGOs, they may not receive understandable, transparent, and complete responses. When there is insufficient public information about how a nonprofit assesses and enforces adherence to its code of ethics – and the sanctions if someone fails to comply – potential donors will not know that they can trust the organization. Thus, NGOs need to be more accountable to demonstrate that they are an organization with meaningful ethics, and they can be trusted. A potential donor who does not receive a prompt and satisfactory response may well become a permanent skeptic and non-donor. The old saying "once bitten, twice shy" applies here. When I was leading Foster Parents Plan, we established a twenty-four-hour standard with accountable responses for every donor communication, and I understand this standard has been strengthened to even a faster time now.

A new mandate for nonprofits: Send communications that do not ask for money

According to the 2015 Edelman Trust Barometer[12] "survey respondents found concern that NGOs were too focused on money, losing touch with the public, using public funding poorly, corrupt, or incompetent." Ed Williams, chief executive of Edelman U.K. and Ireland said at the launch of the public relations firm's 15th annual trust survey: "There's a feeling that NGOs are now acting too much like business. They're too focused on fundraising and the money."

If the public believes nonprofits focus too much on communicating about money, maybe they are right. At least 95% of the appeals I receive focus on asking for money, some even looking like a bill or indicating how much more I should give. One recent appeal from a very large public organization contained an introduction about program information, then the rest of that page and the entire second page focused on fundraising. Then I recalled that this nonprofit had sent me an acknowledgement and thank you letter for my last $500 contribution but not before a full six months after I sent the gift!

I cannot recall receiving many communications about a charity's information, education, advocacy, or results without an appeal for money. The one exception for me is a neighborhood association in Providence, Rhode Island, which distributes frequent newsletters about what is happening in the community and only one annual appeal.[13]

Nishigaki's second key conclusion based on her research is that NGOs need to *demonstrate* they can be trusted, because the organization is transparent, competent, reliable, honest, and actively communicating – and not give potential and current donors the experience of always being asked for money. Non-fundraising communication is essential.

I saw an excellent version of this approach when I consulted with Medicines for Malaria. The organization had a comprehensive communications program about malaria, advocacy, research, and progress. The executive director always insisted to "under-promise and over-deliver" by never exaggerating in the organization's communications. They did great work and received high trust and high respect. He oversaw the growth of their income from $5 million to $20 million in the three years we worked together and then to $65 million a few years later, adhering to the six qualities stated above.

When I worked at Foster Parents Plan, we developed excellent and involving educational materials. The first educational program was called, "See me. Share my world." This was designed to give children in American classrooms engaging information about children in other, less affluent countries. The initiator of that program, Jaya Sarkar, then developed a program called Buffalo Banks & Borewells about overseas development. A series of eight newsletters, each talking about a project in detail, went to a test group of donors. It informed them about the complex but important process of development in less developed countries. There were no fundraising appeals.

In its smart approach, the project also had a control group of similar donors who did not receive the educational materials. The donors who received the educational, non-fundraising communications developed a much better understanding of the program and responded with higher giving levels and higher retention rates than those in the control group. The project continued after the grant for several years and led the organization to continue to provide similar information about the complexity of international development in ongoing communications. The educational program enhanced fundraising through communications using the four mechanisms (transparent, under-promise, consistent, competent). It demonstrated that non-fundraising, educational materials are important in their own right and also have positive influence on fundraising results.

When surveys show that a majority of individuals believe NGOs are too money focused, it means that NGOs are failing to communicate and inform them sufficiently about the full story of what they do and are just asking too many times for more money. To gain trust and respect, NGOs must make certain their key publics know about *all they do*: their ethics and accountability, the needs they are addressing, the strategies for programs they use, the results they achieve, the multiplier effect from volunteers, what they achieve through advocacy, the supporting work through information and education, and how they maintain their independence and support civil society development (not just asking for money). A quarterly newsletter, reports from the various directors, photos and reports from the field, advocacy engagement, media interviews, and other public relations activities are all important. These could be great projects for volunteers from local schools and universities. With social media, these don't have to be expensive activities, and information, education, and advocacy can be effective program support activities.

My takeaway from Nishigaki's research is that nonprofit leaders really must dedicate themselves to a lot more work in public communications to get people to trust and respect them. A relevant finding in the 2022 Edelman Trust Barometer is that "Distrust is the default" for a majority in 24 countries with 59% of respondents reporting "My tendency is to distrust until I see evidence that something is trustworthy" versus "My tendency is to trust until I see evidence that something is untrustworthy."

Especially noteworthy is a statement by Richard Edelman for the Davos Agenda that "It's possible to break the cycle of distrust and rebuild public trust through factual information and demonstrable progress."

Key point: To gain trust, an NGO must be: 1) transparent and trustworthy, 2) competent and achieving impact, 3) consistent and reliable, 4) honest and not overpromising, and 5) actively communicating and not always fundraising.

The Giving Environment: New Models to Engage Donors: Survey Research on US Donor Participation[14] in 2022 by the Indiana University Lilly Family School of Philanthropy reinforces everything you have read thus far. The report advocates "offering subscription-based giving opportunities to donors and prospects" with "curated content and ongoing multi-channel engagement" (5). Those of us familiar with the sponsorship model of fundraising with monthly contributions and regular personal feedback from sponsored children or communities know the power of regular giving commitments and personalized feedback. NGOs like Save the Children and Plan International have been using this effective model for many decades.

"The U.S. nonprofit sector currently averages a 44% donor retention rate. Imagine the impact on nonprofit organizations, their missions, and the sector, if nonprofits increased their average retention rate from 44% to that of the for-profit Subscription as a Service 'SaaS'-based averages of 70% … ." The report continues: "The problem is that nonprofits generally tend to treat recurring donors the same as one-time donors and overlook the fact that these donors are truly invested in the future of the organization" (5).

These are really smart marketing approaches and excellent advice, and they need to be based on the more fundamental trust and impact factors as well as the communications factor. The report recognizes this with key findings about trust, content, and purpose. This is a natural lead into the first challenge for NGOs in this chapter.

CHALLENGE #1: NGOs must communicate more about all they do for beneficiaries and for society (not just fundraising)

The five steps presented in the key point can build on the Six Key Attributes for NGOs I presented in my first book, *Make a Better World*. These attributes include: promoting its vision for a better world, educating key publics about what it does, advocating for action related to its vision, providing services to implement its mission, maintaining its independence of action, and being a voluntary non-governmental organization.[15]

An NGO's non-fundraising communication can elaborate on each of these six key attributes through:

1   Programs, services, strategies, and evaluation used to achieve impact
2   Public relations and media promotion of their vision for a better world
3   Educational materials and programs they provide about their cause
4   Advocacy they do with government, business, and others for the cause
5   Independence in the vision, mission, values, and culture and the board of directors
6   Activities in civil society as a private, voluntary, non-governmental organization

NGOs need to step up to these new responsibilities to communicate and inform donors and the public about solutions, impact, and accountability (do not just ask for money). When current and potential donors see your nonprofit working in these ways, they will have more respect for all you do. Such communication informs and educates about your cause, improves your connections with potential donors, and enhances your separate fundraising appeals. I call them *comprehensive accountability communications or reporting* about ethics, impact, and other organization activities.

If donors just keep getting more fundraising appeals without the other communications, they can easily say, "This is just a fundraising organization." Your activities and results in services, information, education, advocacy, and accountability for a better world and the benefits of your independent voice and private, non-governmental status are great things to talk about in media interviews, conference presentations, newsletters, blogs, and other public relations materials:

- How your board of directors adds value to your work
- How you manage to help your beneficiaries and partners
- How you know your work is effective with lasting impact
- How you benefit from your independent and voluntary status
- How you promote and support the development of civil society
- How you demonstrate responsibility, transparency, and accountability
- How you advocate for governments and corporations to adopt better practices
- How you work to be efficient and keep costs to a minimum and still be effective
- How you inform and educate the public, young people, and educational institutions

To have trust in your organization, the public needs to know more about your vision for a better world, the work you do, the results you get, and how you behave.

Here's the proof communications help

The 2021 Edelman Trust Barometer finds a big difference in responses for rating trust (an average of the percent trust in NGOs, media, government, and business referred to as a Trust Index) between the more informed public (index of 62% who trust) and the mass population (index of 44% who trust) – a Trust Gap of 18% points. What makes the more informed public more trusting than the mass population? Based on my years in marketing, I believe that 18 point gap is persuasive support for more communication about what you do and how you do it, about your information, education, and advocacy activities, and about your ethics, impact, and accountability.

When I was vice president of fundraising at Save the Children, we focused on awareness and understanding and, according to Gallup polls, significantly increased both in my time there, with awareness rising from about 15% to 75%. Not surprisingly, donor support also increased as a result.

At Foster Parents Plan, we conducted regular donor satisfaction and feedback surveys, provided a quarterly newsletter, engaged in extensive TV and print media information and education, supported volunteers around the country to do local promotion, and involved our donors in advocacy with the U.S. government to support international development. These strategies helped us triple income from $10 million to $30 million in only ten years! More involvement in more activities strengthens your donor relationship with your organization.

Key point: Unimpeachable ethical behavior is imperative, but it's not enough to gain trust. People need to be reassured regularly through communications that don't ask for more money but are about all the organization is doing to make a better world.

The first of my Iron Rules of Fundraising is that "Fundraising is not about money. It's about who you are, what you do, and why I should trust you."[16]

If current donors and potential donors don't know what results your nonprofit is achieving as a direct result of their donations, they are highly unlikely to continue donating or begin to donate. It is amazing to me that nonprofits so often fail to provide first-class customer service and responsiveness and substantive and heartwarming reports on their results (results that are measurable and tangible with lasting impact). It is basic management to know what your supporters want from you – regular donor satisfaction surveys give you the answer and treating every donor as unique and special gives you success. Results are always one of the top two expectations, but you need to know much more about what your donors expect.

Stan Rapp, who was head of our advertising agency where I was working, actively involved in our advertising, and later my mentor and friend, taught me how to treat a large number of donors as unique individuals by learning more about them and placing them in a segment of people with very similar interests and expectations. His book *MaxiMarketing* (co-written by Thomas L. Collins), shows how to get into "a one-to-one relationship with the consumer"[17] (30) and, as he told us in our planning sessions, how to create "segments of one" of similar donors. It works!

Communication from the charity back to the donor is so important – it completes the feedback cycle, so the donor can know the donation was worthwhile. This means NGOs need to be close to their donors – they must know them, listen to them, and communicate well with them. I often say to my clients (NGO leaders including fundraisers) that donors give because of the value they receive from the nonprofit they support. This may sound odd, but it's true. If donors do not receive value from their support, why would they continue to give?

It's helpful to keep in mind the challenging business model of every nonprofit: An NGO must request money from one group (donors) in order to support another group (program participants or beneficiaries). This is why it's so important for donors to receive value from their support, so they will continue giving.

Who defines the value that donors want? The challenge for you is to find what each donor wants in the relationship and then to provide it (as long as what the donor wants is within your values and mission). Fundraisers should ask: "What are your expectations and how can we work together to make your dreams come true?" This is a profound message, really awesome, for donors to hear. It is for them to say how they get value from their relationship with the organization. The best fundraisers are skilled at finding answers to these questions through regular feedback from and involvement with their donors. Again, at Foster Parents Plan, we gave high priority to providing real value to donors by finding out what they valued individually, placing them in a segment with other donors who had the same expectations, and then providing them the feedback in a way that was satisfying and not too costly. This communication strategy was built into our strategic and operational plans, a component of every staff member's work and evaluation, and a part of our organizational culture. We called it commitment to customer service.

Key point: Nonprofits need to raise their focus and ability to understand what their donors consider value and then provide it.

CHALLENGE #2: Nonprofit leaders must step up and speak out as authorities on the needs in society, the many roles of NGOs, and progress toward important goals

Next, nonprofit leaders – including staff directors and board members – need to upgrade their personal credibility and increase activity as spokespersons for those they serve and for their organization's varied activities. This is not about fundraising; it is about all you do and your authority in what you do; it's about your role in society. The public needs to know more about the needs you see and the solutions you implement, the innovations you have achieved, the information and education through the media, how you are strengthening your board and how they help, and so much more about your competence and your desire to do the right things efficiently and effectively.

The encouraging finding in the 2021 Edelman Trust Barometer is that people care more! The COVID-19 pandemic brought to everyone's attention the plight of others and, as a result, people believe the following issues are more important for the country to address than last year: Improving healthcare (70%), addressing poverty (62%), improving the education system (62%), addressing climate change (61%), combatting fake news (60%), protecting individual freedoms (59%), closing the economic and social gaps (58%), and addressing discrimination and racism (53%). They are ready to hear more from you.

However, the situation changed partway through the pandemic. A headline from an Edelman IP press release reads: "2021 Edelman Trust Barometer Reveals a Rampant Infodemic is Fueling

Widespread Mistrust of Societal Leaders." The significance of declining trust in societal institutions including NGOs is that gaining trust is even more important now than before the COVID-19 pandemic struck. The press release continues: "With a growing Trust Gap and trust declines worldwide, people are looking for leadership and solutions as they reject talking heads who they deem not credible. In fact, none of the societal leaders we track – government leaders, CEOs, journalists, and even religious leaders – are trusted to do what is right, with drops in trust scores for all."[18]

The challenge to NGO leaders is significant as highlighted in this statement from the Edelman.com website that: "the 2021 Edelman Trust Barometer reveals an epidemic of misinformation and widespread mistrust of societal institutions and leaders around the world. Adding to this is a failing **trust ecosystem** unable to confront the rampant infodemic, leaving the four institutions—business, government, NGOs and media—in an environment of information bankruptcy and a mandate to rebuild trust and chart a new path forward."[19]

Unfortunately, as you can see in the "Spokespeople lose credibility" bar chart, the 2021 Edelman Trust Barometer data show that when forming an opinion of a company, respondents rated NGO spokespeople below academic experts, company technical experts, people like yourself, and CEOs (Figure 3.4).

Nonprofit leaders must step up to new responsibilities to gain more credibility based on their solutions, impact, and accountability (not just asking for money). As "a person like yourself," volunteers have high credibility and can also step up as NGO spokespeople. Some NGOs have developed extensive local and even national volunteer networks to support their activities through public awareness, local events, and even word of mouth.

Today, there is also a resounding need for nonprofits to do more. NGO spokespersons, both staff and volunteers, should always be communicating about so much more about what they are doing to tackle the issues raised to new awareness about poverty, discrimination, and racism; violence against women and people of color; rising income inequity, education, and healthcare; climate change; threats to democracy and freedom; and, of course, your own specific solutions, accountability, and lasting impact.

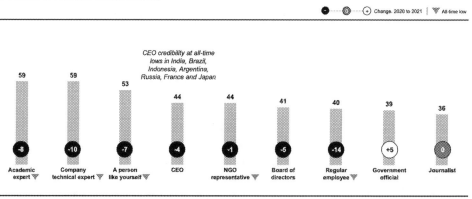

Figure 3.4 Spokespeople Lose Credibility. Bar chart from the 2021 Edelman Trust Barometer.

The public needs to know about your organization's vision for a better world, your work to inform and educate people about the cause you support, and your advocacy for action by government, business, and the public to support that cause – as well as the specific, immediate results and long-term impact you achieve along with the accountability you provide.

CHALLENGE #3: Corporate CEOs should step up and speak out as business leaders and advocates for NGOs about the importance of civil society

Today, there are growing demands for new responsibilities for corporate leaders. The Business Council and some economists and corporate leaders are saying corporate responsibilities must now include a higher level of care for employees, communities, customers, and the public at large as well as earnings for stockholders. This flows from extensive criticisms of the model of capitalism that only focuses on stock value and high CEO salaries and bonuses (Figure 3.5).

For the good of society, I believe corporate leaders have new responsibilities to speak up. As seen in the "CEOs must lead on societal issues" image, a significant number of respondents in the 2021 Edelman Trust Barometer want CEOs to lead and speak out on important societal challenges. Many corporate CEOs are board members, major donors, and leading volunteers for charities. These leaders should step up to new responsibilities to inform and motivate the public about the value of nonprofits in civil society and what their companies are doing to contribute to the communities where they work, care for their employees and customers, support the wellbeing of society and our planet, and protect equality, freedom, and democracy (all important factors to assure business success).

The 2022 Edelman Trust Barometer further reinforces this expectation with most respondents saying: "CEOs should be personally visible when discussing public policy with external stakeholders or work their company has done to benefit society" and they "Want more, not less, business engagement on societal issues" of climate change, economic inequality, workforce reskilling, access to healthcare, trustworthy information, and systemic injustice.

CEOS MUST LEAD ON SOCIETAL ISSUES

I expect **CEOs to publicly speak out** about one or more of these societal challenges

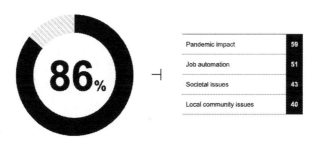

Figure 3.5 CEOs must lead on societal issues. Image from the 2021 Edelman Trust Barometer.

Most nonprofits have highly engaged and committed business members on their boards of directors and advisory committees – nonprofit leaders should be encouraging these business leaders to speak up for civil society in their capacity as board members to:

1   Embrace the expanded mandate for CEOs to lead on societal issues
2   Lead with facts and highlight the results of your own NGO
3   Promote the important roles of nonprofits
4   Encourage other CEOs to find partners in the NGO world
5   Share that business is more than profits; it's people and planet

Trust is precarious

Trust flows from competence and ethics, and communication is the only way for people to know about your organization's competence and ethics.

To review, this chapter put forth three critical challenges for nonprofits:

- CHALLENGE #1: NGOs must communicate more about all they do for beneficiaries and for society, not just about fundraising.
- CHALLENGE #2: NGO leaders must step up and speak out as authorities on the needs in society, the many roles of NGOs, and progress toward important goals.
- CHALLENGE #3: Corporate CEOs should step up and speak out as business leaders and advocates for NGOs about the importance of civil society (Figure 3.6).

Questions for implementation

1   How much do you communicate with your donors when not asking for money?
2   What problems have you actually seen in your nonprofit in management ethics, program effectiveness, finance efficiency, fundraising accountability, or governance policy?
3   What actions will you take to address the problems you have identified?

Please share your answers to these questions with the author at www.NGOFutures.com. Include your name, email, position, and organization, which will be kept confidential. (Figure 3.7).

Activities for Trust and Respect

- NGOs must take steps to demonstrate they are ethical and can be trusted (not just nice claims without backup)
- NGOs must take steps to demonstrate they really get results in their programs (not just nice examples and photos)
- NGOs must communicate more about their accountability and all they do for beneficiaries and for society (not just fundraising)

Figure 3.6 The three essential activities for trust and respect are ethical behavior, program impact, and accountable communications. Infographic by the author.

"I'm thinking about new steps to make our code of ethics more meaningful."

"And let's improve our communications about all we are doing."

Figure 3.7 People working to plan their ethics standards and communications to donors. Artwork by Sawyer Phillips.

Notes

1 "2021 Edelman Trust Barometer," accessed July 2, 2022, https://www.edelman.com/trust/2021-trust-barometer.
2 "2022 Edelman Trust Barometer," accessed July 2, 2022, https://www.edelman.com/trust/2022-trust-barometer.
3 See the discussion of the NGO business model in the Introduction.
4 "2022 Edelman Trust Barometer report."
5 Princeton Survey Research Associates, *BBB Wise Giving Alliance Donor Expectations Survey*, Washington, 2001.
6 "2020 Edelman Trust Barometer Spring Update: Trust and the Coronavirus," May 20, 2020, accessed July 2, 2022, https://www.edelman.com/research/trust-2020-spring-update.
7 "2022 Edelman Trust Barometer report."
8 Ken Phillips, *25 Proven Strategies for Fundraising Success: How to win the love and support of donors* (NGO Futures LLC, 2021), 133–137.
9 "2021 Edelman Trust Barometer Spring Update."
10 "2022 Edelman Trust Barometer report."
11 Dennis Jaffe, "The Essential Importance Of Trust: How To Build It Or Restore It," *Forbes*, December 5, 2016, accessed June 25, 2022, https://www.forbes.com/sites/dennisjaffe/2018/12/05/the-essential-importance-of-trust-how-to-build-it-or-restore-it/?sh=53e82cb64fe5.
12 "2015 Edelman Trust Barometer," accessed July 2, 2022, https://www.edelman.com/trust/2015-trust-barometer.
13 *West Broadway Neighborhood Association*, accessed July 2, 2022, https://www.wbna.org.

14 *The Giving Environment: New Models to Engage Donors: Survey Research on US Donor Participation*, Indiana University Lilly Family School of Philanthropy (January 2022), 5, accessed July 7, 2022, https:// scholarworks.iupui.edu/bitstream/handle/1805/27564/NewModels2022.pdf

15 Ken Phillips, *Make a Better World: A practical guide to leadership for fundraising success* (NGO Futures LLC, 2020), 129–131.

16 Ibid., 159–161.

17 Stan Rapp and Tom Collins, *Maxi-Marketing: The New Direction in Advertising, Promotion, and Marketing Strategy* (Plume, 1989), 30 *inter alia.*

18 "2021 Edelman Trust Barometer Reveals a Rampant Infodemic is Fueling Widespread Mis-trust of Societal Leaders," January 13, 2021, accessed July 2, 2022, https://www.edelman.com/trust/2021-trust-barometer/press-release.

19 2021 Edelman Trust Barometer," accessed July 2, 2022, https://www.edelman.com.

Bibliography

1 "2015 Edelman Trust Barometer." Accessed July 2, 2022. https://www.edelman.com/trust/2015-trust-barometer.

2 "2020 Edelman Trust Barometer Spring Update: Trust and the Coronavirus," May 20, 2020. Accessed July 2, 2022. https://www.edelman.com/research/trust-2020-spring-update.

3 "2021 Edelman Trust Barometer." Accessed July 2, 2022. https://www.edelman.com/trust/2021-trust-barometer.

4 "2021 Edelman Trust Barometer Reveals a Rampant Infodemic is Fueling Widespread Mistrust of Societal Leaders," January 13, 2021. Accessed July 2, 2022. https://www.edelman.com/trust/2021-trust-barometer/press-release.

5 "2022 Edelman Trust Barometer." Accessed July 2, 2022. https://www.edelman.com/trust/2022-trust-barometer.

6 *Edelman.* Accessed July 2, 2022. https://www.edelman.com.

7 Jaffe, Dennis. "The Essential Importance Of Trust: How To Build It Or Restore It." *Forbes*, December 5, 2016. Accessed June 25, 2022. https://www.forbes.com/sites/dennisjaffe/2018/12/05/the-essential-importance-of-trust-how-to-build-it-or-restore-it/?sh=53e82cb64fe5.

9 Phillips, Ken. *Make a Better World: A practical guide to leadership for fundraising success.* NGO Futures LLC, 2020.

8 Phillips, Ken. *25 Proven Strategies for Fundraising Success: How to win the love and support of donors.* NGO Futures LLC, 2021.

10 Princeton Survey Research Associates. *BBB Wise Giving Alliance Donor Expectations Survey.* Washington, 2001.

11 Rapp, Stan, and Tom Collins. *Maxi-Marketing: The New Direction in Advertising, Promotion, and Marketing Strategy.* Plume, 1989.

12 *The Giving Environment: New Models to Engage Donors: Survey Research on US Donor Participation.* The Indiana University Lilly Family School of Philanthropy. January 2022.

13 *West Broadway Neighborhood Association.* Accessed July 2, 2022. https://www.wbna.org.

Chapter 4

How to earn trust and implement the seven imperatives for meaningful ethics to be trusted and to increase funding

If we believe in people's ability and potential to help, the question is: How do we gain their respect and trust and, thereby, their financial support? The answer is to take responsibility.

CIVICUS, the global alliance of civil society organizations, advocates that "civil society organizations need to take responsibility for driving the accountability standards of the sector, rather than waiting for donors or government to step in."[1] Leading INGOs (International NGOs) created *Accountable Now* to support civil society organizations to be transparent, responsive to stakeholders, and focused on delivering impact.

The good news is that a wide variety of organizations – InterAction, the Maryland Association of Nonprofit Organizations, the National Council for Voluntary Organizations, the International Federation of Red Cross and Red Crescent Societies, the state of Rhode Island, the International Committee on Fundraising Organizations, the Association of Fundraising Professionals, and many other associations and individual NGOs – have taken on this responsibility.

How can your nonprofit demonstrate ethics and accountability – qualities that will have a positive impact on your fundraising? This chapter presents five priorities for action.

PRIORITY #1: Make sure your nonprofit is functioning well – An absolute requirement

The executive director overseen by the board of directors is responsible to fulfill the obligations required by governmental authorities and to provide timely reports on the organization. A review of the status of all such obligations and reporting should be on the agenda of the annual meeting of the board. The executive director or finance director should take action as needed to ensure this action is implemented, because such compliance is essential for success in fundraising as well as adhering to the ethical standards of fundraising professionals.

Special obligations for nonprofits

Most countries have laws that provide special status for charities as non-governmental organizations established for the public benefit. These organizations receive certain advantages such as tax-deductions for their donors, eligibility to receive grants from foundations, and no taxes on their income, property, or purchases. Accordingly, they have certain requirements for registration with and reporting to government authorities and complying with certain standards regarding their purpose, governance, and behavior. As a result, NGOs have special obligations to the authorities and to the public as well as to their donors and participants.

Complying with such laws and requirements is a clear obligation for nonprofits to be observed without fail. They are the beginning steps to assure public trust. I often remind NGO leaders that:

DOI: 10.4324/9781003335207-6

1   *Responsibility* is doing what you say you will do.
2   *Accountability* is reporting or accounting what you have actually done.
3   *Foundations of success* are being both responsible and accountable.

Key point: Nonprofit non-governmental organizations have been created to serve the public good; they receive special legal status and certain specified fiscal benefits as a result. This entails ethical, legal, financial, and reporting obligations by the organization to government authorities and the public.

Nonprofit roles and responsibilities

The first steps in providing information to the public and to donors can be guided by the five essentials and the six key attributes of nonprofits that I included in my first book, *Make a Better World*.[2] I have presented these two concepts in scores of countries with numerous clients and with thousands of participants in training workshops. They apply in different cultures and different contexts and are among what I call the "fundamentals of nonprofits."

Here are the five essentials for nonprofits – NGOs should demonstrate value, results, cost, ethics, and accountability:

1   Value or mission – What do you do? How important is your NGO to society?
2   Results or effectiveness – How much and how lasting an impact is achieved?
3   Cost or efficiency – How do you manage? What is the cost to get the result?
4   Ethics or trustworthiness – How well does everyone behave in everything?
5   Accountability or transparency – How responsible and accountable is it?

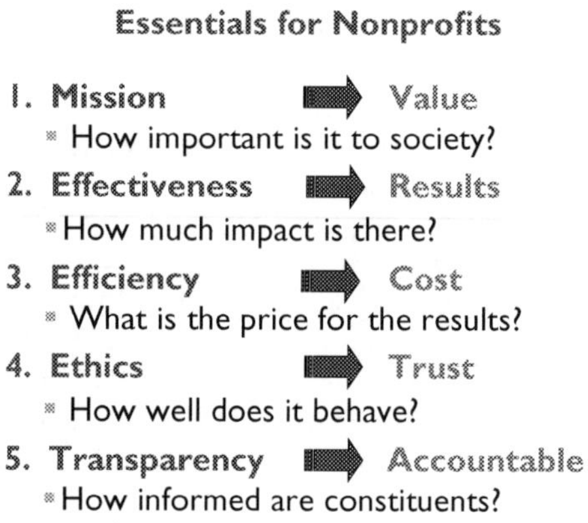

Essentials for Nonprofits

1. **Mission**   ➡ Value
   ＊ How important is it to society?
2. **Effectiveness**   ➡ Results
   ＊How much impact is there?
3. **Efficiency**   ➡ Cost
   ＊ What is the price for the results?
4. **Ethics**   ➡ Trust
   ＊ How well does it behave?
5. **Transparency**   ➡ Accountable
   ＊How informed are constituents?

Figure 4.1 The five essentials for nonprofits. Infographic by the author.

Here are the six key attributes for nonprofits – NGOs should be active in six important ways to achieve their vision and mission:

1   Promote awareness and the importance of your socially worthwhile cause.
2   Educate the public to increase understanding about your cause.
3   Advocate to society, business, and government to increase action for the cause.
4   Provide services to benefit partners and the beneficiaries in your programs.
5   Build its work on voluntary contributions and donated time.
6   Maintain and exercise its independence of action and free voice (Figure 4.1 and 4.2).

Key Attributes of Nonprofits

1. **Providing** services **important to society**

2. **Promoting** a socially worthwhile vision

3. **Educating** the public about this vision

4. **Advocating** to all sectors of society

5. **Independent** status and voice

6. **Private** voluntary **not-for-profit**

To succeed, earn trust and achieve impact.

Figure 4.2 The six key attributes for nonprofits. Infographic by the author.

Excellence in governance and management – A first priority for trust

As fundraiser, executive director, board member, and consultant for NGOs for six decades, I have seen how excellence in governance and excellence in management are prerequisites for success for NGOs.

To deserve more donor trust, nonprofits must have excellent leadership (board members and executive director), top-flight management (department directors and unit heads), well-functioning internal operations (strategic planning, strategies, and processes), and ever-growing organizational capacity (culture, learning, monitoring, and mentoring) to identify and solve significant social problems. It is quite simple: To be trusted, you need to show you are well governed and well managed to get things done and, of course, to do so without financial mismanagement or any other wrongdoing.

The board of directors, of course, has a unique responsibility to assure the trustworthiness of the organization. A fundamental role for the board is to establish or approve a code of ethics and monitor its implementation (and to make sure that staff does this, as well). It is also the board's responsibility to ensure good performance and behavior of the executive staff and to have the board's own code of conduct, too.

The issues of governance activity and fundraising were important when I served on the Committee on Standards of the Better Business Bureau Philanthropic Advisory Service (PAS) (now the BBB Wise Giving Alliance) from 1978 to 1982. I was then vice president for fundraising at Save the Children and had participated in many meetings with PAS staff about standards and was invited to join the committee. After many meetings of the committee, we agreed to expand and strengthen standards on governance, financial management, and fundraising, all with the aim to assure trustworthiness.[3]

As an example of the failure to function well, I was astounded to hear from participants during a 2021 virtual session with the well-known consultant and author Roger Craver that many of the NGOs participating in that session failed to utilize their marketing data or know what their donors really expect from organizations they support. In my work as a fundraiser and, later, as executive director, we routinely surveyed to learn donors' interests and expectations and analyzed the cost to attract new donors by various media and messages, then tracked their retention rates and lifetime value to enable us to optimize our marketing results. Managing acquisition and retention of donors is a priority for basic good management – and for earning trust. We believed that donors who discontinued may have done so because of something we did or did not do and that it was our responsibility to do better.

PRIORITY #2: Achieve real impact for beneficiaries and results for society

It is easy to exaggerate and talk about thousands of people saved, millions fed, everyone helped, and so forth. However, nonprofits (on behalf of their donors and the public) need to understand clearly the progression from *outputs* to *outcomes* to *impacts*.

- *Outputs* are the immediate results from a program.
- *Outcomes* are what happens next.
- *Impacts* are the lasting results.

It is the lasting results that matter in terms of life changes for the participants in the program. Donors especially want to see the benefits their donations make possible. I included *impact for beneficiaries* as one of the must-have strategies for every nonprofit in my book, *25 Proven Strategies for Fundraising Success.*[4]

It is an *output* to say our organization provided food to thousands of children; it is an *outcome* to report that the children had better nutrition and were healthier; and it is a real *impact* to report that the children had better school attendance, higher graduation levels, and better employment prospects. Of course, in an emergency, providing food is an essential service as it keeps people alive, and this should be done with an eye for longer term impacts, for example, providing training in nutrition or farming. See the case studies in chapters 15 and 16 for examples of lasting impacts.

From this book, the *outputs* are knowledge, motivation, tools, and challenges that you get here in these chapters. These outputs may be important, but they are without value if everything stops there. It is what you do with those outputs that become the *outcomes*, that is, how the information you read changes your behavior, how you are motivated to do more, how you use the knowledge and tools, and how you rise to the challenges you'll face. The next level, I hope, is the *impacts* of ethical behavior throughout your organization, better results in your programs, more money, more volunteers, and more people helped.

Unfortunately, all too many nonprofits report on the immediate outputs they achieve without looking at the real impacts. The efforts to extend microcredit to people in developing nations is an eye-opening illustration. In the first phase, the loans were generally given to men – the outputs were the number of participants and number of loans. The excellent repayments, their successful businesses, and the good profits were excellent outcomes. But evaluators eventually found that the money was often spent at the local bar and did not raise the quality of life for families – not a good result! Even though the outputs and outcomes appeared to be excellent, the impact on families was minimal. In the second stage of microcredit, the loans were more often given to women who, it turned out, had the same successful outcomes in terms of payback rates, business success, and profits. And they were found to use the money on education, healthcare, housing, and other benefits for their children. These were the real results, the positive and lasting impacts that donors want to see (Figure 4.3).

When I again served as a member of the Standards Review Panel for the Better Business Bureau Wise Giving Alliance two decades ago, one of the major issues we addressed was the need to demonstrate results. Based on my real-world experience as a fundraiser, executive director, and consultant, I was the most vocal advocate that organizations must focus more on measuring and reporting on the impacts they achieve. As a result of research I was conducting then on how NGOs evaluate themselves, I knew that program evaluation should be a top priority, and working in Europe at the time, I met with evaluation agencies in France, the Netherlands, Switzerland, and the U.K. that were looking at program impact as the next challenge for NGOs.

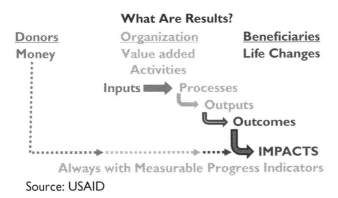

Source: USAID

Figure 4.3 **A chart showing different levels of results: Outputs, outcomes, and impacts. Image by the author based on the United States Agency for International Development materials.**

After the Standards Review Panel considered the complexity of measuring impact for the wide variety of NGOs in the U.S., we concluded that to be in good standing, the board of an organization must periodically review and address the nonprofit's monitoring and evaluation systems to assure good results. This became a required standard for American charities to be in good standing at the BBB Wise Giving Alliance. Now, many years later, I believe that evaluation agencies need to press even harder on nonprofits to improve their evaluation of measurable and tangible impacts of their work with more sector-specific requirements. (In Part II, you will learn about the concept of *strategic evaluation*, which all NGOs can and should be implementing.)

Key point: Public opinion polls and donor surveys almost always find that a top concern by donors is: "What are your results?" and the conviction by non-donors is: "I don't believe they achieve anything." Clearly, achieving lasting impact for beneficiaries and society is the primary reason why nonprofits exist and why people donate.

PRIORITY #3: Adopt and enforce a meaningful organization-wide code of ethics

Nonprofits must adopt their own unique code of ethics and live by those ethics day by day. Such codes lay out the standards that everyone in the organization must follow. This is not a brief statement based on a one-page template. This is a detailed, meaningful code of ethics that is customized to your organization. Thus, it provides an appropriate statement to potential donors that "We adopted and adhere to a *meaningful code of ethics*, and you can count on us to behave properly."

If you don't have a meaningful, effective code of ethics, it is very possible and maybe even probable that someone, somewhere, somehow will do something to create serious problems in your organization, and then publicity will follow and donors will flee. Often it is the attempt to cover up bad behavior that gets the most adverse and persistent publicity. A review of all the data presented earlier in this book should suffice to convince board members and senior staff to move forward with a meaningful code of ethics to protect the organization and its image.

Commitment is the first important input for success. For example, I was the expert advisor and advocate for ethics in a conference in Sinai, Romania, in 1994, for leaders of NGO resource centers in the newly independent nations in Eastern and Central Europe to develop a model code of ethical standards for NGOs in the region. Other experts from the International Center for Not-for-Profit Law provided guidance on the laws needed for a viable civil society sector. Major donors from other countries covered all the costs. The background information and process were good. The participants' drafting of the code of ethical standards over three days was excellent, and they approved the final version of a strong model code. The World Bank published and praised the code in a major volume of recommendations on ethics and laws for NGOs.[5]

But it was a failure! No one paid attention to the code of ethics after the meeting. So what happened to a great output? It was apparently not promoted and was largely forgotten in the fourteen countries that participated in the conference. The motivation for a code came from outside donors rather than from the NGOs themselves. My lesson from this experience is that the initiators and drafters of a code of ethics must be committed to the process for its own sake. They have to own it.

What is a *meaningful code* of ethics?

Many nonprofit leaders will claim they are already doing everything including their ethics rather well, and that may be. Most larger and prominent NGOs have their own codes of ethics. However, much more needs to be done to increase public trust. Not only does an NGO need to be committed to a meaningful code of ethics, but it has to implement it in a meaningful manner. Here are seven imperatives to make your organization's code of ethics meaningful and effective:

First, a code of ethics (describing moral standards) – sometimes called a code of conduct (describing expected behaviors) – is needed as a set of rules and expectations of how an organization *expects and requires* board members, staff, and volunteers to work. The code presents the core values and ethical principles within the organization and informs employees about their responsibilities and appropriate behavior within the organization and toward participants, donors, and others. Leadership responsibility to assure ethical behavior at all levels of the organization needs to be emphasized. It covers all components of the organization's work.

Second, the code needs to be operationalized – and made clear what it means. Codes of ethics can be too general or vague. They state nice ideals but lack the specifics to be convincing. For instance, one code of ethics for an NGO states that "We respect human rights." Another testifies that "We tolerate no harassment, no harsh or inhumane treatment." And another communicates that "We are accountable for our behaviors, actions, and results." In each case, the terms are vague; there are no specifics. How can you know an NGO has respect for human rights? To what extent is one's action considered harassment? What is accountability for behavior? These terms are important to include in codes of ethics, but operational definitions need to be established for those in the organization and the public to understand the significance behind these impressive words. How can a board member, employee, or volunteer comply if the terms are vague and subject to different interpretations? If unethical behavior is found, how can the code be enforced?

Third, how are codes assessed and compliance confirmed? Even if an organization has clear guidelines for its code of ethics, it is uncertain whether or when or how the behavior of board members, employees, and volunteers is actually assessed. What is the process? If assessments are conducted, how valid are they?

Fourth, if an employee, volunteer, or program participant is mistreated or abused or sees unethical behavior, he or she may not be able to reach out safely in the organization to file a complaint. The individual might not receive needed support, and the inappropriate behavior continues. Thus, having a clear process for safely submitting complaints and a commitment and practice to address them fairly and promptly is essential for the person involved, potentially for others as well, and certainly for the organization as a whole.

Fifth, how can donors trust your self-assessment and claims of good behavior? A verification step is needed. A peer review or some other external confirmation is important to gain trust and fully ensure the code of ethics is effective. One suggestion is to have the NGO's financial auditors review and confirm that code procedures were followed, infractions and abuses were assessed, and warranted sanctions were applied.

Sixth, sanctions. If anyone disregards the rules and expectations, it must be clear that the individual will face serious consequences (which must be stated in the code). This information is especially important for the public to know as well, since it shows the organization truly follows its values in everything it does.

Seventh, just as important, at the next level, is to communicate the code with its assessment and sanctions processes. Strong standards against harassment, discrimination, and other inappropriate behavior are now expected, and nonprofits should communicate this widely to managers and their staff, board members and other volunteers, beneficiaries and participants, partners and contractors, and donors and the public. A short statement, for example, in the auditor's report that the organization "correctly followed all procedures in its code of ethics" would be impressive.

Without the relevant communication, the public cannot know if the organization is functioning properly, effectively, efficiently, responsibly, and accountably. Implementation of the code of ethics is an indispensable way potential donors can evaluate whether they can trust an organization to use their money – or not.

To support the seven imperatives, it is important to make sure the executive leadership and the board of directors strongly support the process and involve everyone to get their input and commitment for the final code of ethics and its ongoing implementation. It may be helpful to add the concept of integrity or something similar into your organization's high-level statements on values and culture as well as provide ongoing information and guidance on your code of ethics, even training when it is needed (Figure 4.4).

In my experience, it takes just one person – and I mean exactly that – just one person to start this process. Subsequent chapters provide further guidance and examples to develop and implement a meaningful, effective code of ethics.

I was pleased when I received the following update on its work in this area including a comment about my own involvement with Save the Children US from its CEO Janti Soeripto:

Meaningful Ethics

1. **A code of ethics with rules and expectations**
2. **Operational explanations of the obligations**
3. **Assessing compliance on a regular basis**
4. **Procedures for complaints of non-compliance**
5. **Reliable verification by relevant experts**
6. **Procedures for sanctions for non-compliance**
7. **Communication of all this to constituents**

These seven imperatives make ethics meaningful.

NGO Futures LLC © 2021

Figure 4.4 The seven components to make ethics meaningful. Image by the author.

"Save the Children, the international non-governmental organization I've been privileged to lead since 2020, has a long tradition of incorporating ethical behavior in all that it does. Its five core values are accountability, integrity, ambition, collaboration and creativity. These core values drive our long-term strategies and short-term goals, and they underpin our mission to inspire breakthroughs in the way the world treats children and achieve immediate and lasting impact in their lives. They also reflect the personal responsibility each staff member has to our key stakeholders – our supporters, the children we serve, and each other as colleagues.

"This tradition stems from our movement's founding in 1919 and was strengthened during your tenure as Chief Development Officer in the 1970s, when you professionalized our fundraising and marketing activities and raised awareness of the importance of quality reporting to supporters on how funds are used.

"Last year, we rolled out a new Code of Ethics and Business Conduct built around five key principles, to which all staff, consultants and Board members must commit in writing.

Principle 1. Safeguarding is at the core of every decision we make
Principle 2. We treat our colleagues with dignity and respect, and do our part to create a safe and supportive workplace
Principle 3. We uphold the trust of the children we work with and of our supporters to act as good stewards of resources
Principle 4. As a trusted voice for children, we speak with care, dignity, and integrity
Principle 5. We raise our concerns, even if we are not sure something bad has happened

"These key principles reflect Save the Children's responsibilities to its key stakeholders – the children and families in our programs, Save the Children staff, our supporters and partners, and the public."

PRIORITY #4: Commit to transparency and accountability and establish an independent Chief Trust Officer in the organization

All nonprofits need to commit to transparency and accountability as natural obligations flowing from their privileged legal status and from the expectations of donors and volunteers.

It is time for leading nonprofits to establish a new position at the top of the organization called Chief Trust Officer or Accountability Director. This would be a position of high status and independence that is like an ombudsman in some countries or the public editor at the *New York Times*.

The individual would hold the position for a specified term such as five years and function as a representative of the public, donors, and beneficiaries. This person would have full access, anywhere and anytime, throughout the organization. The responsibilities would include assuring a strong, meaningful code of ethics (or code of behavior) and prohibition of any conflict of interest, annual review of adherence to the code, monitoring behavior throughout the organization, and assuring corrective action is taken as needed – all based on a commitment to integrity, transparency, and accountability. The Chief Trust Officer would oversee an accountability page of the organization's website and establish procedures for board members, employees, volunteers, program participants, donors, and others to identify problems, submit complaints, review complaints, and act when inappropriate or unethical behavior is found.

A brief report by the Chief Trust Officer would be included in the published annual report by the organization. It would be a stamp of approval on trustworthiness in the same way the financial audit is a stamp of approval on financial management. Ideally, the Chief Trust Officer's conclusions should be that the organization has been honest in what it does and what it says and that it reports accurately on how donor funds have been used and what the organization has achieved.

The Chief Trust Officer would report any problems to the board of directors for prompt and appropriate action.

The concept of a Chief Trust Officer was the main recommendation I presented at the 2015 annual meeting of the International Committee on Fundraising Organizations (ICFO) on "Advancing Trust in the Charitable Sector: Communicating Charity Value and Inspiring Trust."[6] ICFO is the international association of national charity monitoring organizations; its members are the leading charity evaluation agencies from nineteen countries. ICFO has a very clear set of standards recommendations, which are included in its website at www.ICFO.org.[7]

Nonprofits can reach out to new donors, but trust is what it takes to enlist their support. By putting in place a Chief Trust Officer (CTO), an organization would take a major step to ensure everything the organization does reinforces its trustworthiness. The key points are:

- The position would be appointed to a specified term by the board of directors with a direct report to the full board as an independent watchdog to bring to the board any alleged wrongdoing for action. It would be protected from recrimination by the board or management.
- The position should not be combined with another staff position as that would create a potential conflict of interest and would negate the impartiality of being "above it all" for the responsibility.
- The CTO position is recommended for all large NGOs with $25 million or more in revenues and for any NGO that has been criticized for any aspect of its operations.
- Smaller NGOs could partner to retain a person for the position on a shared basis. I expect specialized consulting or audit firms will offer to take on the assignment.

Kitty Holt, Director of Ethics and Compliance at Plan International USA (note her title), has been with the organization since 1993. She provided me with an update on what Plan has done with transparency and accountability since I left the organization just a few months before she arrived. As national Director, I recall starting to press in the 1980s to move the global organization to greater responsibility and accountability with donors. I learned years later that these initiatives at Plan International also influenced other NGOs in a dozen or more countries.

Holt's appointment as Director of Ethics and Compliance in 2011 was a significant step forward for that NGO. She has the responsibility to assure that the organization adheres to all relevant ethical and charity watchdog standards. She commented favorably on the main charity watchdogs that provide important service for organizations and, of course, for donors as well: The Better Business Bureau Wise Giving Alliance's *20 Standards for Charity Accountability*[8], Charity Navigator's *Your Guide To Intelligent Giving*,[9] and Guidestar's *Nonprofit Reports and Forms 990 for Donors*.[10] Each has a different approach to charity ethics in the U.S. and each provides important guidance to donors and NGOs as well.

Holt described three other efforts to share the organization's ethical performance:

- An interagency compliance group: "We have an email distribution list. When there is a compliance question, members often use that list to ask others in the group how they handle a particular situation or if they have samples of certain policies, or the like. The group also holds online meetings to learn from one another or from outside speakers, and the group gets together in-person when at the same conference." This noteworthy compliance group started with eight or nine organizations and has now grown to some seventy participants from forty organizations.
- An interagency meeting for organizations that have child sponsorship programs, which started in the early 1990s: It convenes for several days every eighteen months to share what

is working and not working in their respective organizations. The purpose is to help all the organizations do better, which ultimately helps more children and families around the world.

- Internal positions created specifically for ethics and compliance: She added that many large INGOs (International NGOs) have established positions within their organizations with experienced professionals who focus exclusively on ethics and compliance.

PRIORITY #5: Enable everyone in the organization to step up with responsibility to improve operations, especially to ensure trust and impact

Let me set the framework here for building trust by pointing to the significant potential problems for nonprofits in five key and potentially vulnerable areas: Management and trustworthiness, program and effectiveness, finance and efficiency, fundraising and accountability, and governance and policy. This is based on observations of a multitude of NGOs in numerous countries over many years, plus thousands of discussions with board members, executive directors, program directors, finance directors, fundraising directors, evaluators, support staff, volunteers, and also donors about the problems and challenges for NGOs.

Management leads the organization and must assure its trustworthiness and effectiveness. Effective programs are the *raison d'être* for an organization and must be impactful. Finance assures the efficiency of the organization. Fundraising raises money for the organization and provides accountability to donors. Program includes all the information, education, advocacy, and services to achieve a better world. Governance is ultimately responsible for everything.

➡️ *However, leaders cannot know everything.*

They cannot know everything because they are not involved in detail or the frontline implementation. They should periodically conduct a thorough review, looking for potential problems and improvements in program, management, finance, fundraising, and governance. The board of directors should monitor the process and results of the periodic reviews to assure effectiveness, efficiency, and trustworthiness in these five functions. However, formal meetings may tend to avoid open discussion. Therefore, in a well-functioning organization, a more open process is needed.

All staff should be encouraged to speak up to share concerns and solve problems they see in their daily work. They should be protected through a safe and trusted process. On behalf of donors to sustain their support, the fundraising director should be aware of any internal issues that might reduce the organization's appeal to donors and share the findings with the relevant department directors, executive director, or board of directors for improvements. Inside the organization, it is the fundraising director who knows and represents the donors and can speak on their behalf as their ambassador in management meetings and board meetings. Staff in other functions also know what should be improved and corrected. A key theme is "If you don't know what is wrong, you can't fix it" (Figure 4.5).

I encourage you to adopt or at least advocate for the seven imperatives to create an effective, meaningful code of ethics. This process includes reviewing the current situation, drafting the code itself, providing operational explanations, assessing compliance, assuring a safe complaint process, implementing a reliable verification process, addressing procedures for sanctions, and ensuring clear communication to constituents.

And don't forget about the other four priorities in this chapter: 1) That your organization is well functioning in all you do, 2) that you are achieving real impact for beneficiaries, 3) that

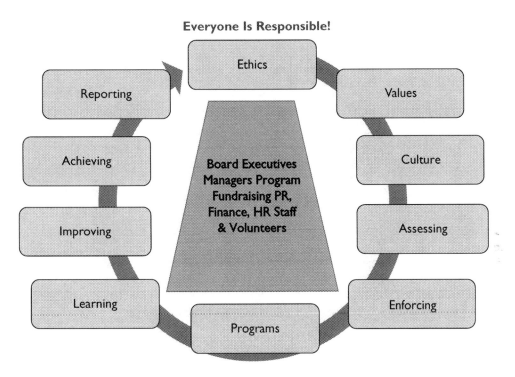

Figure 4.5 Everyone in an organization is responsible to assure good ethics. Image by the author.

there is a process and person who leads in assuring trust, and 4) that everyone is encouraged to identify and step up to correct any shortcomings or more serious problems.

When these are all in place and your organization is well-functioning in all five essentials and all six responsibilities for nonprofits, you will have so much more substance and progress to communicate to donors, so they will not think of you as just another fundraising organization.

Key point: Nonprofits can reach out to new donors, but trust is what it takes to secure and continue their support. You earn trust through excellence in governance and management, real impact for program beneficiaries, the seven imperatives for meaningful ethics, an independent trust officer, and the ability of everyone to take responsibility for trust and impact.

Spotlight on the five priorities

To review, here are the five priorities to demonstrate ethics and accountability – and increase fundraising results:

- PRIORITY #1: Make sure your nonprofit is functioning well in everything it does.
- PRIORITY #2: Achieve excellent impact for beneficiaries and results for society.
- PRIORITY #3: Adopt and enforce an organization-wide *meaningful* code of ethics.
- PRIORITY #4: Commit to transparency and accountability & establish a Chief Trust Officer.
- PRIORITY #5: Enable everyone to step up to ensure trust and impact.

These five key priorities are imperative for all NGOs to improve trustworthiness. You can lead with these initiatives internally and also influence other nonprofits to adopt them as well (Figure 4.6).

Questions for implementation

1 How can you make your organization's existing or new code of ethics meaningful?
2 How do you rate your organization in terms of results and impact?
3 How can you support the concept that everyone should speak up about problems?

Leadership for Ethics and Trust

Ten steps in an NGO to demonstrate your leadership in ethics

1. Adopting a code of meaningful ethics for your own NGO
2. Rigorous approach to self-assessment and self-regulation
3. Confidential internal staff reviews of ethics work
4. Using feedback from donors for internal improvements
5. Verification by external experts of key performance areas
6. Staff recognition or bonus for leadership in ethics and trust
7. Raising the bar internally where you see you are at risk
8. Innovation when following the code becomes routine
9. Promotion with other NGOs to adopt meaningful ethics
10. Public communications about the importance of ethics

20/08/01   © NGO FUTURES 2001   1

Figure 4.6 Ten steps to demonstrate leadership in ethics. Infographic by the author.

Notes

1 CIVICUS, the global alliance of civil society organizations, advocates that "civil society organizations need to take responsibility for driving the accountability standards of the sector, rather than waiting for donors or government to step in" Leading INGOs (International NGOs) created *Accountable Now*. https://accountablenow.org/
2 For a full explanation of the essential roles and key attributes of NGOs, see my book, *Make a Better World*: Ken Phillips, *Make a Better World: A practical guide to leadership for fundraising success* (NGO Futures LLC, 2020), 129–157.
3 BBB Wise Giving Alliance, https://give.org/about-us/our-mission
4 Ken Phillips, *25 Proven Strategies for Fundraising Success: How to win the love and support of donors* (NGO Futures LLC, 2021), 101–106.
5 The World Bank for The International Center for Not-for-Profit Law, "Handbook on Good Practices for Laws Relating to Non-Governmental Organizations," May 1997, accessed July 1, 2022, https://documents1.worldbank.org/curated/en/201351468332690971/pdf/639500WP0WB0Ha00Box0361533B0PUBLIC0.pdf.
6 Ken Phillips, *Advancing Trust in the Charitable Sector: Communicating Charity Value and Inspiring Trust*, Presented at the 2015 Annual Meeting of the International Committee on Fundraising Organizations, Washington, D. C. June 12, 2015.

7 *International Committee on Fundraising Organizations*, accessed July 2, 2022, https://www.icfo.org.
8 "BBB Standards for Charity Accountability," *Give.org*, accessed July 1, 2022, https://give.org/donor-landing-page/bbb-standards-for-charity-accountability.
9 *Charity Navigator: Your Guide to Intelligent Giving*, accessed July 1, 2022.
10 *Candid GuideStar*, accessed July 2, 2022, https://www.guidestar.org.

Bibliography

1 *Candid GuideStar*. Accessed July 2, 2022. https://www.guidestar.org.
2 *Charity Navigator: Your Guide to Intelligent Giving*. Accessed July 1, 2022.
3 "BBB Standards for Charity Accountability." *Give.org*. Accessed July 1, 2022. https://give.org/donor-landing-page/bbb-standards-for-charity-accountability.
4 *International Committee on Fundraising Organizations*. Accessed July 2, 2022. https://www.icfo.org.
5 Phillips, Ken. *Advancing Trust in the Charitable Sector: Communicating Charity Value and Inspiring Trust*. Presented at the 2015 Annual Meeting of the International Committee on Fundraising Organizations, Washington, D. C. June 12, 2015.
6 Phillips, Ken. *25 Proven Strategies for Fundraising Success: How to win the love and support of donors*. NGO Futures LLC, 2021.
7 Phillips, Ken. *Make a Better World: A practical guide to leadership for fundraising success*. NGO Futures LLC, 2020.
8 The World Bank for the International Center for Not-for-Profit Law. "Handbook on Good Practices for Laws Relating to Non-Governmental Organizations," May 1997. Accessed July 1, 2022. https://documents1.worldbank.org/curated/en/201351468332690971/pdf/639500WP0WB0Ha00Box03615 33B0PUBLIC0.pdf.

Chapter 5

InterAction case study – Drafting a code of ethics in a participatory process for greater ownership

This chapter is a case study of the development of a meaningful code of ethics by an association of NGOs. It is based on my own experience initiating and leading the effort when I was executive director of Foster Parents Plan and a board member of InterAction. I present the story here, because it shows how one person can influence a large association and all its members and provide guidance to others for similar activity. The chapter is based on my experience and notes, recent interviews, and research I conducted for Sasakawa Peace Foundation.

As we discuss the development and implementation of a meaningful code of ethics (in this case, it is referred to as standards), keep in mind the ultimate objective: To be able to communicate clearly and honestly to donors and other stakeholders that your nonprofit adheres to the highest level of ethics. As discussed in the previous chapter, having a detailed, customized, and meaningful code of ethics directly impacts trustworthiness, results in a higher level of fundraising success, and enables your organization to deliver a growing program with lasting impact.

Even if your organization already has a code of ethics in place, keep reading. It is important to establish a participatory process, and it is important to create a *meaningful* code of ethics. In my experience, many organizations' existing codes of ethics (or codes of conduct or codes of behavior) are extremely brief, are based on templates and not customized to the organization, and don't address compliance, enforcement mechanisms, or procedures for sanctions.

This case study focuses on InterAction, the American Council for Voluntary International Action, which is an alliance of 200 U.S.-based NGOs working internationally in relief and development. The association's website notes: "Founded in 1984, InterAction is the largest alliance of international NGOs and partners in the United States. We mobilize our members to think and act collectively to serve the world's poor and vulnerable, with a shared belief that we can make the world a more peaceful, just, and prosperous place – together."[1] The NGO members elect InterAction's board members from among the membership (Figure 5.1).

InterAction

- A model for other NGO associations
- Convener, thought leader, and voice for NGOs working to eliminate extreme poverty, strengthen human rights and citizen participation, safeguard a sustainable planet, promote peace, and ensure dignity for all people
- 200+ member organizations bring an estimated $15 billion of private funding to solutions to advance the lives of people in the most marginalized positions.

Figure 5.1 Information about the NGO membership association called InterAction. Sidebar by the author.

DOI: 10.4324/9781003335207-7

Developing the code of ethics (called the InterAction PVO Standards)

As it was being formed, InterAction identified its purpose as working to "enhance the effectiveness and professional capacities of its members … and to foster partnership, collaboration, leadership, and the power of this community to speak as one voice as we strive to achieve a world of self-reliance, justice, and peace."[2] To realize this mission, InterAction would work to:

- Enhance the identity, autonomy, credibility and diverse perspectives of each member agency.
- Provide a broadly based participatory forum for professional consultation, coordination and concerted action.
- Foster the effectiveness and recognition of the private voluntary organizations (PVOs) community, both professionally and publicly.
- Set a standard of the highest ethics in carrying out this mission.

As the fundraising director of Save the Children when InterAction was being conceived in 1980, I volunteered to help draft the above statement of purpose, which became the unifying call for its member organizations. Years later, when I was executive director of Foster Parents Plan (now called Plan International USA) and a member of the InterAction board, I quoted these words at an executive committee meeting: "Set a standard of the highest ethics." I asked my fellow board members exactly how we did that. There was an embarrassed silence as everyone realized the statement was just aspiration or promise with no back-up, no details, and no validity at all. Breaking the silence, the board chairman said that we had a real issue here and, after a dramatic pause, asked me to do something about it.

After careful reflection, at the next executive committee meeting in March 1989, I put forth this proposal: "To establish, as an InterAction project, the development and implementation by 1995 or before, of industry wide standards for PVOs covering governance, financial reporting, fundraising and public relations, management practice, human resources, public policy, and program services." The project was intended to assure good ethical practice and strengthen public confidence in the integrity, management, and effectiveness of InterAction and all of its member organizations. It was based on the importance of establishing a reliable means to ensure the public trust.

InterAction's board of directors approved the proposal and asked me to lead the project. As a clarification, the term *private voluntary organizations* (PVOs) used by InterAction has been replaced by the more common term *non-government organizations* (NGOs).

We created a Standards Committee representing a cross-section of InterAction members to develop the approach to drafting the standards. An important decision was not to draft the standards quickly or rush to completion of the project. Instead, we agreed to provide extensive time for consideration, opportunity for the member organizations to review successive drafts of the code, and encouragement to take issues to the full staff and boards of the many NGO member organizations. All of this was intended to secure the full involvement and complete commitment of the NGO member organizations and their boards, so the effort would be seen as a member-driven code and not something imposed on them. Clearly, a member-driven initiate created in a highly participatory process would lead to greater ownership (and compliance) for all member NGOs.

The most important issue was to secure awareness by the members of the need to develop a code of ethics. The first step I took was a confidential survey of the executive directors of InterAction members, 120 at that time. The survey asked questions about organizational conduct, board effectiveness, financial controls, fundraising practices, risks and vulnerabilities, and ways to put a code of ethics in place.

Respondents overwhelmingly believed the community as a whole was vulnerable in key areas of fundraising, finance, and cost effectiveness. Shockingly, many executive directors (actually 42%) believed there were *serious cases of violation* of ethics by other members! The highest ratings of vulnerability were for fundraising, finance, effectiveness, and management and human resources. But at the same time, and overwhelmingly, the individual executives were convinced that their own NGO was *free of violations* and was maintaining the highest ethical standards![3]

I presented the survey results in a closed meeting of the executive directors of InterAction's members. I said: "You all have very bad opinions of the other organizations in the room, but at the same time you claim for yourself adherence to the highest standards of ethics. Look at the other directors next to you. *They* think *you* are lying! As *you* think they *are*! Imagine what the public would be thinking if they were here! We have some work to do to lift up all our standards!"

Given the feedback from the survey and the resulting frank discussion, the membership strongly endorsed the value of a code of ethics with many supporting comments such as:

- "Trust is a fragile commodity."
- "We should all be held accountable."
- "It is our responsibility to uphold public trust."
- "There should be no reason to hide information."
- "If media or donors request specific information, they should have it."
- "Charities should live by a higher standard, because our existence depends on trust."

Here are two other important points worth considering:

- A full 80% of respondents to that survey – leaders of the member organizations – believed that rather than lowering a standard that is difficult for some members to meet, the ethical standard should be phased in over a period of time to allow everyone to meet and adhere to that higher standard.
- A surprising two-thirds of respondents (68%) reported that they provided no training or information on ethics to leaders, staff, or volunteers in their NGO.

That group of executive directors concluded that a strong code of ethics was urgently needed and that the Standards Committee should move ahead. We agreed on the need to establish high standards and to build on other organizations' codes and professional standards where possible.

We also decided on a phase-in period and not to rush to certification. Eventually, all NGO member organizations would need to be certified, indicating that the NGO meets the high-level standards. We recognized the need for enforcement and chose to create a model code that presented self-certification first, leading eventually to some form of external validation or accreditation. We considered four groups of constituents who benefit from strong standards: the public, program beneficiaries, employees, and donors.

The process of developing the standards (InterAction's term for its new code of ethics) was critical. We were guided by the five stages of standards development recommended by the Ethics Resource Center, now called the Ethics and Compliance Initiative,[4] in Washington, D.C., as follows:

1 Assessment of values and vulnerability
2 Education about ethics awareness

3   Development and review of the code of standards
4   Implementation, guidance, and training for the standards
5   Evaluation

The actual drafting was done by a relatively small group but with broad participation by the other members. Over two years, the committee shared many concepts and considered and responded to many questions and suggestions. We made numerous revisions and circulated five revised drafts to the member organizations with requests for further comment.

The member organizations benefited from their participation in the process. Many members used the evolving standards to continuously improve and strengthen their own internal procedures including even how their board of directors carries out its work. For example, Edward Bullard, founder of TechnoServe, a U.S. NGO member providing assistance in micro-enterprise, found it was a valuable information and involvement process for the organization's self-improvement. He wrote that "Nonprofits have an obligation to make sure programs are cost effective" and stressed that it is particularly important for nonprofits to set rigorous standards for themselves because, unlike businesses, they are not subject to the discipline of the marketplace."

Other members reported that they presented the evolving standards to their boards as a step to implement improvements in governance and management. In fact, thanks to the phased-in, participatory process, the committee communicated high-level ethical standards to the member organizations while giving these NGOs the time and incentive to make continuous improvements throughout their organizations.

A report in *The Nonprofit Times* called it "a move that is likely to be watched closely by other parts of the nonprofit sector" and concluded with a quote from me: "Membership has its privileges and its responsibilities. What one of us does impacts the rest of us through public perception."[5] It was clear that a meaningful code of ethics – adopted by all of InterAction's member organizations – would raise the bar for the entire sector.

As we grew close to adoption of the standards, *The Chronicle of Philanthropy* quoted Peter Davies, then CEO of InterAction: "The community of PVOs stands to gain enormously by having its own internal set of standards against which to measure performance … . A set of standards for the community helps the [board and staff of an] individual agency have an idea of what to aspire to within their own organization."[6]

The project to develop a meaningful code of ethics was completed ahead of schedule. The PVO Standards, now called NGO Standards, were unanimously approved at the annual meeting of the members of InterAction in 1992. A headline in an article in *The Chronicle* cited InterAction for adopting "Ethical Standards for Governance, Finances, and Programs." The article included the entire text of the standards as adopted and quotes me, as chairman of the committee that drafted the standards over the past three years: "The adoption of operating standards, including standards for program results, puts PVOs on the forefront of accountability to donors. Public trust is absolutely essential for the continued ability of our sector to grow and to respond to crises around the worlds. Standards play a critical role in reinforcing that trust."[7]

The InterAction Standards define the financial, operational, and ethical code of conduct for InterAction and its member agencies including substantive sections on:

1   Governance
2   Organizational integrity
3   Finances
4   Communication and fundraising

5   Management practice and human resources
6   Program
7   Public policy
8   Implementation
9   Guidelines

In terms of content of the standards, some of the most important issues identified in the process were active involvement of the governing board, avoidance of conflicts of interest, transparency of the organization, financial integrity, fairness of management, truth in fundraising, and the process and impact of program.

Drafting this code of ethics succeeded, because it was a careful and deliberate process with extensive participation and time for consideration. The approach we took secured strong commitment from all the member organizations. With this careful approach, responsible NGO leaders simply could not say "No" to the development and enforcement of ethical standards for their organization.

Keep reading to discover how other organizations developed and implemented a meaningful code of ethics. When you are ready to develop (or strengthen) your nonprofit's code of ethics, I encourage you to review InterAction's NGO Standards at www.interaction.org/standards/ (Figure 5.2).

Recommended steps to draft and implement a code of ethics

As we progressed, the Standards Committee developed and followed a dozen procedural steps:

1   Include important values as articles of belief and aspiration.
2   Focus on high standards, positive values, and high expectations.
3   Keep standards broad but meaningful.
4   Be reasonable but always aim high.
5   Review existing codes of ethics, codes of conduct, or standards for guidance.
6   Incorporate existing standards of related professions.
7   Implement easier standards first, harder ones later.
8   Require a policy on controversial issues, rather than specifying the policy.
9   Obtain full participation in drafting the code of ethics with multiple discussion drafts.
10 Create a model code of ethics with annual self-certification.
11 Phase in implementation of the code of ethics over several years.
12 Include an enforcement mechanism in cases of noncompliance.

A participatory process results in greater ownership

My InterAction experience indicates that the process of developing a code of ethics is as important as the content of the code itself. The process of discussing the desired elements in a code is a strong educational process and can lead to important changes within your individual nonprofit as well as the multiple member organizations in an association. If we had rushed the process, this would have led to more resistance, less commitment, and little actual change. A rushed process would have undermined our goal of encouraging and

Figure 5.2 The author with the InterAction Standards publication. Photograph by Rebecca Phillips.

guiding all the NGO members to adhere to a higher level of ethical standards throughout their organizations.

Whether you need to implement a code of ethics for your own organization or for a group of organizations, the first step is to develop meaningful standards, the second is to get them implemented, and the third is to establish a means of verification. This is best done by building the supporting culture and involving key constituents. It is important to enforce and

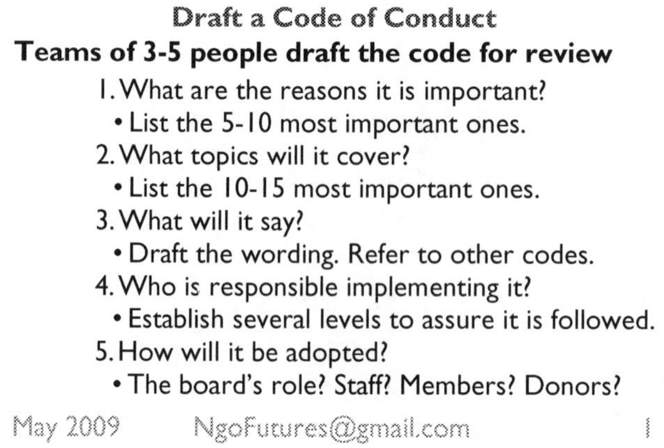

Draft a Code of Conduct
Teams of 3-5 people draft the code for review
1. What are the reasons it is important?
 • List the 5-10 most important ones.
2. What topics will it cover?
 • List the 10-15 most important ones.
3. What will it say?
 • Draft the wording. Refer to other codes.
4. Who is responsible implementing it?
 • Establish several levels to assure it is followed.
5. How will it be adopted?
 • The board's role? Staff? Members? Donors?

May 2009   NgoFutures@gmail.com   1

Figure 5.3 Five steps to draft a code of conduct. Infographic by the author.

audit the code of ethics; include it in orientation, training, and performance reviews; and consider and strengthen it over time. In addition to an annual certification by each member of compliance, InterAction provided a process to review any problems or complaints which, if deemed to be a significant violation of the standards, could lead to revocation of membership (Figure 5.3).

InterAction's experience with the PVO Standards (NGO Code of Ethics)

Self-certification is the basis for InterAction's Standards. Every two years, the executive director or board chairperson of each InterAction member organization is required to review the Standards and certify – formally and in writing – that the organization is in compliance and, if there are any areas in which they are not in compliance, to indicate the improvements they have committed to take. The Standards are also used to review new applicants for membership to InterAction, resulting in approval for membership for some applicants, guidance on changes necessary for others, and rejection for some.

In the years since the InterAction Standards were adopted, the experience has been overwhelmingly positive, and its NGO members have improved their internal way of working based on them. Kenneth J. Giunta, the responsible officer at InterAction for the standards in the 2000s, told me that the Standards "are hugely important. Our members find them very useful, light-years ahead of others. At a recent meeting on standards, he said, members of the media attended and said they look at InterAction members in an entirely different light because of the PVO Standards. We see them as a continuum in a process of self-appraisal and self-improvement."

When donors or journalists see that InterAction has established a robust code of ethics, they can have more confidence that the association and its NGO members are being responsible in their work and accountable to their donors. Giunta added: "Internally, the Standards linked members in the common pursuit of a set of values and ethical code of conduct. Externally, the Standards certify to the public-at-large that members have committed themselves to certain ideals and ways of operating. At a time when public trust in the nonprofit community has been shaken, the Standards are a highly visible, professional statement that enhances credibility with donors, governments, other NGO consortia, and the public at large." I can only add here that these words are even truer now when public trust has been so deeply shaken in recent years.

William Reese, then the CEO of the International Youth Foundation, a leading American NGO, gave me this feedback about meetings with partner organizations in Latin America: "I used our InterAction Standards as not just a list of talking points but an as outline as I went through governance, fiscal, and management issues. We talked about board recruitment and gender/ethnic balance. We talked about governing rules and principles, openness and accountability, fiscal care, and public relations. It reminded me once again that standards are not compliance-oriented straightjackets. In fact, they are high principles and a spirit of doing business."

The Standards have furthered InterAction's position as a leader among NGO coalitions around the world. Coalitions in Canada, Japan, and other countries have used InterAction's Standards as a model for their own standards, and many other coalitions have studied them. Both the Independent Sector and the Committee on International Grantmaking of the Council of Foundations have shared the InterAction Standards with their members, and the European Foundation Center distributed copies at a major conference it hosted. As InterAction notes on its website, it now "proudly heralds the Standards to the larger NGO community, to the media, to donors, and to the international community itself."[8]

InterAction supports disaster response fundraising by informing the media about which of its members are active in responding to that emergency along with the strict standards they follow. Similarly, individual member agencies are free to refer to their compliance with InterAction's high standards in fundraising and educational materials. Funding organizations are aware of InterAction's commitment to excellence though the Standards.

The Standards have been revised when warranted. New topics include transparency, gender equity and diversity, protection from sexual exploitation, safety standards, pharmaceutical and medical donations, food aid, and other important subjects.

Assistance and compliance

As a voluntary association, InterAction's Standards derive their weight and credibility from the collective commitment of the membership. The standards do not supplant the need for each individual member organization to manage its affairs with a concern for program quality and individual and organizational integrity; rather, the Standards are intended to complement the commitment of every member organization.

The implementation process that we adopted in 1992 required:

- Self-certification that an organization meets the Standards is required for membership in InterAction. Each applicant organization accepts responsibility for following the Standards.
- Annual filing of the latest annual report, an audited financial statement, and a statement and checklist – by the chair of the board of directors and/or the chief executive officer of the organization – attesting that it meets the high ethical Standards of InterAction is required and due December 31 of each year (now every other year).
- A Standards Committee shall be elected by the board and shall consist of members of the InterAction board and recognized outside experts.
- The Standards Committee will receive and act upon credible complaints of noncompliance with the Standards.

- In areas where a member organization is not in compliance, it must indicate what improvements it has committed to make to attain compliance.
- Noncompliance with the Standards can result in suspension of a member or denial of a membership application.

Self-certification, which began in 1993, provides an opportunity for dialogue between an organization's senior staff and its board and also encourages members to review their own organizational practices, update and revise existing policies, and draft new ones where they are needed – all with the end goal of improving organizational effectiveness and accountability.

Since 2006, members have been required to participate every two years in a compliance process called Self-Certification Plus (SCP), which provides a mechanism for organizational examination of its own accountability structures and a thorough review and certification of compliance with InterAction's Standards. To date, InterAction member organizations have gone through seven mandatory self-certification processes, each one building on the previous processes while strengthening and increasing their capacity to assure compliance.

The association maintains a resource center with a Standards FAQ and a Standards Guidance document covering many questions about the standards along with a wide variety of resource materials. InterAction staff provides technical support for any member organization seeking to improve its accountability and compliance with the Standards. The association provides resources and learning opportunities for gender and diversity efforts including workshops, recommendations for mentors and consultants, on-site consultations, and materials.

As I reviewed the current Standards on InterAction's website about the standards, I was pleased to read that: "InterAction is especially indebted to Ken Phillips, who served as InterAction's elected chairman of the Board and of the executive committee from November 1990 through November 1992, for his vision and for the skillful way in which he guided the open process to assure full involvement of InterAction's membership."[9]

Key point: The InterAction Standards assure that its member organizations adhere to a high level of ethical standards and have led to continuous improvement in their level of performance. The real results have been greater public credibility and trust as well as increased donor confidence and contributions.

When I asked Bennett Weiner of the Better Business Bureau Wise Giving Alliance about the effectiveness of codes of ethics, he wrote me with this comment: "Regarding the InterAction Standards, my impression is they are very comprehensive and cover items in detail. Regarding whether they are addressing the job intended may be a function of how careful members are in ensuring that they are following these guidelines." So true! The ultimate responsibility for ensuring good behavior rests with the leadership of each organization and the processes for investigation and possible sanctions.

Kitty Holt, director of ethics and compliance at Plan International USA from 2011 to 2022, gave me her view of the InterAction Standards from the perspective of a member organization. "It works if you take it seriously," she noted. "There's a lot of learning that could be done between organizations. We just have to make it more common as policy and practice."

The emphasis on using InterAction's Standards as a learning tool has continued, and complaints are addressed by its Standards Committee. The other good news is that there is a big movement for organizations to work together, an expansion in global standards for NGOs, and more pressure to demonstrate meaningful ethics especially by the charity evaluation agencies. Accordingly, the bigger organizations that comply with these three developments are getting

"We're almost done with our new code of ethics and how to enforce it."

"Let's finish and move on to how we communicate to all our stakeholders!"

Figure 5.4 Image showing people working together to accomplish an important task like drafting a code of ethics. Artwork by Wills Phillips.

better and getting larger. Unfortunately, however, the midsize organizations are getting squeezed, and the smallest are remaining small. You can visit my website at www.NGOFutures.com for key excerpts from the Standards and other guidance.

The challenge is to learn from others, turn the code of ethics into a culture of exemplary behavior, and then monitor the code and culture to assure compliance. If you don't do it right, donors will flee!

For the next levels of accountability, read on! You can do it! (Figure 5.4)

Questions for implementation

1   Have you drafted and implemented a meaningful code of ethics for your own organization? If not, list the actions you will take.
2   What do you need to do to get staff and board members to take your nonprofit's standards seriously?
3   If you are a member of professional associations, have you promoted a meaningful code of ethics for those associations? List actions you can take to introduce or strengthen a code of ethics for others.

Notes

1 See https://www.interaction.org/
2 The author served on a drafting committee in 1979 which drafted the organizational principles.
3 The following references are from the author's personal notes and records.
4 The five stages of standards development from the 1980s are now seven stages. https://www.ethics.org/resources/free-toolkit/decision-making-model/.
5 Jennifer Fisch, "International Relief Groups Develop Standards to Evaluate Themselves," *The NonProfit Times*, June 1991.
6 Stephen G. Green, "International Relief Groups Adopt Ethics Code," *The Chronicle of Philanthropy*, May 21, 1991, 28.
7 Stephen G. Green, "Relief Groups Adopt Ethical Standards for Governance, Finances, and Programs," *The Chronicle of Philanthropy*, December 1, 1992, 33.
8 InterAction NGO Standards, 2. https://www.interaction.org/documents/interaction-ngo-standards/
9 _____, 2.

Bibliography

1 InterAction NGO Standards, https://www.interaction.org/documents/interaction-ngo-standards.
2 Jennifer Fisch. "International Relief Groups Develop Standards to Evaluate Themselves." *The NonProfit Times*, June 1991.
3 Stephen G. Green. "International Relief Groups Adopt Ethics Code." *The Chronicle of Philanthropy*, May 21, 1991.
4 Stephen G. Green. "Relief Groups Adopt Ethical Standards for Governance, Finances, and Programs." *The Chronicle of Philanthropy*, December 1, 1992.

Chapter 6

Three progressive case studies – Developing stronger codes of ethics with external verification

In this chapter, I share three examples of important progression for meaningful codes of ethics. First, the Maryland Association of Nonprofit Organizations (US), which uses self-assessment and peer review. Second, the National Council for Voluntary Organizations (UK), which uses self-assessment and external verification. And third, the International Federation of Red Cross and Red Crescent Societies, which uses self-assessment, expert review, and sanctions when warranted.

Each of these associations or federations sought to implement more meaningful codes of ethics to strengthen their related organizations. A key point is that each realized it needed to supplement internal self-assessment with an independent, external review or verification process for enhanced credibility and accountability. You can learn from their depth of experience as you develop or strengthen a meaningful code of ethics for your own organization or association (Figure 6.1).

Three Case Studies

1. Maryland Association of Nonprofit Organizations (US) – strengthening local NGOs with assessment and peer review
2. National Committee for Voluntary Organizations (UK) –providing external assessment and validation to gain Trust
3. International Federation of Red Cross and Red Crescent Societies (192 National Societies) – assuring good performance with assessment, peer review, and sanctions

Figure 6.1 Three cases by NGO associations and how they improved their accountability. Sidebar by the author.

Maryland Association of Nonprofit Organizations' self-assessment and peer review process

A superb model focused on NGOs is the Standards for Excellence program offered by the Maryland Association of Nonprofit Organizations (MANO) with its practical approach of "Helping organizations through peer review."

MANO's Standards for Excellence Institute exists to promote excellence and integrity in nonprofit management and to strengthen the public's trust in nonprofit organizations in the state of Maryland and other participating states. MANO created Standards for Excellence, an Ethics & Accountability Program for the Nonprofit Sector to help the sector improve. It includes organizational self-assessment, benchmarks, and peer review, which results in accreditation with MANO (Figure 6.2).

According to Amy Coates Madsen, director of the Standards for Excellence Institute: "The Standards for Excellence originated as a special initiative of Maryland Nonprofits in 1998 and

DOI: 10.4324/9781003335207-8

Figure 6.2 Logo of the Standards for Excellence Institute of the Maryland Association of Nonprofits. Permission granted by the Maryland Association of Nonprofit Organizations.

has since expanded into a national program to help nonprofit organizations achieve the highest benchmarks of ethics and accountability in nonprofit governance, management, and operations. The program has been formally adopted by eleven state, regional, and national affiliate organizations and is supported by over 200 licensed consultants and over 100 volunteers with professional experience in nonprofit governance and administration. Since its inception, the program has accredited over 200 individual nonprofit organizations across the United States that completed a rigorous application and review process to demonstrate adherence to the Standards for Excellence: An Ethics and Accountability Code for the Nonprofit Sector."

In 2008, BoardSource named the Standards for Excellence code as "one of the most important milestones in the field of nonprofit governance in the last twenty years." The program has been cited as exemplary at hearings and roundtables before the U.S. Senate Committee on Finance and as part of the Advance America program of the American Society of Association Executives.[1]

Madsen told me: "We wanted to do something positive. As we were considering approaches and launching the initiative, a work group looked at about a hundred self-regulation codes and mapped what was in them. The InterAction PVO Standards were one of our models. It took about two years to write the code and we also developed a set of trainings, resources, and educational materials."

Applications are submitted through an online application portal. There is a three-step review process with a staff review, a peer review, and a committee review. The accreditation process is voluntary. "We believe that as long as an organization is working toward accreditation, we want to work with them for as long as it takes. The goal is to raise the level of these nonprofits," Madsen said.

To participate, an organization pays a modest membership fee and is required to pledge commitment to the Standards for Excellence code's six Guiding Principles, which address the following areas:

• Mission, strategy, and evaluation
• Leadership: Board, staff, and volunteers
• Legal compliance and ethics
• Finance and operations
• Resource development
• Public awareness, engagement, and advocacy

The applicant or member organization completes a self-assessment evaluation based on a checklist of the Standards for Excellence benchmarks to pinpoint what needs to be improved. Assistance, training programs, and resources are offered throughout the process. When ready, the organization submits its application to the Standards for Excellence Institute (or in the case of Ohio, Oklahoma, or Pennsylvania to their local Standards for Excellence licensed partner). After staff reviews the application, it is sent to the peer review step.

The peer review is conducted by people with experience in organizations of similar size but not necessarily the same field. The review is carried out on a strictly confidential basis including a prohibition against dissemination or copying of materials by reviewers. Reviewers receive access to the complete application package, meet to discuss adherence to the standards, and review the application in detail individually using a detailed Standards for Excellence peer review tool. Once the peer review is completed, the application moves next to the Standards for Excellence Council for approval. If denied, an applicant organization may appeal the decision to an Appeals Panel.

The Standards for Excellence program has 67 performance benchmarks in 27 main areas of nonprofit management and governance organized under six Guiding Principle areas. As part of the accreditation process, for example, an organization is asked to describe its conduct in the following benchmark areas:

- Board engagement in planning, approval of the budget, review of expenditure ratios, and annual evaluation of the executive director;
- How the board selects and orients new members; evaluates its own performance; what policies it has for terms of office, attendance, and participation; and prohibition against compensation for board members;
- What the organization's conflict of interest policy covers, what statement is completed (by board, staff, and volunteers), and how the statements are used within the organization;
- What information the organization provides to the public; how the public can provide input to the organization; how the organization reviews its compliance with legal, regulatory, and financial reporting requirements; and how employees can confidentially report suspected financial impropriety or misuse of funds;
- How the organization controls its fundraising, how much it spends to raise funds, how it solicits funds, how it protects donor privacy, and how it honors restrictions placed on contributions by donors;
- How its programs are evaluated, what information is collected (qualitative and quantitative), how outcomes are measured in relation to costs (program efficiency), how outcomes are measured for program participants (program effectiveness), how the evaluation system is used to strengthen and improve the organization, and what evaluation tools are used.

External verification through the three-step review process is required of all applicants. The process is conducted by individuals not associated with the applicant organization in order to provide an *external* assessment. The analysis is a *verification* that the applicant organization meets the Standards for Excellence benchmarks in governance and management. The result is accreditation and the right to use the Seal of Excellence demonstrating trustworthiness, effectiveness, and accountability.[2]

Key point: The lessons from the Standards for Excellence Institute's experience are: The use of standards as a means for self-improvement, emphasis on detailed benchmarks, the self-assessment process, guidance to improve performance, external peer review, and final accreditation with the right to use the Seal of Excellence, which demonstrates trustworthiness.

National Council for Voluntary Organization's self-assessment and external verification process

The National Council for Voluntary Organizations (NCVO) and Charities Evaluation Services (CES), both based in the U.K., merged in 2014. Charities Evaluation Services had been set up by the British government, because it determined it had to trust NGOs. The mission of CES was to improve the effectiveness of the NGO sector, and it provided a support network for voluntary sector organizations that wished to establish evaluation or quality systems. Now under the

Trusted Charity Mark

"The Trusted Charity process consists of an online self-assessment tool, followed by an optional external assessment to achieve the Trusted Charity Mark itself."

National Council for Voluntary Organizations

Figure 6.3 The Trusted Charity Mark is earned by self-assessment and independent external review. Image by the author.

umbrella of NCVO, the organization represents and supports more than 16,000 voluntary organizations of all sizes. In 2020, 3,000 people participated in its training programs and events, three million people visited its website, and its tools were downloaded more than 20,000 times (Figure 6.3).

CES used the following definition (which I still like): "Self-evaluation is a form of evaluation whereby the project itself seeks to understand and assess the value of its work. The project is the judge. The use of self-evaluation techniques allows those people involved in a project – whether they be managers, staff, or users – to reflect upon their practice and to view their project in a different way. In this way the process contributes to the strengthening and development of an organization."[3]

The method is participatory monitoring and evaluation and is applied to all functions of the organization. The self-evaluation process poses these questions:

1   What problem in society do we want to work with?
2   What change do we want to achieve?
3   What must we do to achieve this change?
4   How will we know when change has occurred?
5   Have we succeeded in producing the desired change?
6   What must we do differently to increase our success?
7   What change do we want to achieve?

Key point: The self-evaluation process identifies, supports, and encourages improvement throughout the organization – empowering the organization to strengthen and develop itself even more.

Charities Evaluation Services developed a Practical Quality Assurance System for Small Organizations (PQASSO) covering 16 quality areas, promoting continuous improvement through self-assessment, and helping organizations identify what they are doing well and what they need to improve. These areas cover all aspects of an NGO's work from quality to management, from networking to environmental studies, from user-centered service to monitoring and evaluation. The methodology (discipline) has been used by over 18,000 organizations.

The advantage of self-evaluation or self-assessment is involving the people working on the project themselves in a learning experience. However, the major limitation of self-evaluation is that outsiders see it as less objective and less credible – and that may certainly be so when there is no external review. When NCVO realized that an objective verification of self-assessed quality and credibility was needed, it added an external verification of excellence in governance and operations. It rebranded the discipline as Trusted Charity and launched it in 2019 at an event in the U.K. Parliament. NCVO's website states that: "The Trusted Charity process consists of an online self-assessment tool, followed by an optional external assessment to achieve the Trusted Charity Mark itself."

Trusted Charity areas assessed

1 Governance
2 Planning
3 Leadership and management
4 User-centered service
5 Managing people
6 Learning and development
7 Managing money
8 Managing resources
9 External communications
10 Working with others
11 Assessing outcomes and impact

Key point: The National Council for Voluntary Organizations requires NGOs to complete the online self-assessment and then to undergo an independent external verification to earn the Trusted Charity Mark.

Specially trained members of the sector with support from NCVO conduct the external assessments against the Trusted Charity standards. NCVO states that organizations will improve how they work, have more efficient systems, engage everyone in the process of improving how they work, and provide greater credibility and legitimacy that the organization is well run, accountable, and transparent. Note the emphasis in the Trusted Charity on governance, management, planning, learning and development, and assessing outcomes and impact![4]

International Federation of Red Cross and Red Crescent Societies' self-assessment and external expert review process with the possibility of sanctions

In 2004, when Ibrahim Osman, deputy secretary general at the International Federation of Red Cross and Red Crescent Societies (IFRC or the Federation), called to ask me to come to Geneva, Switzerland, for a two-year contract as head of the Federation's organizational development (OD) unit, I said "No" because my wife Rebecca and I had just returned from eight years in Geneva and were well settled in the United States.

I knew the Federation quite well as I had previously worked as a consultant to support some of IFRC's National Societies (member organizations) in Belarus, Uganda, and other countries as well as having led courses for National Society board members and executives on governance, leadership, fundraising, and organizational development. I also had helped to write and edit keystone IFRC manuals on fundraising, governance, and capacity building. I knew IFRC as a unique and vitally important global organization with special status, a long history, and significant accomplishments … but also with some significant organizational development problems in some of its National Societies.

Just twenty-four hours later and after a discussion with my wife over dinner, I changed my response to "Yes, let's talk." The task was to bring IFRC and the International Committee of the Red Cross (ICRC) closer together in a unified theory of how organizations develop, what the stages of development are, and how to know they are making progress. It was an irresistible opportunity to make a difference in one of the most important federations in the world.

Figure 6.4 Logo of the International Federation of Red Cross and Red Crescent Societies. Permission granted by the Federation.

A few months later we were settled in Geneva, and I was diving into my new role as leader of a small organizational development team. This was an extraordinary workload as the state of development of the Federation's National Society members ranged from very sophisticated to the other end of the spectrum. Fortunately, we were able to identify and recruit a dozen graduate students in Geneva to serve as interns for short-term assignments (Figure 6.4).

With significant help from regional directors and sector specialists in the Secretariat and from ICRC staff and very important input from the leading OD people from National Societies, we were able to develop a comprehensive OD approach, which we called "The Framework for National Society Development for Red Cross and Red Crescent Societies 2006–2008."[5] Informally, we called it *A Common Approach*, because it brought together both IFRC and ICRC in their support for National Societies around the world. Everything we did was built on a set of existing foundational documents including: "Characteristics of a Well-Functioning Society" (1995), "Strategy for 2010" (1999), "Strategy for the Movement" (2001), and "Strategy 2010 Mid-term Review" (2005).

The end product was a substantial policy agreement, which was approved by the governing board for IFRC and then ratified by the 2005 General Assembly and Council of Delegates from the entire International Red Cross and Red Crescent Movement, consisting of the International Committee of the Red Cross, the International Federation of Red Cross and Red Crescent Societies, and 180 (now 192) National Red Cross and Red Crescent Societies.

Based on our work, the Council of Delegates approved new strategic goals for the entire Movement, which confirmed the strategic objective to strengthen the components of the Movement with the following expected results: "A single, common Movement approach to capacity building and organizational development. ... More resources committed to capacity building. ... Common terminology and performance indicators with regard to capacity building, organizational development and planning ... [and] an enhanced sense of discipline and commitment by all components present in a given country to maximize the use of available resources and to work together in a coordinated and effective manner."[6]

All of this would be made possible by related commitments to "monitor external trends and analyze data from relevant sources" and to "promote learning from experience through systematic evaluations of national and international activities, and through a system of knowledge sharing and 'best practice' within the Movement." It was a significant accomplishment!

The operational Framework was a comprehensive policy and action statement for the Movement. It included policy, guidance, tools, and progress indicators in the following categories:

- Foundation (policy, strategy, and legal base);
- People (leadership, governance, management, youth, volunteering, gender, and equal opportunity);
- Organization (assessment, strategic planning, cooperation strategy, project planning process, monitoring and evaluation, relationship development, development in emergencies, and new societies);

- Finance (financial management and resource mobilization);
- Capacity (capacity building, community development, social mobilization, poverty alleviation, and core programs);
- Financial and technical assistance (funding, delegates, consulting skills, stages of development, measurement, results-oriented workshops, organizational change, knowledge management, cultural sensitivity, and inventory of tools).

Looking back on the process of developing and implementing the Framework for National Society Development, I can say now that the essence was strengthening National Societies through identified strategies, guidance, and progressive steps. More than a static document, this significant initiative unified the Federation and ICRC more closely in how they support National Societies in 180 countries to become more effective and more efficient, which is why we selected the name "A Common Approach".

Key points in the Framework are the importance of learning from experience, performance indicators, systematic evaluations, analysis of data, and knowledge sharing. Since then, the Federation has made substantial progress in its management of organizational development and capacity building around the world and has greatly improved the model and guidance we developed between 2004 and 2006.

IFRC's policy states that monitoring and evaluation is both principle and practice. "Monitoring and evaluation (M&E) is an integral part of all IFRC project and programs. This guide promotes a common understanding and reliable practice of monitoring and evaluation for use by National Red Cross and Red Crescent Societies and our humanitarian partners."[7]

I was thrilled to learn in recent conversations with Frank Mohrhauer, director of National Society policy and knowledge development at the Federation, about two significant steps they have taken since 2006. Significantly, they have transitioned from *organizational development* to *National Society development*, a more comprehensive concept. In 2008, the Federation adopted a new constitution, which included a governance tool to address integrity in National Societies and enabled the Federation's governing board to impose certain conditions leading to and requiring integrity with the ultimate sanction of suspension from all Federation activities, rights, and benefits.[8]

A dashboard of eight categories supports this development and takes it far beyond monitoring and evaluation into accountability and continuous learning. This includes the obligations of a National Society in the duties of membership, a requirement to submit information to the IFRC, and a significant shift to evidence and tools to measure sustainability. The Federation is now looking into the possibility to launch a verification system and certain compliance standards.

The new constitution put in place strong systems to support National Society policy and development. In 2010, an Organizational Capacity and Certification Tool was established with eighty-five attributes. The first step is self-assessment by the National Society facilitated by Federation staff, followed by the second step of a global team to review the self-assessment. The National Society is then given the results and taking the appropriate action is up to them. Next, a peer review follows and, if appropriate improvements are made, the governing board certifies the National Society for all Federation activities, rights, and benefits. If a National Society becomes an integrity case in line with the IFRC integrity policy, the governing board can sanction (and has done so) an offending National Society with suspension of the rights, privileges, and funding as a member of the Federation.

As noted in its 2020 Annual Report, "The IFRC utilizes the Organizational Capacity Assessment and Certification Process, to support National Societies to assess their capacities and identify where they would like to improve."[9]

Trustworthiness – Code of ethics and transparency
Program Impact – Meaningful results for beneficiaries
Activities – Communication about all you are doing
Verification – External review of your self-assessments

Figure 6.5 Donors want accountability about an NGO's trustworthiness, impact, activities, and verification. Image by the author.

Mohrhauer cited two other concepts. The first is "learn to change" and the second is "National Society as convener." Underlying these excellent developments in the last 15 years since we broke new ground with "A Common Approach" and the Framework for National Society Development is the challenge to capture learning, so it leads to change and improved performance. As a unique global Movement with activities nearly everywhere, IFRC and ICRC, working together, have a responsibility to promote continuous learning and to bring together all sectors in society to make this a better world.

In the 2020 annual report, IFRC highlighted its commitments to accountability and integrity: "Trust, community engagement, accountability, and integrity were common threads connecting the work of IFRC's general assembly, the council of delegates, and the office of internal audit and investigations." A key strategy is to: "Ensure a strong IFRC that is effective, credible, and accountable … improving transparency and accountability, mitigating risk of fraud and corruption, and enhancing quality of service and value for money for itself and its members."

And "The IFRC's principal objective is to support the work of National Societies. This means helping National Societies to become strong, effective local organizations that are trusted, accountable and capable to carry out programs for vulnerable communities at scale."[10,11]

The Federation has also introduced what it calls the Red Cross and Red Crescent Integrity Line. It is a publically available link where "Anyone can report any incident or misconduct that affects the integrity of IFRC personnel, assets or operations. This includes: fraud and corruption, sexual exploitation and abuse, harassment, child safeguarding, security incidents, health and safety, information security breaches and emblem misuse." Anyone can report by an online link, email, or telephone. Impressive!

Key point: The stories from MANO, NCVO, and IFRC show an increasing emphasis on supplementing self-assessment with external peer review or expert review followed by the possibility of receiving special trusted status or being sanctioned, depending on the external review (Figure 6.5).

It is critical to supplement self-assessment with an independent review

Each of these organizations took a different path to create its standards. A key point was the realization by each that it needed to supplement an internal, self-assessment with an objective, external review or verification process for enhanced credibility and accountability.

"It was not a simple task, but now we have a strong ethics commitment."

Figure 6.6 People in an NGO working together to complete their ethics statement. Artwork by Sawyer Phillips.

To gain trust and respect, it is imperative to find a way, either on your own or in an association, to implement an expert external review process, act on resulting recommendations, and report the results to stakeholders. Whatever role you play in a nonprofit, you should advocate for independent review to assure the highest level of trustworthiness, which will secure increased support from donors.

As a personal note, when I was executive director, I initially used self-assessment as the first step in the annual personnel reviews of managers reporting to me and learned early on that they were overly positive and insufficiently self-analytical. Later, I added the caution that I would add an external review (my own) and that the more honest the self-appraisal was the better the final appraisal would be. I couldn't rely on "internal" self-assessment and had to confirm or correct the information with an "external" review (Figure 6.6).

Questions for implementation

1   How can you apply the lessons from these case studies to your NGO or association?
2   Is your organization conducting a periodic self-assessment of trust-related issues?
3   Is your organization participating in an external review of trust-related issues?
4   Are you communicating to key stakeholders the results of these assessments? If not, what will you do about it?

Notes

1 Praise for MANO's Standards for Excellence Institute, see https://thecentermsu.org/board/.
2 Read more about the Standards for Excellence Institute at http://standardsforexcellence.org/home-2/code/.
3 For information about the National Council for Voluntary Organizations (NCVO) and Charities Evaluation Service (CES), see https://www.ncvo.org.uk/.

4 Read more at https://www.growthco.uk/news/the-growth-company-launches-trusted-charity-mark-after-winning-bid/ (August 18, 2021).
5 Kenneth Phillips et al., "The Framework for National Society Development for Red Cross and Red Crescent Societies 2006–2008," *Internal IFRC documents*, April 2006.
6 International Committee of the Red Cross, "Council of Delegates 2005: Resolution 6," November 18, 2005, 32–34, accessed July 3, 2022, https://www.icrc.org/en/doc/resources/documents/resolution/council-delegates-resolution-6–2005.htm.
7 International Federation of Red Cross and Red Crescent Societies, "Project / Programme Monitoring and Evaluation Guide," September 21, 2021, accessed July 3, 2022, https://www.ifrc.org/document/projectprogramme-monitoring-and-evaluation-guide.
8 International Federation of Red Cross and Red Crescent Societies, "IFRC Constitution":10, 12, 14, accessed July 3, 2022, https://www.ifrc.org/sites/default/files/2021-08/01_IFRC-Constitution-2019-EN.pdf.
9 International Federation of Red Cross and Red Crescent Societies, "IFRC Annual Report 2020," 2021, 49, accessed July 3, 2022, https://www.ifrc.org/sites/default/files/2021-09/20210902_AnnualReport_ONLINE.pdf.
10 Ibid., 17, 29, 42.
11 International Federation of Red Cross and Red Crescent Societies. "Report a concern | IFRC." Assessed November 4, 2022. https://www.ifrc.org/our-promise/do-good/report-concern.

Bibliography

1 International Committee of the Red Cross. "Council of Delegates 2005: Resolution 6," November 18, 2005. Accessed July 3, 2022. https://www.icrc.org/en/doc/resources/documents/resolution/council-delegates-resolution-6–2005.htm.
2 International Federation of Red Cross and Red Crescent Societies. "IFRC Annual Report 2020," 2021. Accessed July 3, 2022. https://www.ifrc.org/sites/default/files/2021-09/20210902_AnnualReport_ONLINE.pdf.
3 International Federation of Red Cross and Red Crescent Societies. "IFRC Constitution." Accessed July 3, 2022. https://www.ifrc.org/sites/default/files/2021-08/01_IFRC-Constitution-2019-EN.pdf.
4 International Federation of Red Cross and Red Crescent Societies. "Project / Programme Monitoring and Evaluation Guide," September 21, 2021. Accessed July 3, 2022. https://www.ifrc.org/document/projectprogramme-monitoring-and-evaluation-guide.
5 Phillips, Kenneth, et al. "The Framework for National Society Development for Red Cross and Red Crescent Societies 2006-2008." *Internal IFRC document*, April 2006.
6 International Federation of Red Cross and Red Crescent Societies. "Report a Concern." Accessed November 4, 2022. https://www.ifrc.org/our-promise/do-good/report-concern.

Chapter 7

Rhode Island case study – Ensuring enforcement and sanctions for more effective codes of ethics

A code of ethics is not simply a nicely written piece of paper with uplifting promises to "strive to do our best," which is shared and then filed and maybe forgotten. Instead, a meaningful code of ethics must be a living document that is regularly reviewed, assessed, and used to ensure full compliance. And without question, it must have teeth. It must address accountability and include specific details about compliance, enforcement, and appropriate sanctions.

This chapter presents another personal story of stepping up to improve ethical behavior through independent review of inappropriate behavior based on established standards and powerful sanctions. Although it is about a state in the United States, it will provide insights for nonprofits as well (Figure 7.1).

After moving to Rhode Island for a new position as executive director of Foster Parents Plan, I came across a huge funeral procession with crowds of people on the street watching with respect and sadness as the funeral party passed. I think there were even prominent politicians walking in the lead. I asked a woman next to me who the procession was honoring, and she said, "Oh, he was a nice guy. He always took care of everybody." I asked her what he did, and she said, "Oh, he ran a coin operating store. He's a great guy, always helping everyone. He's a *Patriarca!*"

Later, I learned he was the head of the New England mob crime family for 20 years and "controlled more than five thousand underworld operatives throughout New England, running his shadowy empire from a vending machine company on Atwells Avenue," according to Phil West's book *Secrets & Scandals: Reforming Rhode Island 1986–2006.*[1] My understanding was that you had to get his approval to rob a bank, hold up a liquor store, steal manhole covers, bribe judges, pay off elected officials, or engage in any other illegal activity in Rhode Island.

I began to discover that corruption in Rhode Island state politics was extreme. State contracting and purchasing projects were dominated by conflicts of interest. Flipping houses (buy low, sell high) provided huge gains for politicians. Bribery was a common practice. The state's affordable housing agency, its statewide credit union association, and other agencies were deeply corrupt. People absconded with millions of dollars. The chief justice of the Rhode Island Supreme Court had previously served as defense lawyer for the New England mob! There was clear evidence that he was "on the take." In 1986, facing certain impeachment for outrageous corruption, he resigned. One governor, two Supreme Court justices, several mayors, several state legislators, and some agency directors were found to be among the many corrupt officials in the 1980s and 1990s.

"Between 1986 and 2006 Rhode Island ran a gauntlet of scandals that exposed corruption, aroused public indignation, and moved thousands to march on the State House. ... Flawed government structures had spawned corruption in all three branches of Rhode Island state government."[2] Those are the opening lines in West's book, which includes extraordinary detail from the time I lived in Rhode Island and witnessed incredible and pervasive corruption in the

DOI: 10.4324/9781003335207-9

Rhode Island

- One of the 50 states in the United States of America
- From 1663 to 1843 the people of Rhode Island were governed under a Royal Charter granted by King Charles II of England
- First American colony to renounce allegiance to King George III on May 4, 1776
- The state legislature has a 75-member House of Representatives and a 38-member Senate
- The current Rhode Island Constitution was adopted in 1986 and has the strongest ethics commission

The State of Rhode Island General Laws

Figure 7.1 The constitutional highlights for the state of Rhode Island. Sidebar by the author.

state. Clearly, ethics reform was needed to combat and, ideally, eradicate the rampant corruption of state officials. (The other quoted items in this chapter are from West's book.)

Corruption was in the news, and an open Constitutional Convention had been scheduled for 1986. This Convention was to have people from the general public as delegates rather than politicians. I stepped up because of my conviction about the importance of ethics in government just as much as, or even more than, in civil society organizations. The Convention was based on elections of 100 delegates, one from each state representative district. An astounding 565 candidates – ordinary citizens who had chosen to step up – gathered the necessary signatures to be eligible, and I was one of them. On election night, I was a clear winner!

All sections of the State Constitution were up for discussion and presentation to voters for approval or rejection. When we convened on January 6, 1986, the first business was organizing how we would work. I naturally chose to be on the Convention's committee on ethics. We worked many evenings for many months that year. We got expert advice, conducted research, debated many options, and drafted a proposed constitutional amendment on ethics in government. As the secretary of the committee on ethics, I had the responsibility of capturing the views of the committee members, suggesting and writing down proposed wording, and recording our conclusions.

We proposed a dramatic new approach to improve ethics in government through a new and truly independent Ethics Commission, which would establish standards, investigate the actions of any government official or government employee in the entire state, and take appropriate action. First, we established the principle that "The people of Rhode Island believe that public officials and employees must adhere to the highest standards of ethical conduct, respect the public trust and the rights of all persons, be open, accountable and responsive, avoid the appearance of impropriety and not use their positions for private gain or advantage. Such persons shall hold their positions during good behavior."[3]

Then our resolution, if passed, would direct the General Assembly to establish an "independent non-partisan Ethics Commission" that would "adopt a code of ethics, including, but not limited to, provisions on conflict of interest, confidential information, use of position, contracts with government agencies and financial disclosure."[4]

We knew that politicians on their own would *not* create and adhere to a stringent code of ethics that would address accountability, include mechanism for enforcement, and authorize severe sanctions; therefore, the independent, non-partisan Ethics Commission would have that responsibility. Then we determined that "All elected and appointed officials and employees of state and local government, of boards, commissions and agencies shall be subject to the code of ethics."[5]

To make the code of ethics meaningful, we also decided that our resolution would empower the Ethics Commission "to investigate violations of the code of ethics and impose penalties, as provided by law; and the commission shall have the power to remove from office officials who are not subject to impeachment."[6] As the historian and ethics leader Phil West writes in his book, "By conferring both the authority to create the new code and the power to enforce it, they were proposing the strongest government ethics agency in the United States."[7]

Our committee unanimously endorsed the above components of our ethics reform as our proposed constitutional amendment. The entire Constitutional Convention approved our proposed amendment, which was included on the ballot in the November 1986 statewide vote. Rhode Island voters approved our Ethics and Government Amendment and, as West summarized, "The convention's innovative proposal to combat corruption became part of the Rhode Island Constitution."[8] I was proud to be part of this effort!

The wording of the amendment is now contained in Article III Qualifications of Office in the Rhode Island Constitution:

- "Section 7. The people of the state of Rhode Island believe that public officials and employees must adhere to the highest standards of ethical conduct, respect the public trust and the rights of all persons, be open, accountable and responsive, avoid the appearance of impropriety and not use their position for private gain or advantage. Such person shall hold their positions during good behavior."
- "Section 8. The General assembly shall establish an independent non-partisan ethics commission which shall adopt a code of ethics including, but not limited to, provisions on conflicts of interest, confidential information, use of position, contracts with government agencies and financial disclosure. All elected and appointed officials and employees of state and local government, of boards, commissions and agencies shall be subject to the code of ethics. The ethics commission shall have the authority to investigate violations of the code of ethics and to impose penalties, as provided by law; and the commission shall have the power to remove from office officials who are not subject to impeachment" (Figure 7.2).

We were just regular citizens but did important work, so it was no surprise that state politicians immediately began to undercut what the voters had just approved. In fact, the resistance extended for years, especially trying to disempower the new non-partisan Ethics Commission. The politicians themselves wanted to "draft and enforce" their own code of ethics. Clearly, this would have meant a complete nullification of meaningful standards, enforcements, and sanctions with only some ghost ethics remaining! A central theme of West's book is the relentless efforts of legislators, governors, and judges to undermine the Ethics Commission's authority.

I continued my support for the ethics amendment as an elected board member (1987–1991) of Common Cause Rhode Island, an advocacy agency established to promote good government. The leadership of Common Cause Rhode Island and its many partners and allies worked tirelessly to overcome the opposition to actual implementation of the approved amendment and confirm that the new Ethics Commission – and not the politicians – would do the ethics work.

Finally in 1992, the Rhode Island Supreme Court, with a new chief justice, unanimously endorsed the totality of the work of our committee on ethics as ratified by the voters. I was rather pleased to read that in their decision: "The justices flagged a comment from delegate Ken Phillips, who had proposed that the Conflict of Interest Commission or its successor agency [i.e., the new Ethics Commission] should 'draft, promulgate, and implement' the code of ethics."[9]

Figure 7.2 The author holding a copy of the 1988 Rhode Island Constitution. Photograph by Rebecca Phillips.

Phil West summarized that "this decision marked a watershed in Rhode Island's history that would go a long way toward establishing the Ethics Commission's power."[10]

Nevertheless, the battle continued with resistance from lawmakers and politicians including a series of governors: Packing the commission with legislative and executive puppets, slashing the commission's budget, appointing members who sabotaged rules, and challenging the commission's jurisdiction over members of the General Assembly. Only a further constitutional amendment led by John Marion, executive director of Common Cause Rhode Island, and approved by voters in 2016 finally solidified the Ethics Commission's authority. That year 78%

of voters supported the amendment to "restore the Ethics Commission's authority to police ethics violations by members of the General Assembly."[11]

West wrote me in 2022 that "Extraordinary in its scope, the Rhode Island Ethics Commission remains unique among the fifty states in its power to investigate conflicts-of-interest complaints against all public officials in the state: legislative, executive, judicial, both statewide and in municipalities."[12]

Whereas Rhode Island was widely known as one of the most corrupt states in the mid-1980s, now 35 years later, it ranks as one of the least corrupt! In his book, West cites Chicago's Better Government Association (BGA), which rates states on their laws on integrity, accountability, and transparency: "In 2002 and 2008, the BGA ranked Rhode Island second in the nation."[13] In 2013, the BGA headline was "Rhode Island Ranked #1 in National Integrity Index."[14]

Another good government organization, the Coalition for Integrity, published its 2019 ratings of Enforcement of Ethics Rules by State Agencies with this conclusion: "Colorado, Florida, Minnesota, and Rhode Island scored 100 on transparency of ethics enforcement (on a scale of 0–100). Their ethics agencies produce annual reports which compile statistics on the number of complaints received, dismissed, resolved with a finding of no ethics violation, resolved with a finding of an ethics violation, and they make the decisions of the ethics agency publicly available in easily accessible fashion."[15]

Another ranking by the States With Anti-Corruption Measures for Public Officials (S.W.A.M.P.) Index in 2020 concludes: "Three states, Washington (80), Rhode Island (78), and the District of Columbia (76) land at the top of the score chart."[16]

The lesson I draw from Rhode Island's struggle to get ethics and enforcement right is that it takes leadership and persistence. The decades-long progress was the result of ethical political leaders and tenacious attorneys general who never gave up to get what was needed and was finally delivered – the ethics reforms that the voters approved, which began with the Constitutional Convention of 1986.

At my 81st birthday celebration, Phil West, who wrote the definitive book on corruption and ethics in Rhode Island, praised my "vision which went far beyond what any expected in dismantling the culture of corruption that had long made Rhode Island – in the words of Lincoln Steffens – 'a state for sale.'" Then he presented a copy of his book to me with the following author inscription: "To Ken Phillips – Visionary ethics leader of the 1986 Constitutional Convention."

Key point: For meaningful ethics, we concluded that they must include independent review of compliance, ability to gather information as needed, and authority to apply meaningful sanctions in case of clear violations of the code.

Learn from the Rhode Island experience to achieve meaningful ethics

Here are the requirements we included in the state's constitutional amendment approved by the voters. There are lessons for nonprofits as well as other states and even countries to gain the trust of donors (and voters):

1 A meaningful code of ethics is necessary to assure good behavior, transparency, and accountability.
2 The code includes essential ethical standards and procedures for implementation.
3 Independent experts review and confirm compliance or noncompliance with the code.
4 The ability to gather information without restriction is essential for validation.

5   The possibility of sanctions is needed to assure adherence to the code of ethics.
6   Key stakeholders are informed about the code, related processes, and conclusions.

Whatever your position is in your nonprofit, you may need to advocate for these steps to assure trustworthiness. Remember, even if your NGO already has a basic code of ethics or code of behavior, your organization deserves a *meaningful* code of ethics that includes impartial review and sanctions – a code of ethics that has teeth. A meaningful code of ethics directly impacts your level of trustworthiness, your donors' confidence in your program's impact and, in my experience, fundraising success (Figure 7.3).

Questions for implementation

1   Do you think Rhode Island would have cleaned up its corruption without a strong code of ethics and sanctions?
2   Do you see a pathway to step up to put a strong (or stronger) code of ethics in place?
3   How do you relate the Rhode Island case to your own organization or city or state? Or NGO?

"This is awesome!"

Figure 7.3 Image of a young person expressing joy when something awesome is done. Artwork by Sawyer Phillips.

Notes

1 H. Philip West Jr., *Secrets & Scandals: Reforming Rhode Island 1986–2006* (Rhode Island Publications Society, 2014), 13.
2 Ibid., ix.
3 *Annotated Edition. Constitution of the State of Rhode Island and Providence Plantations: Done in Convention at Providence on the Fourth Day of December, A.D. 1986, Section 7* (The Office of Secretary of State, 1988), 15–16.
4 Ibid., 16.
5 Ibid.
6 Ibid.
7 H. Philip West Jr., *Secrets & Scandals: Reforming Rhode Island 1986–2006*, 5.
8 Ibid., 7.
9 Ibid., 165.
10 Ibid., 166.
11 "Rhode Island Ethics Commission Amendment, Question 2 (2016)," *Ballotpedia*, accessed July 4, 2022, https://ballotpedia.org/Rhode_Island_Ethics_Commission_Amendment,_Question_2_(2016).
12 Phil West, Email from Phil West to author, June 17, 2022.
13 H. Philip West Jr., *Secrets & Scandals: Reforming Rhode Island 1986–2006*, x.
14 Ibid.
15 "Enforcement of Ethics Rules by State Ethics Agencies: Unpacking the S.W.A.M.P. Index," *Coalition for Integrity*, September 12, 2019, 1, accessed July 4, 2022, http://unpacktheswamp.coalitionforintegrity.org.
16 "States With Anti-Corruption Measures for Public Officials (S.W.A.M.P.) Index," *Coalition for Integrity*, November 18, 2020, 11, accessed July 4, 2022, https://www.coalitionforintegrity.org/swamp2020/.

Bibliography

1 Annotated Edition. *Constitution of the State of Rhode Island and Providence Plantations: Done in Convention at Providence on the Fourth Day of December, A.D. 1986, Section 7*. The Office of Secretary of State, 1988.
2 "Rhode Island Ethics Commission Amendment, Question 2 (2016)." *Ballotpedia*. Accessed July 4, 2022. https://ballotpedia.org/Rhode_Island_Ethics_Commission_Amendment,_Question_2_(2016).
3 "Enforcement of Ethics Rules by State Ethics Agencies: Unpacking the S.W.A.M.P. Index." *Coalition for Integrity*, September 12, 2019. Accessed July 4, 2022. http://unpacktheswamp.coalitionforintegrity.org.
4 "States With Anti-Corruption Measures for Public Officials (S.W.A.M.P.) Index." *Coalition for Integrity*, November 18, 2020. Accessed July 4, 2022. https://www.coalitionforintegrity.org/swamp2020/.
5 West, H. Philip Jr. *Secrets & Scandals: Reforming Rhode Island 1986–2006*. Rhode Island Publications Society, 2014.
6 West, H. Philip Jr. Email from H. Philip West Jr. to author, June 17, 2022.

Chapter 8

Twelve lessons to earn trust – Clarity, assessments, sanctions, reporting, and more

The following lessons are intended to encourage you to play a leadership role in your own organization to develop, strengthen, and follow a meaningful code of ethics – whether you are a leader, manager, or fundraiser. This is all necessary for your organization's success (Figure 8.1).

I first learned these lessons – what I call trust lessons – as a young fundraiser when I found something was missing or wrong or when other departments resisted giving me the information or cooperation I needed to assure fundraising success. As I gained more experience in learning what donors really wanted, I became more insistent and demanding on their behalf to get what was needed from top management (especially in finance and program), field workers and volunteers, and even the executive director and the board of directors. This included evaluation data that proved program impact, ongoing commitment to program innovation and improvement, cost-saving initiatives that could be quantified and reported to donors, and factual success stories with supporting data. Without their support, I could not have been as successful as I have been in fundraising, developing new strategies, and supporting capacity building and board development.

I know that mid-size and small NGOs and community associations have very different challenges compared to large nonprofits with strong track records and large marketing budgets and with universities and hospitals with their strong reputations, huge revenues from tuition and fees for service, and donations from affluent alumni and grateful family members.

The vast majority of NGOs struggle to gain public awareness, secure external support, find new donors, and afford needed fundraising staff. For them, gaining trust is probably the best place to focus their attention to increase fundraising success. Ever-greater fundraising success supports better programs, so they can continue to grow, have more lasting impact, and make a better world.

LESSON 1: Both financial support and volunteer support for nonprofits depend on trust

In a world in which nearly all nonprofits receive insufficient financial support, it is imperative to put in place a process to earn the trust of donors in your organization. Everything depends on excellent behavior of everyone involved in the organization. You need a sterling image and a meaningful code of ethics as part of your presentation to donors, authorities, partners, and the public to demonstrate you are worthy of their support. They are giving their money or time to you to help someone or something else, and quite simply, they will not do this if they don't trust you. People have to trust to give.

DOI: 10.4324/9781003335207-10

What is Trust?

TRUST = Assured reliance on the character, ability, strength, or truth of someone or something

ASSURED = characterized by certainty or security; guaranteed

Merriam-Webster dictionary

Figure 8.1 Definitions of trust and assurance of trust. Image by the author.

LESSON 2: Board members, staff, and volunteers need clear ethical standards to assure they are doing things in a proper way and to be held accountable

The value of a meaningful code of ethics is that it raises the level of an NGO's performance and increases public confidence and support. Having a code of ethics is the first step to demonstrate trustworthiness to the public just as program evaluation is the first step to demonstrate program impact. Some nonprofit directors may think the organization does not need a code of ethics, but experience says it is better to have this in place. The objection that "We don't need new standards; our behavior is already good" can be countered with "Then there is no reason for you to resist them."

A strong code of ethics provides standards for responsibility, organizational integrity, fundraising honesty, financial correctness, administrative efficiency, program effectiveness, transparency, and public accountability. Donors have been saying what they want in poll after poll for the 50 years I have been tracking public opinion about charities. Donors want ethical behavior, good results, and accountability before they contribute.

LESSON 3: Board members, staff, and volunteers should be involved in a participatory process to develop, apply, and assess the code to assure ethical behavior

The process of developing, reviewing, and updating a code of ethics is as important as the standards themselves, because participation raises awareness and creates consensus around important ethical standards. It gets everyone more involved and more committed than imposing the final standards. Implementing, explaining, and enforcing the code of ethics are all effective components to make it effective. And the process continues with annual assessments and occasional improvements to the code. Include "assuring our code of ethics" in every job description and performance review.

LESSON 4: The board of directors should draft and affirm its own written code of ethics

Board members are volunteers from companies, partner organizations, or other professions who bring specific expertise to the board. The board's code of ethics must be different from the NGO's general code of ethics. The board's code includes requiring unblemished reputation of its members, regular participation at board and committee meetings, and prohibition of any self-dealing, financial benefit, or conflict of interest.

If a member has a close connection or a potential conflict, he/she should automatically be excused from discussion of the issue or step down from the board. Nonprofits are different from businesses, and I have seen that we often need to educate business members of nonprofit boards that NGOs have more stringent standards of conduct to assure the nonprofit does not lose the public's hard-won trust.

Since board members of a nonprofit serve as volunteers and without compensation, there should be *no* transactions and *no* privileged information from which a board member might receive personal financial benefit. The board of directors must avoid even the appearance of a conflict of interest in expenditures or financial benefits from privileged information. Each board member should sign an annual attestation confirming compliance to the code.

LESSON 5: Every organization should have a system to encourage and act on complaints, concerns, and whistleblowing about possible infractions

Responsive customer service to donors is the first step, so they know that any concerns they may have are welcomed and will be addressed. A suggestion box or other system for employees, volunteers, and participants to make confidential suggestions and complaints is another needed step. Acting on such concerns is imperative, as is assuring protection to anyone reporting abuse or other violation of the code of ethics. Periodic questionnaires to donors, staff, board members, volunteers, and program participants are important to uncover any concerns about delicate or serious matters, so those can be addressed. Such questionnaires are tailored to the different groups.

If there is a program strategy that is failing; misuse of funds; violation of privacy; conflict of interest by a board or staff member; harassment or abuse of an employee, volunteer, or program participant; or any other infraction of the code of ethics, the senior management or board committee must take appropriate and remedial action. Safe and confidential feedback can prevent problems from becoming bigger or from continuing. It is so much better to correct something before it becomes a public scandal!

LESSON 6: Individual NGOs and NGO associations must be serious about their codes of ethics

Codes of ethics need to be made operational to ensure they are clear and understood by all concerned and can be assessed and enforced without argument. When individual nonprofits and their networks clearly define their standards for staff and volunteers, the clarity will lead to better behavior, smoother operations, and improved results.

Since the reason NGOs exist is for their program results, it is appropriate to involve program participants or their representatives in planning, implementation, evaluation, and even review of the nonprofit's fundraising messages, use of funds, and ethical behavior. When this is communicated to stakeholders, trust will increase. Updates on ethics and accountability are "good news" in reports to donors and on websites.

LESSON 7: An organization should be prepared to deal with a scandal

Scandals do happen in nonprofits, and it is wise to be prepared. Cover up and inaction are often worse than the infraction itself. It is important to have a crisis management plan including designated personnel who are ready to respond quickly and correctly. The best response is to take prompt action to correct the problem, share you what you have done, and communicate the policies or other initiatives the organization puts in place to prevent a recurrence of the problem.

When there is a scandal about another nonprofit, it is time to take stock and review your own situation. A scandal in another NGO may present an opportunity if you are ready to promote your standards – your code of ethics or code of behavior – as an example of accountability without criticizing the other organization, of course. Unfortunately, a scandal in other NGOs can reflect poorly on yours, too. It is smart to present your organization as one that adheres to excellent standards.

The cover up of a scandal is the worst possible strategy. It may initially "protect" certain higher officials but it will almost always multiply the negative publicity. The correct strategy is to admit it was wrong, state what you have learned, and commit to how you will behave in the future.

LESSON 8: Nonprofits and their NGO associations benefit by developing a culture of sharing about ethics

I have seen so many times that people working in NGOs everywhere in the world resist sharing their experiences and lessons learned, even their successes, and especially their failures. On the surface, this appears to make sense. Why would you want to give away your "secrets or failures" to your competitors?

However, I have found again and again that I learned more by sharing with colleagues even if they were competitors in the marketplace. In this reciprocal sharing and learning, competitors can be your best colleagues and teachers. It is a matter of building trust for mutual benefit, but you may have to lead with the sharing before it becomes reciprocal. Leadership in a trust-building and sharing process can reap significant results.

LESSON 9: It has often been the initiative of one person to introduce and generate support for a code of ethics for an NGO or association

A code is something that almost everyone believes in and will support, especially when you say that it is "needed to secure the funding we all want for our programs." It is possible for one person, in a nonthreatening manner, to initiate a plan to develop a code of ethics by referring to the expectations of external constituencies such as donors, potential donors, authorities, and others who want to see a clear statement confirming the organization's good behavior. It is difficult for anyone in the organization to say, "I don't support good ethics."

If your initiate a process to develop (or strengthen) a code of ethics and do so without being critical of others, everyone else will jump on board for the good of the organization.

LESSON 10: The fundraising director can take the lead in all these activities when there is need to do so

Without this leadership, the chances of fundraising success are significantly diminished. The fundraising director or anyone with fundraising responsibilities can step up to urge improved performance and good ethics by everyone associated with the organization. A fundraiser can say to others, including senior directors and board members, "If you want me to succeed, I need your help. I need you to do these things, so I will have a stronger case to present to our prospective donors, so they can trust us." Turn your program and finance directors into allies to make your NGO attractive to donors.

LESSON 11: You can play a role at the national level and become known as an advocate for strong codes of ethics for all nonprofits

In every book in my *Civil Society Series*, I consistently advocate for everyone – and I mean everyone – to step up as a leader, no matter your role in the organization. As a leader when you are not the boss, you can advocate for a meaningful code of ethics, compile and promote good practices, organize confidential peer reviews, conduct surveys to learn more about donor needs and expectations, enforce existing self-regulation codes, and even develop new standards where the sector is vulnerable.

Become an advocate for trust. Your enthusiasm and leadership will enable you to make your nonprofit a model and leader in the field, facilitate improvements in the civil society sector, and move to ever-higher levels of responsibility and accountability in your own work.

LESSON 12: To gain a full measure of trust, an organization needs self-assessments, external verification, enforcement, sanctions, and reporting to support a code of ethics

When implementing a code of ethics, the big challenge to make it meaningful is to address the issues of assessment, verification, enforcement, and sanctions. Self-regulation works when it is taken seriously. If the review process becomes routine, it may become ignored. It requires these external components to ensure meaningful ethics:

- *A watchdog within the organization* – Someone who will monitor compliance, organize self-assessments, and create a strong whistleblower policy.
- *External review and verification* – This can be reliance on serious peer review or external accreditation.
- *Enforcement and sanctions* – These are needed to assure ethical behavior and provide assurance to key stakeholders.

Key point: As a fundraiser, I have often led efforts for a strong code of ethics and justified the effort by communicating that I was the contact with donors. I understood what donors needed and was able to assure everyone how essential trust is to donors and fundraising success.

Years ago at an Association of Fundraising Professionals conference in Connecticut, I gave the keynote.[1] After reviewing what I considered the low level of charitable contributions in the United States, I presented the four reasons for non-giving and highlighted that charities must:

1   Scale up evaluation to prove program effectiveness and results to prove lasting impact.
2   Raise ethical standards higher and present more credible evidence of integrity.
3   Make contributing more valuable for donors through excellent donor service.
4   Pursue fundraising seriously and increase the effort in fundraising.

I based these four recommendations on the in-depth research I did for the Sasakawa Peace Foundation in Japan about how leading international NGOs evaluated their programs and themselves. After completion of this research, my analysis of why NGOs were not raising more money resulted from four issues: 1) unproven results to participants in the programs or beneficiaries of the services, 2) the taint of scandal in the NGO sector and questions of trust in the NGO, 3) weak value experienced by the donors after their support, and 4) insufficient effort in staff and budget to generate the needed funds. When an organization performs

Crisis of Confidence in NGOs

Issues identified in research as the basis for lack of public confidence

1. PROGRAM	**Impact for Participants**
2. ETHICS	**Trustworthiness**
3. COMMUNICATION	**Impact on Donors**
4. EFFORT	**Fundraising Investment**

Based on research by the author for Sasakawa Peace Foundation on "International NGO Evaluation Methodologies For Capacity Building, A New Paradigm for International NGOs."

Figure 8.2 There is a crisis of confidence in NGOs: Impact, trust, communications, and fundraising effort. Infographic by the author.

to high standards in these four areas, it becomes a model that people can trust and want to support[2] (Figure 8.2).

Twelve realities to consider

I seriously hope these stories and models have inspired you to work to increase public trust in nonprofits in general – and for yours in particular. This is what is needed to achieve larger financial support for your nonprofit and, therefore, greater improvements in society.

Ultimately the question is this: How does the average donor and especially the average non-donor know whether to trust a given charity? Be sure to use the worksheets in Chapter 9 (and on my website at www.NGOFutures.com) to guide you and your colleagues through a process as I have done with individual organizations, associations, and even the state of Rhode Island.

Here are some reminders about what is important when it comes to trust and, consequently, the need for a meaningful code of ethics:

1 Nonprofit organizations provide services as well as information, education, and advocacy for the betterment of society. There are also the five essentials for nonprofits: mission, effectiveness, efficiency, trustworthiness, and accountability. When working well, they bring out the best in people for their caring and helping through donations and volunteer support.[3]

2 Charitable giving in the United States has been stuck at 2% of disposable income for decades. Giving by middle and lower income families has been declining. It is only contributions by the super-rich that have increased the total overall giving amount in recent years (even though this has not kept pace with their soaring wealth).[4]

3 In its *2020 Donor Trust Special Report on Charity Impact*, the Better Business Bureau Wise Giving Alliance reported that "63.6% of respondents rated the importance of trusting a charity before giving as essential" and that only "18.6% of respondents report as highly trusting a charity."[5]

4 In its *2021 Donor Trust Special Report on Charity Impact*, the Better Business Bureau Wise Giving Alliance concludes that "Charity trust was most frequently selected as a very important aspect in the giving process" and "Charity impact was the second most popular choice."[6]

5   The frequent questions from donors about "Can I trust you?" and the frequent findings from surveys about the trust level for nonprofits pose urgent challenges to board members, executives, managers, and fundraisers – as a priority![7]

6   In the lead-up to the InterAction NGO Standards, I found it remarkable that almost all the executive directors believed their NGO was above reproach, yet a majority of them had a negative assessment of the others. Is it time for self-reflection?[8]

7   The InterAction NGO Standards provide a model on how to lead the process to create a code of ethics for organizations and associations in a participatory process that engenders greater ownership. This case study and others covered in this book show it is possible to create a meaningful code of ethics for your NGO and other member organizations.

8   When I returned from the global Red Cross Movement meeting and told the international regional directors that they now had a mandate to evaluate the National Societies, they all said, "No way!" What worked was the subsequent governance policy that required self-assessment with an external review followed by possible sanctions by the international board of directors.[9]

9   The story of government corruption in Rhode Island says a lot that nonprofit leaders should understand. It was only when we put in place an independent Ethics Commission with the power to investigate and apply sanctions (in this case, remove the person from office) that corruption was dramatically reduced. You cannot rely on those involved in bad behavior to improve on their own.[10]

10 The process of assuring trust has progressed over recent decades from just having a code of ethics to monitoring compliance with self-assessments, and then to peer review and even external review of compliance, and ultimately to applying serious sanctions for noncompliance.

11 The Better Business Bureau Wise Giving Alliance and other watchdog agencies, the Rhode Island Constitution, InterAction and its members, the Maryland Association of Nonprofit Organizations, the International Federation of Red Cross and Red Crescent Societies, the National Council on Voluntary Organizations, and many individual NGOs and NGO associations have played indispensable roles in setting standards, applying rigorous assessments, getting independent expert verification, and taking action when violations are uncovered. You can learn more by exploring these leading organizations and their codes of ethics.

12 Finally, people really do care and do want to help and the money is there, so it is up to individual NGOs to work hard to gain the public trust. You will earn credibility with donors and increase fundraising success.

The Introduction and PART I presented the importance of ethics for trust, chapters 1, 2, and 3 presented market realities for nonprofits and the need for improvements in ethics, chapter 4 presented five priorities and seven imperatives for ethics to be meaningful, chapters 5, 6, and 7 provided instructive case studies, and this chapter and chapter 9 show the work you need to do to earn trust (Figure 8.3 and 8.4).

Five Priorities for Trust
    1. Make sure your organization functions well.
    2. Achieve excellent impact for participants.
    3. Adopt and enforce a meaningful code of ethics.
    4. Commit to accountability and communication.
    5. Enable everyone to step up with responsibility to ensure trust and impact.

Figure 8.3 Five priorities for trust. Infographic by the author.

There is a crisis of confidence in nonprofits

Four challenges for trust from chapters 1, 2, and 3

1   Nonprofits need to recognize that trust levels are not high enough.
2   They need to "get things done" for their beneficiaries and society.
3   Nonprofits need to take responsibility for the low levels of trust.
4   They need more non-fundraising, informative communications.

Five priorities for trust from chapter 4

1   Make sure your organization is functioning well.
2   Achieve real impact for participants and results for society.
3   Adopt and enforce a meaningful organization-wide code of ethics.
4   Commit to transparency and accountability and appoint a Chief Trust Officer.
5   Enable everyone to step up with responsibility to ensure trust and impact.

A good catch is rarely a coincidence.
"We can learn from others."

Figure 8.4 We can learn from others who are more trusted. Artwork by Sawyer Phillips.

Questions for implementation

1   What is the public trust level for your nonprofit? If you don't know the answer to this question, what do you need to do to find out?
2   The Pew Research Center has listed three components to build trust: competence, honesty, and benevolence. How would your donors rank your organization in these areas?
3   What will you do next in your nonprofit to generate increased public trust?

Notes

1 "So Much Money – So little for Charity: Why Charities in Affluent America Aren't Generating More Support," AFP CT Association of Fundraising Professionals conference (Connecticut Philanthropy Day, Hartford, CT, 2001).
2 *Considering International NGO's Evaluation*, published in Japanese by the Sasakawa Peace Foundation, Tokyo, 2001.
3 See the six key attributes and five essentials for an NGO presented in chapter 4.
4 See the data presented in chapters 1 and 2.
5 BBB Wise Giving Alliance, "2020 Donor Trust Special Report on Charity Impact."
6 BBB Wise Giving Alliance, "Charity Impact: 2021 Give.org Donor Trust Special Report," *Give.org*, accessed July 4, 2022, https://www.give.org/docs/default-source/donor-trust-library/donor-trust-report---charity-impact.pdf
7 See chapter 3 for the call to action for nonprofits.
8 See the survey result in the InterAction case study in chapter 5.
9 See the three progressive case studies in chapter 6.
10 See the Rhode Island case study in chapter 7.

Bibliography

1 BBB Wise Giving Alliance. "2020 Donor Trust Special Report on Charity Impact."
2 BBB Wise Giving Alliance. "Charity Impact: 2021 Give.org Donor Trust Special Report." *Give.org*. Accessed July 4, 2022. https://www.give.org/docs/default-source/donor-trust-library/donor-trust-report---charity-impact.pdf
3 Phillips, Ken. *Considering International NGO's Evaluation*, published in Japanese by the Sasakawa Peace Foundation. Tokyo, 2001.

Chapter 9

Worksheet for ethics and trust

Meaningful ethics are essential for your organization to earn the trust of donors (Figure 9.1).

Meaningful Ethics
1. **A code of ethics with rules and expectations**
2. **Operational explanations of the obligations**
3. **Assessing compliance on a regular basis**
4. **Procedures for complaints of non-compliance**
5. **Reliable verification by relevant experts**
6. **Procedures for sanctions for non-compliance**
7. **Communication of all this to constituents**
These seven imperatives make ethics meaningful.
NGO Futures LLC © 2021

Figure 9.1 The seven essential elements for Meaningful Ethics. Infographic by the author.

Questions before implementation

1   What is your assessment of your organization's current practice in ethics, transparency, and accountability for trustworthiness?
2   What are the findings from surveys of your current donors, lapsed donors, and others?
3   How will you use the model codes from InterAction, MANO, NCVO, IFRC, Rhode Island, ICFO, evaluation agencies, the Association of Fundraising Professionals, and other organizations?
4   What can you do when a board member, staff member, or volunteer violates your code of ethics?

Drafting a meaningful code of ethics (or code of conduct) for your organization

This is the action step for nonprofit ethics and building trust for your organization. Situations vary, but this can be an outline of some of the key steps to take. The process of developing (or strengthening) a code of ethics for a nonprofit should follow these proven approaches:

1   Collect stories of nonprofits' shortcomings and scandals in your own country or sector of activity to give you an actual and relevant baseline for action.

DOI: 10.4324/9781003335207-11

2   Gather information about what other nonprofits and their associations have as a code of ethics, code of conduct, code of behavior, or standards including advice from relevant watchdog nonprofit associations and resource centers.

3   Make your case that you need to establish a code or expand a current code to increase trustworthiness, which will help your organization increase fundraising success.

4   Remind everyone that greater success in fundraising enables an expanded program with greater results.

5   Recruit allies within your organization especially the executive director, finance director, program director, key board members, and others to support your initiative.

6   Communicate how a code of ethics can show that your organization is responsible and accountable, prevents problems and improves work, gains donor trust and more funding, and provides a defense if needed.

7   Secure formal endorsement from executive leadership and the board to develop a code as a key step to involving other staff.

8   Create a small drafting team to assure broad-based and ongoing involvement in the process and to generate important participation and relevant suggestions.

9   Reference the examples in this book and customize your code of ethics to fully and accurately represent your nonprofit.

10   Build your work on proven steps for developing standards including identifying problems, assuring shared values, obtaining broad participation, being reasonable, and aiming high.

11   Conduct confidential interviews or surveys of current and potential donors, staff, board members, long-term volunteers, and other stakeholders to collect their views on important behavior they expect from you.

12   Be completely transparent about the process and share the plans, ideas, and drafts within the organization and repeatedly ask for suggestions and actual wording to use.

13   Provide time for participants to reflect and develop consensus on appropriate standards and terminology and to include suggestions from others wherever appropriate. A participatory process results in greater ownership.

14   To create a meaningful code of ethics, include key topics such as organizational integrity and good behavior, informed and independent governance, transparency and accountability, truthful fundraising appeals, use of funds according to donor expectations, sound and professional financial management, well planned and measured program effectiveness, fair and honorable treatment of employees, adherence to best practices in all aspects of work, accurate and timely reports, avoidance of even an appearance of conflict of interest, prohibition against discrimination, abuse, and harassment, and steps for self-assessment, external review, and possibility of sanctions. Review other organization's codes of ethics, codes of behavior, or codes of conduct for other important topics to include.

15   Secure management and board approval to adopt a meaningful code of ethics and the commitment to monitor and validate compliance of your nonprofit's code of ethics.

16   Communicate the code widely within the organization including discussions at staff meetings and recruitment and orientation for new staff and board members.

17   Implement the code with care including phasing it in over a reasonable time period, if needed, providing opportunity for feedback and conducting periodic assessments and enforcement.

18   Build a culture of accountability through personal example, reinforcement, discussion in staff meetings, a recognition and reward system, and annual plans and evaluations.

19   Verify compliance with the standards annually by staff, volunteers, and board members and conduct periodic audits to assure accountability.

20 To ensure a strong code of ethics, support it with self-assessment, peer review, external monitoring, and application of sanctions to demonstrate full commitment to meaningful ethics, good behavior, and full accountability.

21 Review the code periodically and make improvements based on feedback on issues and concerns, suggestions for improvements, and your own evaluations.

22 Include the code on your website and in your statements to the public along with your nonprofit's vision, mission, values, culture, and positioning as key elements of trustworthiness.

23 Keep in mind that a strong code of ethics is critical in order for donors to recognize that your nonprofit is worthy of their trust – and their donations.

24 Share the code with other nonprofits and NGO associations as a model and encourage them to adopt their own tailored code of ethics.

Key point: In all your planning and all your implementation, please do remember to focus on creating an awesome experience for both donors and beneficiaries. They will love you (Figure 9.2).

WORSHEET: Develop your own code of ethics for your organization	
Steps to success:	Who will do what and when:
Research issues and report	
Involve everyone in the process	
Review other codes for guidance	

(Continued)

Draft the code	
Circulate and improve the code	
Adopt and confirm the code	
Share and publicize the code	
Assess compliance annually	
Have external verification	

(Continued)

Include clear sanctions	
Step up to lead other NGOs	
Report to stakeholders	

Why You Need a Code of Ethics

1. **Shared values and common direction**

2. **Public responsibility**

3. **Donor trust**

4. **Prevention**

5. **Improvements**

6. **Defense**

You are under a magnifying glass!

Held by the public, authorities, donors, media, others, even your staff and volunteers

20/08/01   © NGO FUTURES 2001

Figure 9.2 Six reasons you need a code of ethics. Image by the author.

Part II

Strategic evaluation for respect

Chapter 10

Strategic evaluation for impact

Donors Have Expectations
Nonprofits must demonstrate their
1) **Value** **(Mission)**
2) **Results** **(Effectiveness)**
3) **Efficiency** **(Cost)**
4) **Trustworthiness** **(Ethics)**
5) **Accountability** **(Communication)**
Give your donors confidence!
Based on the author's paradigm for the Five Essentials for NGOs.

Figure 10.1 Donors have expectations that organizations must meet. Infographic by the author.

The following statements were made by actual nonprofit leaders. Which statement best describes your organization's attitude toward evaluations?

- "We did a great evaluation for our major donor. They loved it. Then we filed it and never had to look at it again."
- "We learn so much from our evaluations. We always find ways to improve what we do. Our donors love to see our regular evaluations and continuous improvements."

PART II in this book covers a key theme in my *Civil Society Series* on how to make this a better world. The comprehensive series enables you – the nonprofit director, community leader, fundraiser, or volunteer – to know what to do and how to do it to make real change in your organization, company, or community to get better results. The themes covered so far in three previous books are: leadership and fundraising principles; strategic planning, strong values and energizing culture; and proven strategies for fundraising, and now in this book ethics for trust and evaluation for impact along with communication for accountability and engagement.

Underlying all I have written is the conviction that people can – and must – step up to operate at all levels in an organization and in all areas of society. Few of us will be historic leaders, but most of us can lead from where we are right now in society – where we work or study, where we live and shop, and where we meet friends and family.

I want to repeat a statement I quoted in the introduction: "NGOs across 40 countries represent $2.2 trillion in operating expenditures. That figure is larger than the gross domestic product of all but six countries."[1] Further, as reported by the Johns Hopkins Center for Civil

DOI: 10.4324/9781003335207-13

Society Studies, "Nonprofits also generated the third largest payroll income of any U.S. industry in 2017, behind only manufacturing and professional services."[2] Note that this definition of nonprofits includes universities, hospitals, and other healthcare organizations as well as non-governmental organizations (NGOs). To put it mildly, the work of nonprofits is huge and important, but too many people remain unconvinced (Figure 10.1).

Data about trust and impact and donations are clear and convincing

Nonprofits need to respond to the findings of reports and surveys about the influence of trust and impact on donations. As the introduction to PART II in the book, I draw on six reports that confirm the correlation, as well as on previous chapters in this book and my own research.

1   In an excellent monograph titled "Philanthropy and Digital Civil Society: Blueprint 2022"[3] in the *Stanford Social Innovation Review*, Lucy Bernholz, senior research scholar at Stanford University's Center on Philanthropy and Civil Society, provides important recommendations. After citing the dramatic impact of the COVID pandemic (and I would add the largest war in Europe since World War II), Bernholz argues that "Only big changes will lead to positive futures" (5) and that "Shaping the future is more than just leaving certain assumptions and structures behind; it is about making explicit our dreams and hopes for a better world" (7). She moves on to challenge governments, corporations, NGOs, the wealthy, and everyone to accept the need for change and work for a better future.

2   In her 2021 monograph "Philanthropy and Digital Civil Society: Blueprint 2021"[4] in the *Stanford Social Innovation Review*, Bernholz had raised a number of complex and challenging issues. For example, "Today's tax policies are toxic and use the promise of philanthropy to justify inequality. In the United States today, this toxic tax code permeates our soil and prevents us from growing into an equitable society. Our current tax laws starve our schools, hospitals, transit, and elder care systems. They allow individuals to become trillionaires and corporations to pay nothing" (18).

    She refers to "the basic human instinct to give and care for others" (10). She argues that "In its proper role in democracies, civil society creates alternatives to dominant commercial and government systems. These alternatives can be powerful enough to shift the dominant systems, proven by examples as diverse as the Voting Rights Act, environmental protections, and universal design" (22). She points out that "The enormous growth of nonprofits and philanthropy since the end of World War II has limited our imaginations about where society's good works happen. But these entities have never made up the whole of civil society. In addition to the informal activities like mutual aid networks that have always been there, numerous new options have come knocking at the door since the turn of the 21st century" (34). She is referring to the great variety of significant civil society actions and financial and volunteer support mechanisms led by informal groups, community associations, individuals, and spontaneous popular protests and advocacy for change.

All that Bernholz describes in these two most recent monographs reinforce, to me, the importance that trust and impact have for people deciding what they will do and who they will support. When they have personal connections, they trust them and believe they will do everything well. When they are in a group protesting and advocating together, they have high trust and commitment that the group is doing the right thing.

Trust and impact are frequently top themes in Independent Sector and BBB Wise Giving reports and conclusions as well as in the Edelman Trust Barometers highlighted in chapter 3.

3   The Independent Sector's 2022 report *Trust in Civil Society: Understanding the factors driving trust in nonprofits and philanthropy on trust*[5] concludes that "Public trust is the currency of the nonprofit sector. The public's belief that nonprofits will 'do the right thing' is one of the central reasons the sector exists" (4). Further, it finds that "Consistent with past waves, integrity and purpose contribute most to trust for both nonprofits and philanthropy. Distrusters in both sectors point to perceived mismanagement of funds and instances of corruption and scandals. Neutral trusters say financial transparency and proof of impact is necessary for them to see an organization as trustworthy" (6).

4   The BBB Wise Giving Alliance *Donor Trust Report 2020. The Pandemic and a Three-Year Retrospective*,[6] finds that "While trust is still considered highly important in the giving process, our results suggest that reliance on trust as a giving indicator has eroded in the past 3 years." However, "63.6% of respondents rated the importance of trusting a charity before giving as essential." But only "16.8% of respondents report as highly trusting a charity" (7). Especially noteworthy is that of "factors signaling a charity as trustworthy in 2020," respondents rated "Accomplishments shared by the organization" at the top (11).

5   The next BBB Wise Giving Alliance *Donor Trust Report | 2021. Profiles in Charity Trust and Giving*[7] opens its Summary of Results with "There is ample space to build trust in the sector, with 63.0% of respondents rating the importance of trusting a charity before giving as 9 or 10 (Essential) on a 10-point scale, and only 18.5% of respondents highly trusting charities."

Note also the finding that "As exemplified by 2020 results, donors with higher contribution levels are more likely to report high trust in charities" (6). It is important for nonprofit leaders to see the correlation between high trust and high donations.

There is more. In the detailed findings of this report, "high trust" was important to 73%, 70%, 65%, and 63% of respondents in 2017, 2018, 2019, and 2020, respectively and "having high trust" was indicated by only 10%, 19%, 17%, and 18% of respondents in those same years (13). Significantly as in the 2020 report, "When asked what most signals that a charity is trustworthy," the #1 top factor was "Accomplishments shared by the organization" (45).

Based on its own surveys, the Wise Giving Alliance is worried about the erosion of donor participation. "Our survey results suggest that the decrease in donor participation rates identified by Indiana University continued during 2020 — even as total contributions from individuals continue to increase. This is a worrisome trend as we strive to build a diverse and inclusive charitable sector" (53).

6   A third very important report from the BBB Wise Giving Alliance is its 2021 *Donor Trust Special Report on Charity Impact*[8] which "delves into how individual donors perceive charity impact and how important charity impact is in their giving decisions" (40). A key finding is that "Only 53.3% of survey participants report knowing what a charity means when talking about 'impact.' The remaining respondents (46.7%) said they do not know (19.1%) or are not sure (27.6%) about what charity impact means" (4).

When asked about the importance of impact, "30.7% of respondents rated 'information on the charity's impact' as a very important (9 or 10 on a scale of 1 to 10) aspect in their giving process. While that is a significant portion of respondents, other aspects were rated similarly (and sometimes with higher importance). For example, 39.5% of respondents rated how much they trust the charity as very important; and 28.2% rated financial ratios as very important" (5).

As for immediate versus long term results, "Respondents indicated that both immediate and long-term results are important, but more respondents said long-term results are highly important (31.9%) than immediate results (20.7%)" (5).

Respondents rated trust the most important factor at 40% and impact as the second most important factor at 31% (12). "The relatively high importance attributed to long term results as compared to immediate results also held across giving levels but was most marked among higher donors" (15). "We asked potential donors to rate the importance of program volume and program quality. Both volume and quality are important, but more respondents said program quality is highly important than program volume" (17).

➡ *The guidance to nonprofit leaders is clear! The BBB conclusions are significant (30–31):*

"Optimistically, charity impact information can help individual charities improve or become more efficient, and it can help impactful charities attract support. At a macro level, charity impact information has the potential to help direct social investment toward more effective organizations."

"Our survey finds that, although people care about immediate results, volume of programs, and the accomplishments of their own contributions, they attribute higher importance to long-term results, depth of programs, and the overall accomplishments and capacity of the organization."

"Results also show that the donating public does not have a clear understanding of the term 'charity impact.'"

"Our findings are also a call to keep things in perspective. While it has become a common assumption that donors seek and want to support highly impactful organizations, survey results show that this is an incomplete picture. Specifically, while donors say they care about charity impact, they care even more about overall charity trust and continue to think financial ratios are important. On top of that, our survey shows the importance of targeted communications."

"BBB's Give.org considers efforts to identify best impact measures and to improve an organization's mission-driven work to be most successful when done as an introspective exercise of the charity's board and staff. With attention to charity impact mounting, the need to be thoughtful and precise in charity communications is also rising. As mission-driven organizations, charities have an obligation to monitor their effectiveness and seek to improve their 'impact'."

"As mission-driven organizations funded by public contributions, charities have an obligation to monitor their effectiveness, seek to improve their impact, and communicate results. With that in mind, some of the BBB Standards for Charity Accountability are dedicated to verifying whether the charity's governing board evaluates the success and impact of the organization, and to ensuring that the charity communicates recent program service accomplishments (among other important information) to potential supporters." (33) In fact, that was the recommendation in 2003 of the Standards Review Panel for the Wise Giving Alliance to add a requirement on program evaluation, coming from the evaluation sub-committee which I chaired.

In a panel discussion led by Art Taylor, President and CEO of the Better Business Bureau Wise Giving Alliance about its 2021 *Donor Trust Special Report on Charity Impact*, several panelists emphasized that people report they feel a high responsibility to make a difference but don't know how to do that. Well, it's the responsibility of the leaders in every charity to let potential donors know how they can make a difference!

➡ *You cannot grow your organization without proving your trust and your impact.*

Lessons about Evaluation

1. The results that matter are measured, long-term, sustained impacts.

2. Design with Indicators, Monitoring and Evaluation, and Learning are core management functions.

3. NGOs should regularly use self-assessment for internal learning.

4. NGOs should focus more on documenting, sharing and using Lessons Learned.

From a 2001 study by the author for the Sasakawa Peace Foundation on "International NGO Evaluation Methodologies for Capacity Building, A New Paradigm for International NGOs"

20/08/01   © NGO FUTURES 2001   1

Figure 10.2 Clear lessons from research about results that matter, designing the process, assessing your progress, and sharing lessons learned. Infographic by the author based on his research for the Sasakawa Peace Foundation.

After Yayoi Tanaka, Chief Program Officer of the Sasakawa Peace Foundation, asked me to conduct research into how leading international NGOs were evaluating their results and ethics, we selected two dozen of the best NGOs for the research. The research concluded with clear recommendations on the importance of designing the process with best practices, achieving results that matter, assessing yourself, and sharing lessons learned.[9] These were pressing issues two decades ago when I did that research and they are still pressing issues today. The Foundation's book, *Considering International NGO's Evaluation* based on my research, was published in 2001[10] (Figure 10.2 and 10.3).

The many articles and reports in PART I also demonstrate how philanthropy is stressed in the United States.

When NGOs have first-rate evaluation and learning as well as first-rate ethics and accountability, they can achieve very significant benefits for the wellbeing of society. They can create and demonstrate new approaches and new projects in their own work that can be adopted by other NGOs and by local, state, and federal governments. Throughout history, NGOs and others in the civil society sector have often been the innovators and entrepreneurs for social change and improvements. We need more of this! Donors expect it! Results matter!

In these next chapters, I address how to achieve and communicate more impact with answers to the following questions:

1   Why should organizations conduct strategic evaluations?
2   How can they develop evaluation reports that actually matter?
3   How can they use evaluation for effectiveness, learning, and accountability?
4   How do organizations improve themselves internally?
5   How do they work better with their partners?
6   Who is responsible?

As an executive, manager, fundraiser, staff member, or volunteer with answers to these questions, you will have a pathway for your organization or a personal initiative to learn more from experience and to improve results, account better, raise more, and achieve more. Throughout my 60 years working with nonprofits, regardless of the position I held (as beginner, fundraiser,

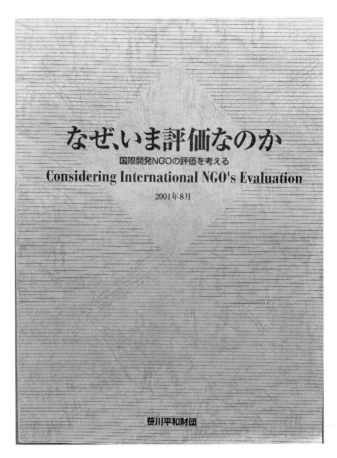

なぜ、いま評価なのか
国際開発NGOの評価を考える
Considering International NGO's Evaluation
2001年8月

笹川平和財団

Figure 10.3 Cover of *Considering International NGO's Evaluation* based on the author's research. Photograph by Rebecca Phillips.

executive, board member, consultant, or volunteer), I always felt it was my responsibility and my prerogative to encourage and then insist that executives, program staff, finance staff, board members, and others recognize that without donors there was no program and that they must, for the good of the organization and the benefit for the program beneficiaries, build into their plans, as a priority, making the organization more attractive to donors through better management, better trust, better programs, better evaluation, better impact, and better reporting. I truly believe everyone in a nonprofit organization has this responsibility and prerogative. It makes a better organization!

> *The questions are evident: Why do you exist? What is your impact? Why should I trust you?*

Philanthropy in America is in deep crisis

The 2021 data from Giving USA[11] paint an even worse picture than I had imagined. Giving failed to increase, organizations are increasingly relying on wealthy donors and foundations, and fewer Americans are donating. This raises three huge concerns: First, the rich are playing a disproportionate role, some would say hijacking, American philanthropy, and their views do not always, or maybe rarely, reflect those of the vast majority of the population. Second, what happens if more Americans lose faith in nonprofits and conclude that wealthy donors are giving enough? Third, what happens when the stock market crashes?

Based on research by Bernholz, Edelman Trust Barometers, Johns Hopkins Center for Civil Society Studies, Independent Sector, BBB Wise Giving Alliance, and others, it is clear that NGOs need to step up to a higher level of performance in response to global and local needs, such as poverty, job loss, COVID response, climate change, inequality, prejudice and racism, violence, hate in social media, and other social ills. Civil society actors should be more powerful forces in society, and they can accomplish more only by getting better at proving their impact and demonstrating their trustworthiness.

Let's be perfectly clear: Donors want to know what impact or results an organization achieves. The reports cited above in this chapter make the case that trust and impact are absolutely critical to NGO growth and success and that substantial change is needed in the sector. Recall the conclusions in chapters 1 and 2 that nonprofits are not increasing their share of the national market and not growing enough to meet pressing needs. If donors do not have confidence in your impact, they will not consider you worthy of their support. To get them to consider donating or volunteering, you must upgrade what you do to achieve real impact and communicate that reliably so you will be seen as effective, accountable, and trustworthy.

As my high school calculus teacher wrote after presenting a theorem, QED or *quod erat demonstrandum*, that the argument has been proven.

➡️ *The most important issues for donors are trust and accomplishment. QED.*

In my workshops, I often compare fundraising with courtship or with marriage. If you read a survey saying that trust in marriage was higher than trust in government and news media, would you really be impressed? If you did a survey of your neighbors or your family or any group and found that 16.8% or 18.5% or !0%-19% of respondents (see research above) said they were "highly trusting", what do you think the future holds?

➡️ *What more do you need to lead the changes needed?*

As I write this, my daughter, who is founding a new NGO for adult literacy, wrote me: "My top advisor told me the thing to remember is that people feel good when they donate to a good cause, so when you ask people to get involved or give money, you're helping them to feel good."

I agree and add these thoughts:

- Caring and helping others are the highest human values.
- The Sustainable Development Goals show what is needed.
- Trust, impact, and communications are keys to success.
- The world and our planet need YOU to step up now.
- Your donors will feel good when you do!

Key point: In a world with so many problems for people and for planet, it is the private, nonprofit, non-governmental organizations, and the many individuals and informal groups that constitute the *caring, volunteering, and helping sector*. These individuals and organizations are at the top of the pyramid of human values (Figure 10.4).

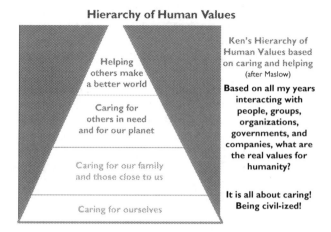

Figure 10.4 The hierarchy of human values for caring and helping. Image by the author.

Notes

1 Adam Jezard, "Who and What is 'Civil Society'?," *World Economic Forum*, April 18, 2018, accessed June 25, 2022, https://www.weforum.org/agenda/2018/04/what-is-civil-society/.
2 Chelsea Newhouse, "NEW REPORT: Nonprofits—America's Third Largest Workforce," *Center For Civil Society Studies Archive*, May 2, 2018, accessed July 4, 2022, http://ccss.jhu.edu/2015-np-employment-report/.
3 Lucy Bernholz, "Philanthropy and Digital Civil Society: Blueprint 2022," *Stanford PACS*, December 2021, 5,7, accessed July 4, 2022, https://pacscenter.stanford.edu/publication/philanthropy-and-digital-civil-society-blueprint-2022/.
4 Lucy Bernholz, "Philanthropy and Digital Civil Society: Blueprint 2021," *Stanford PACS*, December 2020, 10, 18, 22, 34, accessed July 4, 2022, https://pacscenter.stanford.edu/publication/philanthropy-and-digital-civil-society-blueprint-2021/.
5 Independent Sector, "Trust in Civil Society—Understanding the Factors Driving Trust in Nonprofits and Philanthropy," May 2022, 4, 6, accessed June 27, 2022, https://independentsector.org/trust.
6 Better Business Bureau, "Donor Trust Report 2020: The Pandemic and a Three-Year Retrospective," *Give.org*:7, 11, accessed July 4, 2022, https://dev.give.org/docs/default-source/donor-trust-library/2020-donor-trust-report.pdf.
7 Better Business Bureau, "Donor Trust Report 2021: Profiles in Charity Trust and Giving," *Give.org*:6, 13, 45, 53, accessed July 4, 2022, https://www.give.org/docs/default-source/donor-trust-library/2021-donor-trust-report.pdf.
8 BBB Wise Giving Alliance, "Charity Impact: 2021 Give.org Donor Trust Special Report," *Give.org*:4–5, 12, 15, 17, 30–31, accessed July 4, 2022, https://www.give.org/docs/default-source/donor-trust-library/donor-trust-report---charity-impact.pdf.
9 Ken Phillips, "International NGO Evaluation Methodologies for Capacity Building: A new paradigm for international NGOs" (Personal papers from research for Sasakawa Peace Foundation, 2001).
10 Sasakawa Peace Foundation, *Considering International NGO's Evaluation*, published by the Foundation, 2001.
11 "Giving USA Annual Report on Philanthropy," accessed July 4, 2022, https://givingusa.org.

Bibliography

1 Bernholz, Lucy. "Philanthropy and Digital Civil Society: Blueprint 2022." *Stanford PACS*, December 2021. Accessed July 4, 2022. https://pacscenter.stanford.edu/publication/philanthropy-and-digital-civil-society-blueprint-2022/.
2 Bernholz, Lucy. "Philanthropy and Digital Civil Society: Blueprint 2021." *Stanford PACS*, December 2020. Accessed July 4, 2022. https://pacscenter.stanford.edu/publication/philanthropy-and-digital-civil-society-blueprint-2021/.

3   BBB Wise Giving Alliance. "Donor Trust Report 2020: The Pandemic and a Three-Year Retrospective." Give.org. Accessed July 4, 2022. https://dev.give.org/docs/default-source/donor-trust-library/2020-donor-trust-report.pdf.

4   BBB Wise Giving Alliance. "Donor Trust Report 2021: Profiles in Charity Trust and Giving." *Give*.org. Accessed July 4, 2022. https://www.give.org/docs/default-source/donor-trust-library/2021-donor-trust-report.pdf.

5   BBB Wise Giving Alliance. "Charity Impact: 2021 Give.org Donor Trust Special Report." *Give.org*. Accessed July 4, 2022. https://www.give.org/docs/default-source/donor-trust-library/donor-trust-report---charity-impact.pdf.

6   "Giving USA Annual Report on Philanthropy." Accessed July 4, 2022. https://givingusa.org.

7   Independent Sector. "Trust in Civil Society—Understanding the Factors Driving Trust in Nonprofits and Philanthropy." May 2022. Accessed June 27, 2022. https://independentsector.org/trust.

8   Jezard, Adam. "Who and What is 'Civil Society'?" *World Economic Forum*, April 18, 2018. Accessed June 25, 2022. https://www.weforum.org/agenda/2018/04/what-is-civil-society/.

9   Newhouse, Chelsea. "NEW REPORT: Nonprofits—America's Third Largest Workforce." *Center For Civil Society Studies Archive*, May 2, 2018. Accessed July 4, 2022. http://ccss.jhu.edu/2015-np-employment-report/.

10 Phillips, Ken. "International NGO Evaluation Methodologies for Capacity Building: A new paradigm for international NGOs." Personal papers from research for Sasakawa Peace Foundation. 2001.

11 Sasakawa Peace Foundation, *Considering International NGO's Evaluation*, published by the Foundation, 2001.

Chapter 11

Problems with monitoring and evaluation – Resistance and donor mandates

Overcoming resistance to monitoring and evaluation

The best organizations routinely plan, implement, evaluate, and learn from evaluation. That is certainly the reason they became the best organizations – and the biggest. Others fail to evaluate and fail to learn. Why? Reasons given range from "We already know what to do" to "We don't have funding for it." Those who don't conduct ongoing, honest evaluations will pay a serious penalty – for themselves, their beneficiaries, and their donors. Almost without question, the nonprofit will stagnate and eventually be in crisis.

I had my own eye-opening experience with failure to closely monitor a project in my own organization. A manager was responsible for writing the annual report, a large job for our growing organization. I did check in with him occasionally with, "Harold, how's the report coming along?" His reply always was, "It's good."

Well, my monitoring was completely superficial, and the week before the final draft was due, I asked him again. This time his reply was, "I'm so sorry, Ken. I've had problems. I haven't even begun." This project was now a crisis, because we had to meet a mandated deadline to submit our annual report. We went into overdrive (and overtime) with another writer. A clear lesson for me – monitoring has to get into the details of the process with an objective view of actual, real progress in order to be valid and to be able to make needed corrections before it's too late. As U.S. president Ronald Reagan said while negotiating with Soviet premier Mikhail Gorbachev in the 1980s, "Trust, but verify."[1]

Key point: *Monitoring* is the process by both implementers and supervisors to keep looking at a project's progress from plan to completion, identifying any problems or shortfalls, and making necessary adjustments or corrections to stay on target.

Key point: *Evaluation* is the process by an independent specialist to examine a project after completion, consult with those involved including beneficiaries, identify successes and failures and reasons for them, and provide a "lessons learned" report for use in the future.

Key point: *Mentoring* is a more productive process to assure good results during the implementation of an activity. In the workplace, the supervisor as mentor listens to employees, guides them in their implementation activity, and steers them to greater productivity and achievement of objectives. It is a more supportive process than monitoring which can easily veer into a critical mode.

Key point: Learning is a supportive process of using all experiences to discover what can be done better. It builds on relationships and monitoring, evaluation, and mentoring to improve future performance. It is a commitment to improve rather than judge or just identify what went well and what did not. It turns evaluation into a process that both supervisor and supervised welcome.

➡️ *Properly done, monitoring becomes mentoring and evaluation becomes learning (**M&L**).*

DOI: 10.4324/9781003335207-14

Figure 11.1 People arguing. Artwork by Sawyer Phillips.

Although the methodology and tools required to conduct the typical level of **monitoring and evaluation (M&E)** are widely known in the profession – especially to satisfy a major donor's requirement – many executives and board members are not comfortable with the ongoing process of regular, in-depth monitoring and strategic evaluation. The following comments[2] from interviews with NGO professionals who are experts in evaluation illustrate the problem:

- "A lot of organizations have anxiety about monitoring and evaluation." *Experienced NGO consultant*
- "The term 'evaluation' has long held negative connotations for program managers and staff. It is like 'a report to get us, finger-pointing.'" *Head of evaluation of a mid-size NGO*
- "We keep making the same mistakes thirty years later." *Senior evaluator at a small international NGO*
- "If you don't think of systems as having parts that are faulty, you can't begin to achieve what your vision and mission talk about." *Field evaluator with a well-performing NGO*
- "Evaluation was something so specialized and mystifying that only evaluators themselves could talk about it." *Director of evaluation at a large nonprofit*
- "NGOs don't seem to care about developing the body of knowledge of their profession." *A pediatrician working with an NGO on child health* (Figure 11.1)

While M&E is a reality in most nonprofits (especially to meet a major donor's requirements), people often raise problems with doing it. The issues raised below probably relate more to larger organizations, but smaller ones may also benefit from reviewing them.

1 ***"I take responsibility for my work. I don't need someone looking over my shoulder."*** Staff may see a high degree of monitoring of their work as interference and unproductive. Good supervision conducts monitoring in ways that are both supportive and productive. As such, monitoring can be a welcome mentoring process.
2 ***"What happens if it shows we are not doing something well? What will our donors say?"*** It is a real problem when a board member, manager, or anyone else says this. But what is the alternative? Making the same mistakes over and over again? It is better to know what you are not doing well, so you can correct it. Doing better will attract more donors.
3 ***"Evaluation costs money. We just need to know what the donor wants."*** Some evaluations are expensive. Measuring real results – lasting impact – takes money that could otherwise go to beneficiaries. Yes, this is true, but investment in thorough evaluations will provide important returns to the organization and its beneficiaries immediately and over

time as the learnings are applied in a process of continuous improvement. Donors will appreciate your commitment to improvement, since this directly impacts the quality of your program, results for program beneficiaries and, of course, lasting impact.

4   *"Everyone is afraid of evaluation. They think they can lose their job from a poor evaluation."* Field workers fear for their jobs if the evaluation is not good. The program manager fears the program budget will be cut. Program participants and partners fear the support they receive will be discontinued. The executive director and fundraising director fear donors will turn away. Board members fear having to admit the organization is not as good as they thought it was. Donors fear having wasted their money. With so much fear at so many levels, it is not surprising that regular, in-depth monitoring and strategic evaluation are seen as a nuisance at best and a threat at worst. However, a good leader does all the following: Leads with vision, mission, and values; understands that failure can be a learning opportunity; communicates the benefits of truthful evaluation; and inspires everyone to accept, learn, and improve.

5   *"M&E is often not well planned or integrated into basic operations."* Some evaluators have told me that their management does not see the need to include monitoring and evaluation in the design phase of program planning. Monitoring and evaluation that are added later when the project is underway cannot help to improve operations during a project and fails to lay a solid foundation for the final evaluation process. To get the best possible results, a good manager integrates regular, in-depth monitoring and strategic evaluation as an integral part of planning, which enables mid-course adjustments smoothly throughout the project and builds trust for a smooth final process to understand successes and failures.

6   *"Monitoring and evaluation are multi-faceted, with complex and confusing disciplines."* Many consultants, grantmakers, and NGOs are developing new approaches and tools for advanced M&E. Different donors demand different approaches for M&E to satisfy their own requirements. Initiatives gain favor, then fade into the background. NGOs just began to understand monitoring and evaluation and then self-assessment appeared. After the Logical Framework was promoted, Results Monitoring was next, and then Innovation, and more. There are a multitude of evaluation tools available ranging from simple to complex. A comprehensive context is needed to understand the variety and applicability of various evaluation tools. It is the NGO manager's responsibility to understand which tools are most appropriate to deploy. Smaller NGOs can use simpler tools or partner with other organizations.

7   *"The results of our evaluations are not well used."* Many evaluations are done just to fulfill the terms of a grant. After such an evaluation is sent to the donor, it is filed and forgotten. When evaluation is done just as a report to donors, it will not be used as a learning tool. Professional evaluators and program implementers are frustrated at this lack of commitment to learning. Only when evaluation is seen as an opportunity to learn what worked and what didn't will it be used to make changes, build capacity, and make continuous improvements.

8   *"Program evaluation is especially difficult."* Program progress and results are difficult to measure because of the complex nature of many program services, the difficulty of finding valid indicators, the lag before results are realized, questions about causality and attribution, and unanticipated consequences and unknown influences. However, these challenges of program implementation make it all the more important to evaluate the strategies, assumptions, measurements, and outputs, outcomes, and impacts, so your organization can do more and do it better. Program impact is why you exist. Participants expect it. Donors do, too.

9 **"The findings of program evaluation do not flow upward within an organiza-tion."** Evaluators nod their heads in agreement when I say there is a "glass ceiling" on evaluation issues – too often, leaders take only a superficial glance at the findings. For comparison, *financial management* has a rigorous data-driven process throughout an organization for planning, budgeting, approving, monitoring, reporting, consolidating, and reviewing financial data along with an annual independent external audit according to generally accepted procedures, with lots of management and board time devoted to financial analysis. *Fundraising and marketing* also have a data-driven process for planning, budgeting, approving, testing, monitoring, reporting, consolidating, and reviewing detailed revenue and expense data that inform the next round of marketing, with lots of management and board time devoted to fundraising analysis. However, in many organizations, *program* has traditionally been driven more by conviction than by data. In a smart organization, evaluators have a direct report to the board of directors and such open communication produces the most useful findings. This is what an independent financial auditor does and what a smart fundraiser does. Program needs the same level of evaluation.

10 **"NGOs as a group lack a culture of professional learning."** Unlike most professions such as medicine, many nonprofits lack a culture of continuous learning. Budgets for learning are limited, and while learning may be a desirable objective, it is often deferred.

These ten concerns – and there may be others as well – are powerful disincentives for most organizations to embrace strategic evaluation. However, these disincentives can be overcome through good governance and good management. Who wins with a truthful evaluation? Program participants, staff, donors, society, everyone – provided the findings are *used* to learn and build capacity (not filed and forgotten). The cost of conducting a strategic evaluation is repaid many times over when the information it reveals is used as a learning tool to assure better services in the future. Turning monitoring into mentoring and evaluation into learning will more fully engage staff and dramatically reduce resistance (Figure 11.2).

➡ *Truthful strategic evaluation concludes with lessons learned and results improved.*

My advice on this topic is to stop arguing about it and get to learning. Here are a few approaches:

• "Learning while doing" can be incorporated into the culture of every organization.
• "Changes are made right away" can be prioritized by supervisors through monitoring.
• "Things to keep and things to change" can be highlighted in all evaluation findings.
• "Lessons learned" can be shared for action by all managers in different departments.
• "How have you contributed to learning?" can be included in performance evaluations.
• "Lifelong learning" is a great concept. Your organization can adopt this attitude as well!

In a fascinating process known as *Fail Festivals*, a group of NGOs meet and share their failures. Kitty Holt, Director of Ethics and Compliance at Plan International USA, wrote to me that "Plan participates in *Fail Festivals*, and we have been quite transparent about them, so we can help others and we can learn from them."

My own experience is that NGO workers learn so much from each other when they agree to share. I've seen it in many lively "brown bag" lunch meetings where one organization hosts the space and provides refreshments and invites other participants willing to share. (These are referred

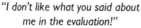

Figure 11.2 The oil of learning and improving. Artwork by Sawyer Phillips.

to as "brown bag" because everyone brings their own lunch.) This is typically a group of professionals from NGOs with similar interests and a desire to improve. It regularly happens with many associations of NGOs such as InterAction and other groups where "competitors" become friends and partners through mutual sharing of successes and failures, while developing plans to get better.

Key point: Donors, authorities, executives, and the public are demanding better results from the funds donated to nonprofits. Attentive monitoring/mentoring, strategic evaluation, continuous learning, and capacity building are the steps to achieve improved results, accomplish lasting impact, and earn greater respect.

During my meetings and discussions with NGO leaders and managers over the years, I am always impressed with their commitment to make the world a better place. The best performing organizations are increasingly using evaluations strategically to improve planning, implementing, monitoring, learning, and building capacity for better results. They give attention to questions such as:

• How can we improve our methods for M&E?
• How can we use mentoring for better results?
• How can we use M&E more effectively in all functions of our organization?
• How can we get useful "lessons learned" and conclusions in our evaluations?
• How can we promote a culture of continuous learning and self-improvement?
• How can we share what we learn and help improve the entire sector?

The benefits of strategic evaluations are in the process and in the results. The process engages staff, volunteers, and participants in the fruitful culture of continuous improvement. The

"It is hard to do this, but I can do it!"

Figure 11.3 Heavy lifting when you have to overcome resistance. Artwork by Sawyer Phillips.

results come from designing what you want to learn and how you will use that learning to build capacity for better performance in the future. Strategic evaluation is internally driven by leaders (at all levels) committed to learn what needs to be continued and what needs to be changed, to teach implementers to do a better job, and to use and share the lessons learned (Figure 11.3).

What's right and what's wrong with donor-mandated evaluation

As a standard step in new consulting assignments with a nonprofit, I always ask the executive director about the organization's recent evaluations. In a surprising number of cases, the answer would be something like, "Well, sure, we have many evaluation reports. We did them, and they were very successful. The donors were happy. Why do you ask?" Then I would ask, "Well, how have they helped your organization? What have you done with them?" And the replies often were: "They did the job. We sent the evaluations to the donors. They served their purpose."

What's wrong with donor-mandated evaluation? Donor-mandated evaluation means the evaluation is done specifically for the donor, following the donor's specifications to meet the donor's needs and secure possible future support. Such an evaluation may even minimize some negatives and emphasize some positives to curry the donor's favor. The evaluation was promised at the beginning of the process to get the grant and, later, done to satisfy the donor.

I consider this type of monitoring and evaluation (M&E) report as simply a *tactical evaluation* – a one-time, limited evaluation specifically carried out to satisfy a large donor's requirement, like a grantmaking foundation or a government agency. When the report is accepted favorably, the reason for the evaluation has been accomplished. Donor-mandated evaluation is of course useful. It is certainly important to show that the organization met the terms of the grant and did well enough to retain the donor's confidence and support.

Evaluation: Strategy or Tactics

- Strategy underlies everything. The right fundraising strategies can be rocket fuel for your strategic plan.
- It is not possible to have effective strategies when you do not have an effective overall strategic plan.
- A clear strategy indicates how you will move forward. Each strategy you identify must address the question, "How will we …?" Strategy is the roadmap that shows how you will achieve the results you desire
- Tactics support strategy and help to ensure the larger, long-term strategy is successful. You need to get both right.
- Money is not the problem. Trust and results are the answer. Strategy is the means. And what can you learn from others?

25 Proven Strategies for Fundraising Success: How to win the love and support of donors by Ken Phillips

Figure 11.4 Definition of strategy vs tactics as a guide to evaluation. Sidebar by the author.

However, donor-mandated evaluation is not useful as an ongoing learning tool that the nonprofit can use to pursue continuous improvement. Although many organizations have adopted more advanced strategic planning processes, unfortunately, many others still see evaluation at its best as a tool to meet a donor's requirements and at its worst as a nuisance and bother to do.

We all know that when we do something for someone else, we use it less than if we do it for ourselves. In the same way, evaluations done for donors may not be well used by the nonprofits themselves. The evaluation is completed, sent to the donor, checked off the list – and often filed and forgotten. This is comparable to going to a doctor, getting a prescription, going home, saying "I saw my doctor," and not filling the prescription. Seriously!

For evaluation to be meaningful for an organization, it should be raised to the strategic level as an approach for learning what to do better in order to build the organization's capacity to achieve its mission. The real value is in learning what to keep and what to change, what to continue doing and what to avoid doing – using both failures and successes as lessons learned to improve performance and to share with others. When evaluation is used in this way it is well worth the increased effort and cost it entails. It becomes *strategic*! (Figure 11.4)

On its website, Charities Aid Foundation, a leading civil society support organization in the U.K., notes: "The only real way to know if you are having an impact, or not, is through evidence." Then the article identifies as a serious problem that "charities tend to view impact reporting as a way to secure more donations. This has led to the rise of 'snake oil salesmanship' and a proliferation of organizations claiming to measure your impact, when in fact they are sharing stories and short-term outcomes, without robust long-term evidence."[3]

In another article on that website, Michael Mapstone suggests some great ways for nonprofits to learn. Highlights include:

- "A 'no blame,' honest, and objective review of lessons learned can provide high-quality learning points that can help to replicate successes and avoid repeating our failures."
- "Learning from organizations with a different culture, context, skills and experience can shift us from our normal perspective and make us see problems, and solutions, from a fresh angle."
- "The most important people to learn from are those we work for – our donors, our clients, our beneficiaries, our wider stakeholders. What are they telling us about our service and their current and future needs?"

- "Articulating our experience to someone who is unfamiliar with our work can help us to view it from a different angle, find new reflections and refine the way we present our organizations and our work to the outside world."[4]

Donor-mandated evaluation versus self-driven evaluation

	Donor-mandated evaluation	Self-driven evaluation
Motivation	Meet donor requirements	Learn and improve
Significance	Tactical, short-term	Strategic, long-term
Real goal	Renewed funding	Organizational development
Objective	Donor satisfaction	What to keep and what to change
Primary user	The Donor	The entire organization
Effort	Minimum required	Do more to learn
Process	Delegate down	Involve everyone
Conclusion	Evaluation done. File it!	Lessons learned. Use them!

Why not more funding for nonprofit organizations?

As I pointed out in the opening chapters, we have a problem. With the affluence and the increase in disposable income in so many countries, it is surprising that charitable giving has not grown more in light of unmet needs in virtually all countries.

I attribute this slow growth in private and public support of NGOs to four basic failures:

1   Results are not convincing. (Results may be good, but they should be better through strategic evaluation.)
2   Charity scandals occur too often. (Scandals may be few, but there should be more processes to prevent such behavior, especially since an organization's scandal can tarnish the reputation of other NGOs in the sector.)
3   Donors are not given sufficient value for their contributions. (Donors get lots of communications for fundraising but not enough for building the relationship.)
4   When monitoring is done as a control and evaluation is done for donors, staff will not be fully engaged compared with mentoring and evaluation as learning.

If donors don't sincerely believe their donations produce meaningful results, if they have an impression of scandal among charities, and if they don't receive other information to build their confidence in the organization, they will find other uses for their disposable income including expensive electronics, new vehicles, and other consumer goods.

Key point: The needs of children, victims of violence, the sick, the poorly educated, those afflicted by disasters, impoverished communities, abused animals, and indeed the earth itself are too important to allow NGO mistakes to continue to give excuses to potential donors not to donate.

Developing a strategic approach to evaluation – evaluation as a process of learning, building capacity, and producing better results for society – is urgently needed by many nonprofits. Strategic evaluation based on regular, in-depth monitoring will mean organizations learn more, results are improved, donors are satisfied, funding increases, programs are broadened, and more people are helped. Such an approach by many nonprofit organizations around the world will inevitably contribute to increased public, corporate, and government confidence in the sector and their increased support for so many worthwhile charitable activities.

"Let's do it."   "I'll help you!"

Figure 11.5 Let's do it – agreement to get it done. Artwork by Sawyer Phillips.

➡️ *The solution is strategy, teamwork, and leadership with* **mentoring and learning (M&L)** *instead of monitoring and evaluation.*

Key point: The real value of evaluations is the organizational learning about what worked and why, what failed and why, what corrections were made and how, what are the long-term benefits and costs of the project, and what to do better in the future. For donors, the real value of such reports is confidence in the NGO (Figure 11.5).

Questions for implementation

1   How can your organization overcome resistance to monitoring and evaluation?
2   How does your organization use evaluations that were done for donors?
3   How has your organization explicitly committed to learning and getting better?
4   What steps will you take to get improvements in these areas?

Notes

1 Suzanne Massie, "The Reagan Years 1984-88," accessed July 4, 2022. http://www.suzannemassie.com/reaganYears.html.
2 Interviews from my research for Sasakawa Peace Foundation about NGO evaluation.
3 Aurelia Kassatly, "Philanthropy: Evidence vs Impact," *CAF*, accessed July 4, 2022, https://www.cafonline.org/my-personal-giving/long-term-giving/philanthropy-evidence-vs-impact.
4 Michael Mapstone, "Is Your Charity Embracing New Ways of Learning?," *Civil Society*, September 13, 2017, accessed July 4, 2022, https://www.civilsociety.co.uk/voices/michael-mapstone-is-your-charity-embracing-new-ways-of-learning.html.

Bibliography

1 Kassatly, Aurelia. "Philanthropy: Evidence vs Impact." *CAF*. Accessed July 4, 2022. https://www.cafonline.org/my-personal-giving/long-term-giving/philanthropy-evidence-vs-impact.
2 Mapstone, Michael. "Is Your Charity Embracing New Ways of Learning?" *Civil Society*, September 13, 2017. Accessed July 4, 2022. https://www.civilsociety.co.uk/voices/michael-mapstone-is-your-charity-embracing-new-ways-of-learning.html.
3 Massie, Suzanne. "The Reagan Years 1984-88." Accessed July 4, 2022. http://www.suzannemassie.com/reaganYears.html.

Chapter 12

From project management to capacity building to strategic evaluation

NGO leaders, especially founders, are strongly mission-driven and have a clear vision of a better society they seek to create. But being mission-driven is both a strength and a weakness for an organization. It is a strength, because it motivates and empowers. It is a weakness, because it may blind the leader who does not want to hear about barriers, problems, or failures in daily work or in evaluation results. Just about every organization I have supported has leaders who say, "We are the best!" Part of my job as consultant for 25 years with more than 75 clients with many repeat assignments was to show them they could be and should be better.

I also found that many leaders who came to recognize the need to improve their performance lacked an approach to use as a regular evaluation process seriously and strategically – that is, to learn and develop. Strategic evaluation is the essential tool to learn, improve, and provide ever-better services to beneficiaries.

Let's step back

Evaluation has long been an essential component in traditional project management, with five basic steps. An evaluation report based on the traditional *project management model* is usually included in most grant requirements, and for many years most NGOs have provided the necessary reports to satisfy the M&E requirements of major donors or grantmakers. The project management model is clear: Plan → Implement → Monitor → Evaluate → Report (Figure 12.1).

Of course, it is the beneficiaries of your work who are the most important stakeholders for evaluation and learning. After all, making this a better world is the reason your organization exists. Their views or the views of their representatives should be at the top of your priorities for consideration in all the steps in good program management. An organization's work is all about changing the reality for its program beneficiaries and, to do that, every organization needs to improve – continuously improve – its programs by building its capacity to do better.

I value the project management model, but I want to place an emphasis on learning and improving, so the model becomes a *capacity building model* with eight steps:

1 Plan or design with logic
2 Implement with data
3 Monitor to discover where to improve
4 Correct as necessary and drive to better results
5 Complete the project or program
6 Evaluate all results and impacts
7 Learn from your findings
8 Improve your project or program to build capacity and do better

DOI: 10.4324/9781003335207-15

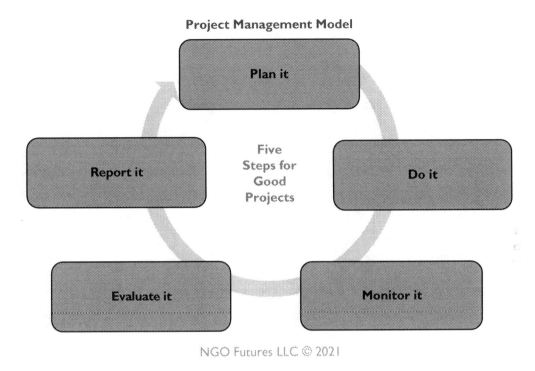

Figure 12.1 The Traditional Project Management Model with 5 steps. Image by the author.

Key point: The ***capacity building model*** creates a positive flow to do better: Planning → Doing → Monitoring → Correcting → Completing → Evaluating → Learning → Improving to build capacity (Figure 12.2).

Building capacity is essential, but the model is not yet complete. The capacity building model is an improvement over the project management model, but it may still be perceived by staff as a review of their own performance – "Monitoring and evaluating what you did or didn't do!" – rather than the more engaging process of mentoring and learning – "So we can do better!"

The next stage is using the *strategic evaluation model*, not only to build capacity, but to engage staff, raise more funds, and expand programs. This chapter introduces you to the eight priority disciplines in strategic evaluation, chapters 13 and 14 develop the model further, and later chapters provide real world examples and in-depth advice for implementation.

What is strategic evaluation?

In this book, you will learn how to start using evaluation in a new, strategic way. I call the actions in strategic evaluation the *eight priority disciplines*, because they are difficult to do well, and it requires discipline to do this. To succeed, you need a culture and practice of continuous learning.

Strategic evaluation is the strategy in which the whole organization uses monitoring and evaluation (M&E) or, rather, mentoring and evaluation, at a more strategic level to improve implementation, learn more from your successes and failures, build needed capacity to do better, engage staff more fully in the learning process, actually achieve more for your program beneficiaries, become more appealing to donors, and raise more money so you can do even more (Figure 12.3).

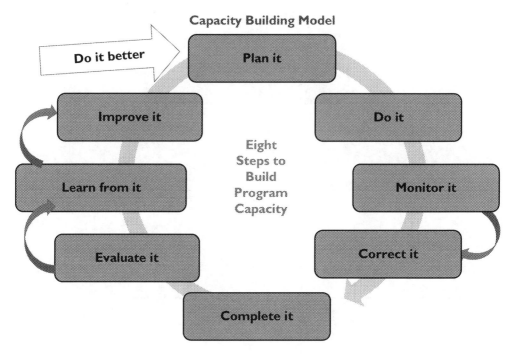

Figure 12.2 The Capacity Building Model with 8 steps. Image by the author.

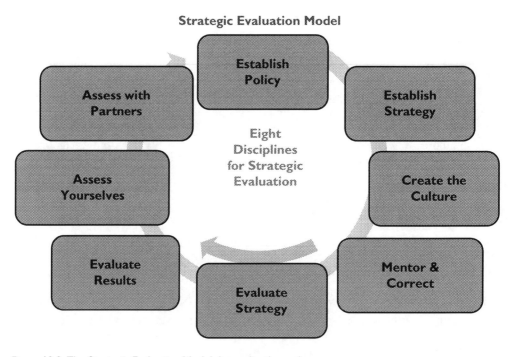

Figure 12.3 The Strategic Evaluation Model. Image by the author.

Strategic evaluation directly helps you to achieve your mission in a much larger way than traditional M&E in the project management model or even the capacity building model. I emphasize the connection between strategic evaluation and fundraising success, because donor respect is essential for continued and increased support! And respect by donors is earned by evaluating, learning, improving, and reporting what you do.

The flow of the *strategic evaluation model* goes from mission to programs to M&E to learning and building capacity and on to better programs, greater fundraising appeal, and substantially greater mission achievement.

Key point: The **flow** for ***strategic evaluation*** becomes a strategy for overall success: Planning → Doing → Monitoring or Mentoring → Correcting → Completing → Evaluating → Learning → Building Capacity → Improving and doing better → Achieving greater impact for participants → Reporting better impact for donors → Raising more support from donors → Expanding programs to help more → and on and on.

The benefits of taking monitoring and evaluation to this new, strategic level of mentoring, learning, and improving are significant. It's actually very simple but too often ignored. Generally speaking, traditional monitoring and evaluation is done to meet the terms of a grant, get good results, provide a good report to donors, and, from employees' perspectives, to admonish their performance. Capacity building evaluation is done to learn and improve. Strategic evaluation is done for that and to develop staff abilities, achieve more impact, increase appeal to donors, raise more money, and provide ever-increasing program services in a continuous cycle of development and growth.

The best organizations are already doing all this and, as a result, they regularly achieve bigger and better program results and unprecedented fundraising growth. Other organizations need to catch up, or they will drop behind. Three of the organizations I worked for years ago when they were still relatively small – Save the Children, Plan International, and Care International – are now generating billions of dollars for their programs. I certainly am not claiming credit for this amazing growth, but I played a role and learned so much in the process.[1]

In particular, smaller and mid-size organizations that are not growing significantly every year need to be especially concerned about this. Just as in the corporate world, the big organizations are getting better and bigger, and all the others need to get much better to survive and thrive. As my board chair at Foster Parents Plan (now called Plan International USA) told me almost every time I saw him, "Ken, organizations that don't grow die. What are you doing to get better and grow faster?" This is not growth for growth's sake; it is growth to make a better world by getting smarter and learning to build your capacities, so your nonprofit can deliver improved programs and help more people.

Jim Rugh, senior evaluator at CARE at the time, said to me that "There is a major gap between technical people who do evaluation and management people who need it." This part of the book will help both sides bridge that gap. NGO executives and board members can learn how to:

- Turn evaluation reports into learning messages.
- Create channels of feedback within the organization.
- Eliminate the "glass ceiling" that evaluators often encounter.
- Enable evaluation findings to flow upward within an organization.

You will learn specific steps to take to your next management or board meeting. You will learn how to help evaluators, managers, and board members communicate more openly and more effectively about learning from mistakes and successes. You will enable others to see evaluation in the new light of strategic benefits, not just as a cost item or extra effort. You will learn the framework to challenge a supervisor who fails to support staff or to listen to evaluation findings. You will see how strategic evaluation helps program staff to achieve greater impact and fundraisers to demonstrate better results to donors.

The origins of these chapters are my 60 years of experience as a fundraiser, manager, executive director, board member, and board chair of large and small nonprofits, as a consultant teaching and learning from NGOs in more than 40 countries, and as researcher and discussion leader with many thousands of interviews with fundraisers, managers, evaluators, and donors about their work.

A priority interest for me has always been how organizations learn to get better. My father always said to me, "Whatever you do, do it well." But what does "well" mean for an NGO? Early in my career, it became abundantly clear that getting better – continuous improvement plus breakthrough thinking – requires effective systems and knowledge of planning, strategy, and capacity building along with the recognition that every organization makes mistakes and can learn from them.

We all know we need to get better in the NGO sector at delivering programs and services, because the needs are urgent as laid out in the Sustainable Development Goals,[2] reports by scientific experts on climate, and regular news coverage of discrimination, abuse, poverty, corruption, and other offenses to humankind. Getting better requires continuous change and improvement, and the top responsibility of NGO leaders is to initiate and manage change to support their mission. As a supervisor and executive director, I always said, "I want to hear from you about problems and mistakes. That's normal as long as you learn from them."

In my book *25 Proven Strategies for Fundraising Success*,[3] the first and most important strategy is *Transformation* whereby organizations progress from new to dependent to developed to scaling up. They do this through good management and strategic evaluation – mentoring, evaluating, learning, and building capacity – in program, marketing, communicating, and everything they do.

With every client organization and in every course I teach, I emphasize the importance for the organization to continue to get better and to grow in order to achieve ever greater impact for its beneficiaries. The world needs better and bigger NGOs, so we can do more to progress toward those profound Sustainable Development Goals. Organization transformation is the way to do that (Figure 12.4).

An added basis for these chapters is the research I conducted for the Sasakawa Peace Foundation on how international NGO organizations evaluate their work. The research report, titled "International NGO Evaluation Methodologies for Capacity Building: A New Paradigm for International NGOs" on how international NGOs carry out and use evaluation as well as what major donors expect in evaluations. An overview of the research was published as *Considering International NGO's Evaluation* in 2001 in Japanese.[4]

My research for Sasakawa and my own empirical research throughout my employment and consulting over the years led me to these two obvious but fundamental conclusions:

1   The board of directors is responsible to establish policy and priority for strategic evaluation.
2   Management is responsible to assure evaluations are strategic and valid and used for learning and improving.

Over the years, I increasingly saw the obvious: Evaluation, when used as a learning step, is essential to develop an organization. Smart NGO leaders focus on building knowledge and skills, partner with other NGOs to increase capacity, and gear up new learning teams to implement improvements identified in the evaluation process.

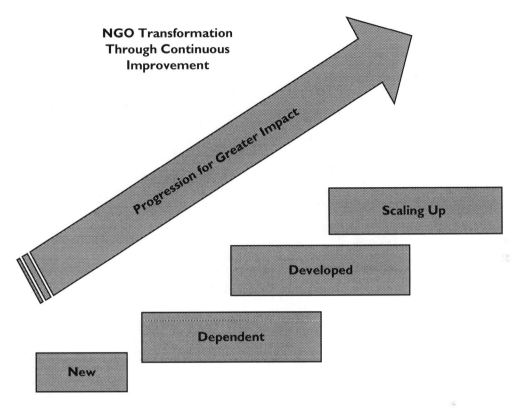

NGO Transformation
Through Continuous
Improvement

Progression for Greater Impact

Scaling Up

Developed

Dependent

New

Figure 12.4 NGO transformation strategy to grow and improve. Image by the author.

Key point: *Results* is a general term for what happens as a consequence of certain actions. There are many levels of results. *Impact* is the term for the lasting benefits for program participants and beneficiaries and for society.

Cautions from examples: Why every nonprofit needs strategic evaluation

The following examples illustrate what can happen when an organization fails to learn from meaningful evaluations.

In this first example, the mission of the organization was to help *at-risk youth* who might be tempted into a life of crime. To show them where such a life could lead, the organization developed a program to expose young minor offenders to convicted prisoners who told them how horrible it was to be in prison. The founders were passionate about the many inspiring success stories – anecdotes from the former juvenile offenders and the program participants who went to college, who got regular jobs, who received recognition for public service.

However, after some years and at the request of a key donor, the organization conducted an evaluation of its long-term results (the lasting impact on participants). Sadly, the evaluation found that a higher percentage of its program participants actually ended up in prison compared to those in the control group! The core strategy of exposing impressionable young people to charismatic former offenders was found to be counterproductive.[5]

Another example was a U.S.-based *drug education* program that had many inspiring stories. Promotion from committed believers enabled the program to expand into numerous American schools. However, an objective evaluation of the effects of the program found real results to be lacking, which led to termination of its funding. Studies concluded that the short-term outcomes of the program were not lasting or were even counterproductive for some participants, and the strategy used in the program was flawed.[6]

Here is a positive example: An in-depth evaluation of the Chicago Child-Parent Center, a *Head Start* program, compared hundreds of children who had been in the program with a comparable group of non-participants 15 years later. The results for the participants were an impressive 29% higher high school completion rate, 42% lower special education placement, 42% less likely to have been arrested for a violent crime, and 51% reduction in child abuse and neglect. Overall, the costs of $6,730 per child in the program paid back an estimated $47,758 in benefits, which included higher earnings and better prospects for the participants as well as lower social costs for the community. This organization used evaluation to prove its impact and make its case for expanding the program.[7]

I know of many good evaluations for other organizations that were used to report to donors but then were simply filed without any long-term learning benefit for the organization. I've asked executives about their evaluation reports, and their answers often were that their reports were great successes because their donors loved them. When I pursued and asked how the findings were used internally to improve the organization or the program, a frequent response was a blank stare.

These stories – and there are many more examples, both good and bad – highlight four lessons.

1   ***Anecdotes are not valid evidence of success*** – The first lesson is that anecdotes of success, although colorful and inspiring, are woefully insufficient as evidence of success and, worse, may be seriously misleading. Yet many organizations rely on them. NGO board members and managers who believe they are successful but do not have hard evidence of lasting impact may, as revealed in the first two examples above, be doing more damage than good.

2   ***Traditional monitoring provides an "early warning system"*** – The second lesson is that internal monitoring and evaluation – and smart managers – should identify any significant problems long before external pressures (such as a donor-mandated evaluation) identify the inherent failure of the organization's program strategy. Ongoing "eyes wide open" monitoring can avoid serious pitfalls in the implementation stage.

3   ***Strategic evaluation that shows significant impact can lead to program expansion*** – The third lesson, as illustrated in the Head Start example, shows how evaluation of long-term results can lead to scaling the program to much higher levels. Throughout the world, there are many examples of successful NGO evaluations that have led to significant expansion of their programs – and even to massive scaling up through widely funded NGO activities and government-funded programs.

4   ***Understand what you are evaluating, so you can communicate results to donors*** – The fourth lesson is to know the difference between outputs, outcomes, and impacts. For example, there is a difference between building a school (outputs), educating kids (outcomes), and graduates having good jobs (impacts).

The better approach for mentoring and learning (M&L) for better results

When it comes to M&E, I believe too many nonprofits use a *tactical* approach of completing the evaluation, reporting good findings to a donor, filing the evaluation, and continuing to do "business and usual" without identifying and integrating lessons learned.

Evaluation, when done *strategically*, is used for organizational learning and capacity building to achieve better results. This approach combines a policy of board-mandated strategic evaluation with supporting disciplines for implementation. Organizations that pursue strategic evaluation apply a higher-level and substantially more strategic approach to monitoring/mentoring, evaluation, and staff development and continuous improvement for the long-term benefit of society.

When vision-driven leaders see evaluation as a strategic tool to develop the organization – and not just a tactic to meet grant requirements – they demonstrate their true leadership. When they see the real benefits that strategic evaluation can bring, they will use the findings to communicate evaluation lessons throughout the organization as well as to current and prospective donors. Staff are more engaged because they see benefits of personal growth and improved performance.

Key point: *Strategic evaluation* uses monitoring/mentoring to make short-term corrections, uses evaluation for learning to build its capacity to do better, and improves results in the future. This impresses donors more than a tactical report.

Although the methodology and tools required in evaluation are widely known among experts in the profession, many (and some would say most) NGO executives and board members are not comfortable with an in-depth, strategic evaluation process. At an international meeting of NGO leaders, an executive said to me, "I want to find a good system for evaluation to put in place – a turnkey approach. What should I do?" This book provides a step-by-step answer to that question.

The strategic evaluation model creates a positive flow to improve programs and increase revenue: Planning → Doing → Monitoring/Mentoring → Correcting → Completing → Evaluating → Learning → Building Capacity → Improving and doing better → Achieving greater impact for participants → Reporting better impact for donors → Raising more support from donors → Expanding programs to help more

Strategic evaluation is internally driven evaluation to learn what to continue and what to change. It shows how to identify, understand, and share lessons learned and how to implement the changes for better programs and operations in the future.

Tactical evaluation is evaluation carried out to meet the particular short-term need for a report to a donor and demonstrate your success. It may or may not contribute to long-term strengthening of the organization.

How do you implement strategic evaluation in your organization? The eight priority disciplines are:

1   *Board responsibility:* Establish strategic evaluation as policy and priority.
2   *Management responsibility:* Implement strategic evaluation as strategy and practice.
3   *A culture of learning:* Assure M&E and lessons learned improve results.
4   *Monitoring:* Mentoring as an effective supervisor for correcting and learning.
5   *Evaluation of program strategy:* Making certain your program strategy is valid.
6   *Evaluation of results:* Knowing what lasting impact you actual achieve.
7   *Organizational self-assessment:* Learning and improving with each other.
8   *Mutual accountability:* Knowing you are working well with partners.

The above list provides a quick summary. In the following chapters, we take a close look at the eight priority disciplines – including in-depth advice to implement these in your organization.

Every nonprofit goes through a life cycle. Without regular monitoring/mentoring, evaluating, learning, and improving, many organizations will stagnate and eventually fail. Yes, monitoring and evaluating are needed to make certain programs are succeeding; however, mentoring and learning are more effective for employee development and engagement and will lead to better results.

Good news! Strategic evaluation will renew a troubled organization and get it on an upward trajectory again. Regular, in-depth monitoring and strategic evaluation can identify shortcomings in a program and can lead to critical corrections as well as identify the successes to continue.

As described earlier in this book, a famous evaluation example was the use of microcredit or small loans, which many NGOs adopted as a strategy to support the economic development of families in low-income countries. The reports for some years highlighted high success rates of the recipients, usually men, using the small loans effectively to higher incomes and get high payback rates, which were excellent outcomes. However, longer term impact evaluations began to reveal that the families were not actually benefitting from these "successful" loan programs as much as expected.

Organizations such as Save the Children, UNICEF, and others looked more closely at who was receiving the loans and discovered that many of the fathers were spending the extra income at the local bar! Rather quickly, most organizations using microcredit switched to awarding loans to mothers, who demonstrated just as good financial success (outcomes) and used the proceeds for better housing, health, education, and other family benefits (impacts).

The Lifecycle of an NGO or Project image shows growth through several stages, then a problem and tailspin downward – that can be avoided by conducting strategic evaluation to learn and make improvements! After ten years of stagnation at Foster Parents Plan, I was brought in as a new executive director to lead the organization back into a growth mode. We applied new strategy, new evaluation, and new learning, and three years later had doubled the income from $10 million to $20 million and on to $30 million in eight years (Figure 12.5).

Remember the story I shared in chapter 5 about the executive directors of 120 organizations who responded in a survey that they believed their competitors (other NGOs) had ethical and

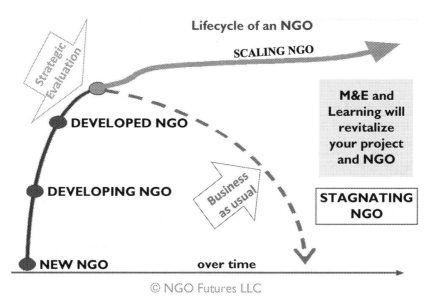

Figure 12.5 Lifecycle of an NGO image. Image by the author.

program failures while their own organization had none? NGOs should beware of the danger of believing they are working so well that they don't need strategic evaluation to assess objectively how well they are really working and learnings to improve continuously.

Every smart leader understands that the organization needs to avoid doing business as usual in order to improve and grow. The Lifecycle of an NGO shows the dangers of doing *Business as usual* and the benefits of utilizing *Strategic Evaluation*.

Questions for implementation

1   Can you describe the evaluation model used in your organization?
2   Where is your organization in the lifecycle of organizations? New, Developing, Developed, Scaling, or Stagnant?
3   What are the outputs, outcomes, and impacts of your program?
4   What will you do to improve in these areas?

Notes

1 See chapter 16 which describes my involvement at Save the Children US and Plan International USA. My work with CARE included strengthening CARE Japan and exploring potential new donor country members.
2 "What are the Sustainable Development Goals?," accessed June 26, 2022, https://www.undp.org/sustainable-development-goals.
3 Ken Phillips, *25 Proven Strategies for Fundraising Success: How to win the love and support of donors* (NGO Futures LLC, 2021), 83–100.
4 Ken Phillips, "International NGO Evaluation Methodologies for Capacity Building: A new paradigm for international NGOs" (Sasakawa Peace Foundation, Tokyo, 2001). An overview of the research was published in Japanese as *Considering International NGO's Evaluation* in 2001.
5 This site has been deleted.
6 Landmark Recovery, "Why the DARE Program Failed," May 18, 2020, accessed July 4, 2022, https://landmarkrecovery.com/why-the-dare-program-failed/.
7 Brian Mattmiller, "Study Shows Economic Benefits of Early Intervention," June 26, 2001, accessed July 4, 2022, https://news.wisc.edu/study-shows-economic-benefits-of-early-intervention/.

Bibliography

1 Brian Mattmiller. "Study Shows Economic Benefits of Early Intervention," June 26, 2001. Accessed July 4, 2022. https://news.wisc.edu/study-shows-economic-benefits-of-early-intervention/
2 Landmark Recovery. "Why the DARE Program Failed," May 18, 2020. Accessed July 4, 2022. https://landmarkrecovery.com/why-the-dare-program-failed/.
3 Phillips, Ken. *25 Proven Strategies for Fundraising Success: How to win the love and support of donors*. NGO Futures LLC, 2021.
4 Phillips, Ken. *Considering International NGO's Evaluation. Sasakawa* Peace Foundation, Tokyo (Japanese language), 2001.
5 "What are the Sustainable Development Goals?" Accessed June 26, 2022. https://www.undp.org/sustainable-development-goals.

Chapter 13

Strategic evaluation – A powerful tool for learning and increasing impact

Strategic evaluation plays a crucial role in learning and building capacity in *all* aspects of organizational performance – program, finance, fundraising, administration, and other functions. My model for strategic evaluation for learning and improving addresses the important questions in practical ways based on real-world solutions and straightforward case examples.

1   What is your NGO actually trying to do?
2   What has prevented it from doing more?
3   What have your evaluations taught you?
4   How do you manage ongoing learning?
5   How does culture support your work?
6   How do you know what to improve?

At workshops and conferences, I challenge nonprofit leaders to think broadly about evaluation and accountability for their own improvement while considering these five key essentials or responsibilities of NGO performance:

1   Value – What is its mission?
2   Results – What is its effectiveness?
3   Cost – What is its efficiency?
4   Trustworthiness – What are its ethics?
5   Accountability – How transparent is it?

These responsibilities reflect the essentials for an organization for its own sense of accomplishment and for donors to be satisfied. In a business transaction, the purchaser is usually the user of the product or service, so he or she can judge the value, quality (results), and cost directly. However, in an NGO transaction, the "purchaser" or donor is not the user or beneficiary of the service. Therefore, the added elements of trust, impact, and accountability are essential to close the loop between the "purchaser" and "user" of the service.

Key point: The significance of strategic evaluation is to learn and build capacity to achieve better impact for beneficiaries and, as a result, to have a stronger appeal to donors.

➤ The best NGOs are already doing this. They are growing to achieve ever-greater impact and are attracting ever-increasing support.

Warren Van Wicklin, an international development consultant specializing in evaluation, said to me with great insight: "Evaluation has two main functions: accountability and learning.

DOI: 10.4324/9781003335207-16

Good evaluations tend to have some of both. If an evaluation is purely for accountability, people feel they are being policed and under judgment, and don't see much upside to the evaluation. On the other hand, if it is only for learning, people can slough off any shortcomings, saying that we've learned our mistakes and will do better in the future. A good evaluation includes both learning and accountability."

What is mentoring? "The purpose of mentoring is to grow by tapping into the knowledge and experience of someone further along than yourself. It's the best way to accelerate your development."[1] "A mentoring program can improve employee retention, create more diversity, help plan for the future, and save on costs for other forms of training."[2] "Employees are happy, engaged, and productive when their individual needs and the needs of the organization are in sync. ... Employees reach their full potential when their job also brings intrinsic rewards—the feeling of doing meaningful work that is connected to their own personal and professional development. ... Mentoring programs have become mainstream. About 70% of Fortune 500 companies have one (although only a quarter of smaller companies do). ... Employees who participated in the program were five times more likely to advance in pay grade. ... Mentees were promoted five times more than those not in the program. ..."[3] "The benefits of mentoring are myriad. For individuals, studies show that good mentoring can lead to greater career success, including promotions, raises, and increased opportunities. Organizations that embrace mentoring are rewarded with higher levels of employee engagement, retention, and knowledge sharing."[4]

With better knowledge sharing, accelerated development, improved employee retention, happier, engaged, and productive employees, more promotions, and greater career success, mentoring is a step up from traditional monitoring. As I described in chapter 11:

Mentoring for Results is a more productive process to assure good results during the implementation of an activity. In the workplace, the supervisor as mentor listens to employees, guides them in their implementation activity, and steers them to greater productivity and achievement of objectives. It is a more supportive process than monitoring which can easily veer into a critical mode.

To become a more supporting, verifying, and learning organization

Here is an example, based on my notes, of progress on the six questions just above during my employment (1982–1992) with Foster Parents Plan (now Plan International USA).

We worked together globally at the senior level to move evaluation forward in response to demands from donors for more accountability about the use and effect of their donations. We identified eight *program sectors* and improved field reporting with both progress data and human interest stories – which helped to convey program results and confirm donors' interest.

We established a new *impact evaluation system* for our global development programs. This included baseline data, progress toward goals, and impacts on program participants. The performance indicators included access to potable water, vaccination coverage, nutritional status, sanitation and waste disposal, housing, formal education, literacy, and income. The finance team allocated budget and required expenditure reports to reflect those same program sectors.

We conducted a *global strategic planning* process, which added a focus on quality, continuous improvement, and ongoing learning as emerging priorities. The progress Plan made in the 1980s from simply beginning to address evaluation to making evaluation meaningful and a priority just ten years later reflects the complexity of this work. The organization identified the purposes of evaluation as institutional learning, improved management, better accountability, and increased community capabilities. We even discussed a *program guarantee*.

In a recent conversation, Donna Jean Rainville, who was director of finance and administration when I was executive director, told me, "I remember important discussions about evaluation, and I took very seriously my trips to the field and in all my other work to look through the eyes of donors to validate if we were doing what we communicated to them." She was an advocate of continuous improvement, and that was the approach we took to continually getting things right for planning and strategy, monitoring and evaluation, learning and development, and being accountable to donors.

In 1996, Plan moved forward and prioritized learning as a program principle: "Drawing upon internal and external sources, Plan will promote learning for itself and its partners in the development community in order to achieve its Mission. Plan will learn from relevant experiences, whenever and wherever this learning supports the achievement of its Mission. By establishing an information system that makes relevant program information available and through networking, Plan will create a learning environment. Plan will both apply and contribute to the learning of the outside world, including the wider development community. This will lead to improving the technical soundness of its programs."[5]

In addition to the organizational approach to evaluation, I also believe in the personal approach. In all my career, I regularly visited program operations to verify our reports and fundraising claims. I learned that conversations with program participants can be misleading, because they want to be appreciative and hesitate to criticize the organization that is helping them. It took a special kind of questioning to get close to reality. I found, for example, that it was useless to ask, "How is the program going? Is the staff really helping? Do you have any complaints?" Instead, I worked to get the person thinking: "Tell me two or three things you really like about the program and how it's going." And then after those answers: "Tell me about a few things that could be better. We want to know, so we can help even more." This was all about supporting, verifying, and learning.

I recall key ideas from Peter M. Senge's book, *The Fifth Discipline: The Art and Practice of the Learning Organization:*[6]

1   Shared vision to aim high;
2   Personal mastery to see reality;
3   Systems thinking to see the whole picture;
4   Mental models to avoid self-imposed restrictions;
5   Team learning by using dialogue and thinking together.

My favorite quote from Senge is: "Through learning we re-create ourselves. Through learning we become able to do something we never were able to do. Through learning we re-perceive the world and our relationship to it. Through learning we extend our capacity to create, to be part of the generative process of life. There is within each of us a deep hunger for this type of learning."[7] This is all about understanding and improving ourselves and others we work with, doing things differently and more creatively, and generating or producing better results. These steps can be affirmed and applied as part of a new learning culture.

Steps to make evaluation strategic – Strategy is about *how* you will do something

Strategy is the *how* of working, which determines how you move forward, what you budget, and what you actually do. Making evaluation strategic means turning the concept (and process) of traditional evaluation into an ongoing, action-oriented strategy that guides *how* you will implement, learn, improve, and achieve better impact. This is a more in-depth approach than a tactical evaluation that is carried out primarily to satisfy a donor's requirement.

In strategic evaluation, all the elements of monitoring and measurement, research and evidence, evaluation and learning, strengthening and collaborating, and internal and external accountability are woven into the organization's strategic and operational plans with goals and objectives with activities and indicators as essential management and supervisory functions. Codes of conduct, mentoring, learning, and honest evaluations are seen as necessary components to improve performance.

As essential strategy, strategic evaluation is about learning from evaluation in order to strengthen your capacity to perform better, get more significant results, operate on less cost, and raise more money – in other words, to carry out your mission better. It should be a hands-on approach to "shake up your organization" (in a good way) for better performance. Organization leaders need to understand the benefits of strategic evaluation and continuous improvement. Managers need to step up their supervision to support the strategy (Figure 13.1).

As I noted in chapter 12, strategic evaluation creates a positive flow to improve programs and increase revenue and expand programs. It sounds complicated but it is just the flow. Like driving a car, it is complex the first time but then it is becomes simple – Open car door, Settle in driver's seat, Attach seat belt, Put key in ignition, Turn the key, Check for other cars, Put in gear, Accelerate, Turn when needed, Be careful, Slow down, Find parking, Park, and Disconnect ignition. That's the flow of driving to get where you want to go safely. It is very hard and challenging the first few times you do it. Then it becomes natural and you are happy to do it well.

The strategic evaluation model creates a positive flow to improve programs and increase revenue: Plan → Do → Monitor/Mentor → Correct → Complete → Evaluate → Learn → Build Capacity → Improve and do better → Achieve greater impact for participants → Report better impact for donors → Raise more support from donors → Expand programs to help more.

Let's see if we can simplify this in the next few sections.

Strategic Evaluation

1. Establish the Policy

2. Implement the Strategy

3. Create a Learning Culture

4. Mentor and Improve Progress

5. Test and Prove Program Strategy

6. Verify Long-Term Program Impacts

7. Conduct Self-Assessments Internally

8. Assess Accountability with Partners

These eight disciplines make evaluation strategic.

NGO Futures LLC © 2021

Figure 13.1 The eight disciplines to make evaluation strategic. Sidebar by the author.

Eight priority disciplines in the strategic evaluation process – Each is a tool for mentoring, evaluating, learning, and improving

The objective here is to inspire, inform, and guide yourself and your organization about the value and use of strategic evaluation. My focus is on the implementation of strategic evaluation, not its origins, theories, or technical details. The following paragraphs present the eight essential, organization-wide steps – which I call priority disciplines – to fully implement strategic evaluation in your nonprofit.

It really is quite simple. Each discipline has its own value and its own use, and each is inadequate on its own. When used together strategically, however, they form an easy-to-use approach to monitor/mentor, evaluate, learn, and improve. Here is a description of each discipline:

1   *Board responsibility: How to make strategic evaluation a policy, priority, and ongoing practice to build your capacity.* This step creates the framework for building capacity and managing change. A policy of strategic evaluation instructs staff leadership to implement the strategy, supports management to conduct full-on honest evaluations, and expects staff to embrace and to use all the findings (both good and not so good) to learn and improve. It is a board responsibility to establish strategic evaluation as policy, priority, and practice.

2   *Management responsibility: How to implement strategic evaluation as essential strategy and practice to build your capacity.* This step carries the policy, priority, and practice into all planning and day-to-day action throughout the organization. Establishing strategic evaluation as essential organizational strategy means including it in all strategic and operational planning, instituting regular monitoring/mentoring, conducting full-on honest evaluations, recognizing that all the findings (both good and not good) are learning opportunities, being dedicated to make the changes indicated, and supporting all staff in implementing improvements to strengthen the organization, so it can perform better, get more significant results, operate on less cost, and raise more money – in other words, to carry out the mission better. The organization's leaders provide a fair share of meeting time for evaluation findings, learning, and knowledge management. It is a management responsibility to implement strategic evaluation as a priority strategy for improvement.

3   *A culture of learning: How to assure your organization is learning to improve results.* This step requires a hands-on approach to achieve a culture of learning. It addresses both vertical and horizontal responsibilities within an organization with the objective of sharing and learning. A culture of learning facilitates progressing to ever-better performance by all managers, staff, and volunteers. It fosters an open environment of discussion and communication about evaluation lessons and improves communication between implementers and managers, evaluators and leaders, and staff and board. It overcomes resistance to accepting there are opportunities for improvement, minor issues to fix, or even serious problems to address. It encourages actions to make needed changes, so results of evaluations are really used to improve processes and results. It is the responsibility of managers to lead the process of identifying and living the desired culture with full and open participation by staff and to prioritize learning as a continuous process for improvement.

4   *Monitoring or, rather, mentoring: How regular mentoring and learning (M&L) along with correcting let you know how your program is progressing.* Effective monitoring and evaluation (M&E) enables staff to assess progress, make

midcourse corrections, and achieve established objectives. I advocate using *mentoring and learning (M&L)* as a better process than monitoring and evaluation. An ongoing M&L process is a management tool to know if your program is progressing as planned and to provide regular guidance on program implementation. Embracing monitoring/mentoring and evaluating/learning throughout the planning and implementation cycle enables you to build staff engagement and facilitate staff development. By identifying *meaningful, manageable, measurable, and motivational progress indicators* (4MPIs) more clearly, everyone can check regularly on progress, make midcourse corrections, develop staff, and achieve established objectives. Both managers and supervisors are responsible for thorough implementation of M&L in program and other functions.

Key point: To live a learning culture, build staff competence, and achieve better results, monitoring needs to become mentoring and evaluation needs to become learning. Supportive mentoring and learning evaluation facilitate staff development, commitment, and better work, but harsh monitoring and fault-finding evaluations will not.

5   ***Evaluation of program strategy: How to assure your program strategy is valid.*** The evaluation of program strategy, also called the concept evaluation approach, tests a program strategy or approach to determine if it is valid and effective to continue and use more widely. As an essential first step, this discipline tests a program strategy or concept to determine if it works, so you can be confident in using it more widely. A second step is refinement and further innovation and then testing variations to improve the results. Organizations using a new program strategy without evaluating its effectiveness may be wasting funds on an ineffective program – or may actually be harming program participants. The program director and independent evaluators are the individuals responsible for validating that the chosen program strategy is working better than alternatives.

6   ***Evaluation of results: How to know the long-term impacts that your program achieves.*** This step, evaluation of long-term results, proves to yourself and others that you have done really well in your overall programs. Evaluation of results verifies the long-term impacts your program has actually achieved. These impacts are much farther along and more significant than the program objectives measured in traditional M&E and the findings in evaluation of program outcomes. Evaluation of results is the essential component of evaluation that moves your organization's thinking beyond immediate outputs and shorter-term outcomes to identify the longer-term impacts. This is what demonstrates that you have made the most excellent use of funding in your programs. It is what donors really want – proof of your impact and assurance that their contributions will achieve the long-term results they expect. The executive director and independent evaluators are the individuals responsible for validating long-term impacts of the organization's work.

7   ***Organizational self-assessment: How to know if you are doing well internally.*** Self-assessment evaluation is a candid, internal analysis for learning and improving in all aspects of the organization's work by management, board, staff, and volunteers. Organizational self-assessment lets your organization discover how it is doing internally: what should be preserved and what should be changed. In addition, it empowers you to learn and improve from each other. Self-assessment is the ultimate in candid analysis for learning and improvement by those who know the processes, achievements, and problems best (management, staff, board, volunteers, and participants or their representatives, too). Managers and supervisors are responsible to lead the self-assessment process and to assure candid input by all, no harm to anyone for honest participation, and serious consideration of the findings.

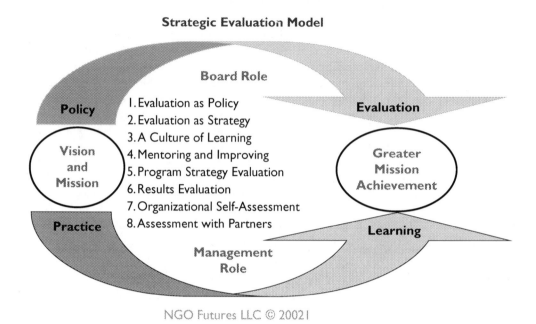

Figure 13.2 Strategic Evaluation Model with eight disciplines. Image by the author.

8   ***Mutual accountability: How to know if you are working well with your partners.*** As the funding process goes from donor to organization to beneficiary, mutual accountability becomes more complex as it should involve everyone in the overall business model from donors to society. This step – accountability with partners – shows how well you and your partners are collaborating and how to make needed improvements. This accountability examines goals, values, communication, cooperation, and relations among partners in order to make improvements rather than ignoring any potential difficulties with each other. Partners include grantmakers and other donor segments (or their representatives), universities and other NGOs involved in your work, program partners and collaborators, your beneficiaries or their representatives, and even representatives of the broader society such as interested media, relevant experts, and other influencers. Everyone in an organization is responsible for productive accountability with partners (Figure 13.2).

Take a moment to study the *Strategic Evaluation Model* image. On the left of the chart is the vision and mission and on the right is the mission achieved through implementation, evaluation, learning, and improving. The eight disciplines in the middle comprise a comprehensive approach to effective evaluation for mentoring, evaluating, learning, and improving. Arching above all is the board's responsibility to make strategic evaluation a priority policy and practice, and underlying all is management's responsibility to implement evaluation as a priority strategy.

With a culture of learning, the entire organization – leaders, staff, and volunteers – will be enabled to utilize the other five disciplines: monitoring and evaluation (now mentoring and learning) for better results, assuring the program strategy is effective, demonstrating the long-term impact achieved, improving their own activities and behaviors, and working well with partners.

Key point: Both board and management must take specific steps to assure commitment to the process, accuracy in evaluation, acceptance of problems, learning from evaluation, and using the learning to build capacity. Having a learning culture is critical to success.

My previous books in the *Civil Society Series* address the topics of stepping up to leadership and the fundamental principles of fundraising, strategic and operational planning with strong values and energizing culture, and proven strategies for fundraising. These are the essential underlying steps to support what this book presents about trust and impact.[8]

The next chapter provides in-depth advice and action steps, so you can integrate the eight priority disciplines into your organization with the goal of continuous monitoring, mentoring, evaluating, learning, and improving. The case studies in chapters 15 and 16 show how NGOs have actually developed and used various approaches or disciplines to monitor, evaluate, learn, and improve.

Are YOU up to this challenge?

A great organization accepts leadership from all levels. A self-confident executive director encourages leadership initiatives from staff at all levels. A smart fundraiser knows it is often necessary to step up to leadership within the organization to make sure everyone is doing everything possible to make it an effective organization that achieves its mission, benefits participants, behaves well, and is attractive to donors.

As I have written elsewhere, the time to step up is *now*, and you can do that through realistic steps everyone can take. Whoever and wherever you are, you can do it … and you must to make this a better world (Figure 13.3 and 13.4).

Six Realistic Steps to Leadership

Simple steps to lead that everyone can take

1. **Networking with others**
   ➤ So you have potential partners and allies.

2. **Seeing what needs to be done**
   ➤ So you can focus on important matters.

3. **Seizing opportunity**
   ➤ So you can take advantage of circumstances.

4. **Stepping up when you hesitate**
   ➤ So you will actually decide to lead in new ways.

5. **Persisting in spite of roadblocks**
   ➤ So you will achieve the results that are needed.

6. **Running meetings well**
   ➤ So you will be known as someone who gets things done well on time.

Always based on positive values for a better world!!

Figure 13.3 Six realistic steps to leadership. Image by the author.

"That's a really good suggestion. Thanks. Who's next?"

Figure 13.4 People planning what to do. Artwork by Sawyer Phillips.

Questions for implementation

1   Where will the leadership come from to implement strategic evaluation?
2   Can you identify how each of the eight disciplines will lead to greater impact?
3   Can you progress from monitoring to mentoring staff? From evaluation to learning?
4   How will you move forward to use these different disciplines?

Notes

1 "What is the Purpose of Mentoring Programs?" Matthew Reeves, CEO of Together, April 22, 2021, https://www.togetherplatform.com/blog/what-is-the-purpose-of-mentoring
2 "Using Mentoring in the Workplace to Improve Employee Retention," BizLibrary, accessed August 23, 2022, https://www.bizlibrary.com/blog/employee-development/workplace-mentoring/
3 "Improve Workplace Culture With A Strong Mentoring Program," Naz Beheshti, Forbes, January 23, 2019, accessed August 23, 2022, https://www.forbes.com/sites/nazbeheshti/2019/01/23/improve-workplace-culture-with-a-strong-mentoring-program/?sh=10b3f60676b5
4 "Mentoring Matters: Three Essential Elements Of Success," Mary Abbajay, Forbes, January 20, 2019, accessed August 23, 2022, https://www.forbes.com/sites/maryabbajay/2019/01/20/mentoring-matters-three-essential-element-of-success/?sh=444701d845a9

5 "Plan International Program Directions [internal staff document]," July 1996, accessed July 4, 2022, https://plan-international.org.
6 Peter M. Senge, *The Fifth Discipline: The Art & Practice of The Learning Organization* (Crown Business, 2006).
7 _____, 13.
8 Ken Phillips, *Make a Better World: A practical guide to leadership for fundraising success* (NGO Futures LLC, 2020); Ken Phillips, *Strategic Planning and Culture for Nonprofits: Clear and doable steps to create motivating plans and the supporting culture you need for success* (NGO Futures LLC, 2021); Ken Phillips, *25 Proven Strategies for Fundraising Success: How to win the love and support of donors* (NGO Futures LLC, 2021).

Bibliography

1 Abbajay, Mary. "Mentoring Matters: Three Essential Elements Of Success," Forbes, January 20, 2019, accessed August 23, 2022, https://www.forbes.com/sites/maryabbajay/2019/01/20/mentoring-matters-three-essential-element-of-success/?sh=444701d845a9

2 Beheshti, Naz. "Improve Workplace Culture With A Strong Mentoring Program", Forbes, January 23, 2019, accessed August 23, 2022, https://www.forbes.com/sites/nazbeheshti/2019/01/23/improve-workplace-culture-with-a-strong-mentoring-program/?sh=10b3f60676b5

3 Phillips, Ken. *25 Proven Strategies for Fundraising Success: How to win the love and support of donors.* NGO Futures LLC, 2021.

4 Phillips, Ken. *Make a Better World: A practical guide to leadership for fundraising success.* NGO Futures LLC, 2020.

5 Phillips, Ken. *Strategic Planning and Culture for Nonprofits: Clear and doable steps to create motivating plans and the supporting culture you need for success.* NGO Futures LLC, 2021.

6 "Plan International USA." *Charity Navigator.* Accessed July 4, 2022. https://www.charitynavigator.org/ein/135661832

7 "Plan International Program Directions [internal staff document]," July 1996. Accessed July 4, 2022. https://plan-international.org

8 Reeves, Matthew. "What is the Purpose of Mentoring Programs?" Together, April 22, 2021, https://www.togetherplatform.com/blog/what-is-the-purpose-of-mentoring

9 Senge, Peter M. *The Fifth Discipline: The Art & Practice of The Learning Organization.* Crown Business, 2006.

10 "Using Mentoring in the Workplace to Improve Employee Retention," BizLibrary, accessed August 23, 2022, https://www.bizlibrary.com/blog/employee-development/workplace-mentoring/

Chapter 14

How to implement the eight priority disciplines in strategic evaluation for better programs, more funding, expanded programs, and more engaged employees

You first read about the eight priority disciplines for strategic evaluation in chapters 12 and 13. This chapter takes a deep-dive into the eight priority disciplines, offering detailed advice and action steps to implement them into your organization, so you can develop a process of continuous monitoring/mentoring, evaluating, learning, and improving.

As you will recall, the first two disciplines address the responsibilities of the board of directors and the management team to implement the strategy. These are the two indispensable disciplines to launch a strategic evaluation strategy, which leads to learning and building capacity. I use the term *discipline* intentionally as it means "control gained by enforcing obedience or order; orderly or prescribed conduct or pattern of behavior; SELF-CONTROL; training that corrects, molds, or perfects the mental faculties or moral character; a field of study; a rule or system of rules governing conduct or activity."[1] Yes, board and management do have to set rules, train people to follow the rules, and take action in cases of disobedience.

Let me share what John Baguley, the British NGO consultant and author, recently wrote to me: "Donors here are increasingly expecting impact analysis, which is driving M&E." Another colleague working in the European Union said almost the same thing: "Everybody is looking at results." Many nonprofits are doing great things but, as you have read earlier in this book, public trust in NGOs is really quite low. That's why you can never lose sight of the two critical questions that donors ask: "Can I trust you? What is your impact?"

The eight priority disciplines for the strategic evaluation process are listed below. The following paragraphs offer substantial advice and action steps based on decades of experience, so you can implement the eight priority disciplines in your organization and achieve a continuous process of monitoring, mentoring, evaluating, learning, and improving. After you read these next pages, focus on the case studies in chapters 15 and 16 to see the actual experience of other NGOs in improving their approach to making evaluation more strategic (Figure 14.1).

The Disciplines in Strategic Evaluation

1   **Board responsibility:** Establish strategic evaluation as policy and priority.
2   **Management responsibility:** Implement strategic evaluation as strategy and practice.
3   **A culture of learning:** Assure learning behavior day by day to improve results.
4   **Monitoring:** Mentoring to be an effective supervisor for correcting and learning.
5   **Evaluation of program strategy:** Making certain your program strategy is valid.
6   **Evaluation of results:** Knowing what lasting impact you actually achieve.
7   **Organizational self-assessment:** Learning and improving with each other.
8   **Mutual accountability:** Knowing you are working well with partners.

DOI: 10.4324/9781003335207-17

Trust and Impact for Success

Figure 14.1 Trust and Impact lead to raising more funding and helping more. Image by the author.

DISCIPLINE 1: Board responsibility – Establish strategic evaluation as policy and priority

In my experience with NGOs, a good board accepts primary responsibility in six areas:

1   Fiduciary responsibility (trust)
2   Overall guiding policy (rules)
3   Program reach and effectiveness (impact)
4   Financial and fundraising accuracy (integrity)
5   Supporting fundraising (support)
6   Review of the executive director (performance)

In many small organizations, the seventh responsibility of the board is active participation in carrying out the organization's work along with staff and volunteers.

Fiduciary means "held or founded in trust or confidence; holding in trust; and depending on public confidence for value or currency"[2] and trustworthy means "worthy of confidence: DEPENDABLE."[3] Trust is as important for an NGO as it is for a financial agent or bank, because without trust no one would put money in a financial entity or make a donation to an NGO. To warrant the trust of donors, a board of directors must assure that organizational monitoring and strategic evaluation are taking place, that organizational learning and capacity building are effective, and that financial matters, behavior, and accountability are above reproach. Yes, monitoring is still needed even when you adopt mentoring and learning as priorities. Otherwise, a board cannot claim to be responsible.

At your organization's next board meeting – as an executive director, staff member, or board member – you can say (I've done this, and it works):

> "OK, everyone, we're really doing a good job in many areas here, but I still wonder about how effective we are – how much good we're really doing. I just read this guy's book – someone who's worked all his life for organizations like ours – which says that evaluation is the responsibility of the board! In fact, the standards of the Better Business Bureau Wise

Giving Alliance (which he helped to develop) say exactly the same thing. So, I have some suggestions for action today.

First, let's make mentoring and learning a policy and a priority throughout the organization.

Second, we can require regular evaluation reports be given to the board and, of course, we can require measurements of progress in program, fundraising, finance, and all other plans.

And we should evaluate the executive director based on the evaluations and the use of evaluation findings. Naturally, we need to budget for this just as we do for financial audits.

In addition, we should all walk around in the program and talk to beneficiaries to get a better feel for our effectiveness. Let's also get some outside views of our program, informally at first from people doing similar work and later from a formal external evaluation.

Finally, I recommend we plan a retreat a year from now on what we have learned and how we have used the lessons. Our mission is too important not to do all these things. If we do this, I am sure our current and new donors will like it, and I am sure we can raise more funds to expand our good work!"

Action steps for the board of directors

To carry out its board responsibilities, here are nine action steps for the board:

1   ***Establish strategic evaluation and learning as policy and priority for the organization.*** A fundamental responsibility of the board of directors is to establish policy for an organization. If the board says evaluation and learning are important and a priority for management, they will be important. If a board leaves evaluation and learning to management, the board is neglecting its fiduciary responsibility. Although the focus here is on strategic evaluation to improve program, evaluation is just as important in administration, finance, fundraising, and other functional areas.

2   ***Provide adequate funding to conduct strategic evaluation.*** Evaluation does cost money for staffing, research, and related costs, and this requires regular budget allocations. Larger NGOs should have regular staff responsible to oversee evaluations. Smaller NGOs can work collaboratively to afford occasional external reviews. Evaluation done "on the cheap" will produce cheap, insufficient results. Good evaluation that leads to new learning will build capacity and get better results, which in turn will lead to more trust and more funding by donors.

3   ***Make sure evaluation measurements are included in the planning process.*** How else will you know if you have succeeded? What needs to be done to get better? There are four types of measurements you'll need: 1) Are you heading in the right direction as planned? These are measurable progress indicators used regularly throughout the project or activity. They are important to show when midcourse corrections are needed. 2) Are you achieving your objectives? These are the outcome measures for the annual objectives. They confirm whether the activities produced the expected outcomes. 3) Are you producing the desired long-term impacts? These are the results indicators that are the real proof of your work. 4) Are you learning and what are you changing? These measurements look for the shortfalls and failures, so you can know what to change and what to continue as you proceed. Your own planning process identifies the indicators in these four areas. It is useful to include data from competitors and global entities as benchmarking input for planning.

4 ***Make a practice of receiving regular program evaluation and learning reports.***
   Once the board creates the policy and priority, it should require regular measurable
   program progress reports from staff, just as it does for finance and fundraising. Evaluation
   should be incorporated in the strategic plan, annual operational plans, and project
   proposals, plans, and results. Each plan should be able to report progress and achievement
   periodically during the year. If you have specialized staff in evaluation, they should have a
   direct report to the board. This will break the "glass ceiling" some evaluators describe.
   Listen to reports on program and learning just as much as you listen to reports on budget
   and fundraising progress with actuals versus budget comparisons.

5 ***Do your own evaluation – walk around in the program and listen to beneficiaries.*** Look closely at your programs and services. Show your interest, keep it personal, and
   ask questions on a confidential basis: "How are you doing? How is the program helping?
   What more could it do? Have you seen any problems? What else can you tell me?" A more
   formal process is for the board to meet occasionally and informally with program staff
   and with beneficiaries or their representatives. An example from a Washington, D.C., home
   for older adults shows the value of direct board-beneficiary connections. Individual board
   members met for dinner and discussions with the clients. The board members discovered that
   there was need for certain changes in the staffing structure, as they learned about a surprising
   lack of previously unreported supervisory support and ongoing issues with staff burnout.

6 ***Get an outside view of your program.*** You can retain an experienced evaluator for a
   project or ask an expert to offer some views on your effectiveness. The value of the outside
   evaluation is its independence and its experience from working with other organizations.
   Some NGOs have retained university teams to evaluate the program and the learning.
   Board and management could devise a program audit, which is similar to a financial audit
   but focused on program effectiveness and learning rather than financial management. At an
   NGO when I was its executive director, we routinely asked the auditing company to
   provide a management letter with recommendations on a particular issue such as IT
   systems, data security, or performance reviews. A similar management letter could be
   authorized for a program and learning audit. As in the financial audit, the auditing firm
   would have unrestricted access to files and personnel.

7 ***Include evaluation and learning in the executive director's performance
   review.*** These simple questions can be included in the executive director's performance
   review, and the executive director should incorporate them into the performance appraisals
   for other senior staff (concise responses only):

   • Did we achieve our annual objectives? If not, why and what needs to change?
   • How useful and effective were measurable progress indicators? Explain.
   • What evidence is there that we are achieving our desired long-term impacts? Explain.
   • What have we learned this year and how have we used the learning? Explain.

8 ***Take time to reflect at a "lessons learned" retreat for board and management.***
   A board and management "lessons learned" retreat is an ideal input when drafting a new
   three-year strategic plan. It will take time, but board members should confirm their
   commitment to this process as your mission is too important not to do all these things.

9 ***Include experts and practicing professionals on the board.*** Well-performing
   organizations have active and involved board members who bring expertise and experience
   to board discussions and decisions in your program areas, fundraising and marketing,
   finance and administration, and other relevant fields. Everywhere I worked, I always had or
   found new board members who provided valuable advice of all phases of our work
   (obviously at no cost, since board members are volunteers).

Key point: When I served on the Better Business Bureau Wise Giving Alliance Standards Review Panel 20 years ago, we added "evaluate the success and impact of its program(s)"[4] as a key board responsibility. As Naseeb Dajani of Global Harmony advocated, board members should be looking at what is happening as it happens (see chapter 15).

To fulfill its responsibilities and assure that the organization is doing the right things and doing them effectively and efficiently, your board of directors should adopt the action steps listed above as standard operating policy and practice to fully embrace and support strategic evaluation in your nonprofit. It is a matter of improving performance and building trust.

DISCIPLINE 2: Management responsibility – Implement strategic evaluation as strategy and practice

Whereas the board needs to set the policy and priority for strategic evaluation, management needs to assure evaluation and learning are foundational strategy and standard management practice. As strategy, it's important to recognize that strategic evaluation will guide all planning and operational implementation. As standard practice, it will elevate this approach to a high level of responsibility for all managers.

Action steps for managers

To carry out its management responsibilities, here are eight action steps for managers:

1   ***Become proficient in mentoring and learning (M&L) disciplines and their use and benefits.*** Managers and staff realize that candid assessments of their work including learning and capacity building are necessary steps to increased public, donor, official, and participant confidence in their activities. By transforming monitoring into mentoring and evaluation into learning processes, managers will better motivate staff and improve results. Increasing competence in the knowledge and skills of mentoring, learning, and capacity building are important for a manager's own performance and personal development.

2   ***Overcome fear of monitoring and evaluation (M&E) by presenting it as a personal growth and learning opportunity (M&L).*** Good managers know that strategic evaluation is done to facilitate their progress, augment their learning, upgrade their capacity, and improve their results. The best way, in my experience, to overcome fear is to involve people in the planning process, as described below. When people know their voices have been heard and they have been involved in the decisions, they will have greater commitment to supporting the resulting plans including supervisory review and support of their work. They will see M&L as a means for their own personal learning and growth and as a pathway to better achievement of the organization's work. Good management turns monitoring into mentoring which is more accepted by those supervised and more effective than monitoring.

3   ***Include mentoring and learning (M&L) in the goals and objectives in strategic and operational planning.*** Strategic planning establishes the strategic framework and strategic goals for the organization. It is based on a process of research and thinking creatively. It includes vision (your dream), mission (your work), values (your beliefs), culture (your behavior), critical problems (what you must solve), strategies (how you will proceed), and strategic goals (where you want to be in several years). It is based on your situation (strengths, weaknesses, opportunities, threats), stakeholder assessments (donors, beneficiaries, media, others), and other research (competitor assessments, evaluation reports, and lessons learned). M&L should be in every person's plans for the year.

4   ***Find ways to measure progress in learning and capacity building for your own organization.*** Operational plans and project designs need to have *meaningful, manageable, measurable,* and *motivational progress indicators* (MPIs) and also as measurements of completion (the agreed planned objectives). In the planning process, managers can identify indicators of progress, indicators of completion, and indicators for learning and capacity building in their areas of responsibility. Can everything be measured? Yes, everything can be measured, but nothing can be measured perfectly. As either manager or employee, you want to be sure you are achieving something meaningful, something significant for learning, and to know when you have achieved it.

5   ***Implement mentoring and learning as essential ongoing management responsibility.*** The disciplines of mentoring and learning enable managers to check on progress, help make midcourse corrections, improve achievement of objectives, and provide support for learning and capacity building – to get better results. Smart managers will use indicators for M&L regularly as tools for monthly operational progress and improvements in learning and capacity building. Remember, your progress indicators should be measurable, meaningful, manageable, and motivational (MPIs).

6   ***Establish open and honest feedback channels on what is working, what is not, and what to do.*** Strategic evaluation is built on honesty and reliability. Only with honest evaluations and reliable lessons learned (successes and failures) will mentoring (yes, with monitoring, of course), evaluation, and learning succeed to improve your organization's capacity building, performance, impact, and revenues. Managers and others will welcome open communication up and down within the organization and with other constituencies including donors, the media, authorities, partners, colleagues, and participants/beneficiaries. This includes vertical accountability up and down within the organization and horizontal accountability with other departments and other organizations.

7   ***Review a consolidation of lessons learned and actions taken on a periodic basis.*** Periodic reviews of evaluation findings, lessons learned, and actions taken will encourage and enable greater learning and development. Such reviews, when honest and concise and never discursive, stimulate deeper analysis of the lessons, open more discussion about the reporting systems themselves, and lead to improvements in the processes and uses of strategic evaluation. Such reviews inspire greater sharing and learning through ad hoc discussions, learning groups, "brown bag" lunches, performance reviews, and meetings in NGO associations.

8   ***Base professional advancement on individual contributions to learning and building capacity.*** The more staff members learn, the better they will perform. A component in annual personnel reviews should be devoted to the learning process and results. It is good for the individual and good for the organization. The board and top management should also include compliance with professional standards and ethical behavior as a standard practice and make it clear to all involved that this must be rigorously followed and confirmed.

Key point: Utilizing these management steps can assure your organization will continuously learn and build capacity. The approach emphasizes accountability within an organization, bridges the gap between evaluators and leaders, and takes other steps to assure results of evaluations are used effectively.

An essential attitude by the manager is that the ongoing process of mentoring and learning are pathways for improvement, good for both the organization and the individual, and not ways for criticism. Positive and encouraging communication is essential to assure the lessons from M&L and other assessments are utilized to learn and build capacity.

A brief digression on good strategic and operational planning

Good strategic plans are built on the *reality of your situation* and can only do so based on accurate evaluation findings as planning teams consider the past while they draft plans for the future. Inputs from M&E (M&L) and lessons learned are essential in the research phase of planning. Planning should include a management mandate for acceptance and learning with respect to success and failure (what worked well and what didn't work well) by departments, teams, and individuals. As I often reminded staff, "If we don't know where we failed, we can't know what to improve."

Operational plans identify specific *measurable objectives* to achieve strategic goals. For each objective, the plan indicates the activities to be undertaken, who is responsible, when the various activities will be accomplished, and what resources are needed. The operational plan includes meaningful, manageable, measurable, motivational progress indicators (MPIs), which managers use to make necessary adjustments and corrections to assure successful achievement of plans. Learning and capacity building as well as other objectives should be included in every department plan. It is not enough to say you will do well, you must clarify what you will do better and show how you will use learning to get better.

Finding the right things to measure often takes time, conviction, and experience. Sometimes you will need surrogate or indicative measures for what you really want to achieve and how you can use learning to build capacity. In the initial uses of an indicator, it may be necessary to make a best estimate of the measurement for the first time. Based on experience, you get more precise the next time.

Smart managers require *learning summaries* in monthly and other regular staff reports. Good reports from M&E/M&L progress and other assessments include summaries of lessons learned and recommendations for using the learning. These managers will place evaluation and learning in the center of their supervision with clarity of purpose including feedback channels, learning groups, learning sections in reports, and consolidated lessons learned – all framed positively as opportunities to get better. The managers also support external education and training, sharing, and learning with other organizations, and recognize learning as a systematic, continuous, and strategic process for personal growth. All this makes for better learning and improving results.

At a panel discussion at an InterAction Forum called "How Do We Measure What Really Counts?" Dr. Anju Malhotra, a vice president at the International Center for Research on Women, presented that "We should measure the 'what' and 'the how' of development interventions" and noted that managers and implementers "must be closely connected." For managers to use M&E effectively, it is important to have indicators that are, as I've stated before, measurable, meaningful, manageable, and motivational, which is why I prefer the phrase 4MPIs (*Meaningful, Manageable, Measurable, Motivational progress indicators*) rather than KPIs (key performance indicators).

A practice of *open feedback* breaks down a "glass ceiling" between staff and management and any interdepartmental walls, so supervisors and evaluators can reach those who need to hear from them. Many experts say that we learn more from our mistakes than from our successes; however, since evaluation lessons can be received defensively, it is important to assure such reports present findings and recommendations not as criticism, but as *lessons for learning* and building capacity. Honesty and accuracy are important in reports in order to implement changes for the better.

Warning! The tendency to want to look better can distort reports as they go up the organization chain from implementation to the highest levels. An evaluator in a multi-layer, global organization highlighted this problem when she commented at a workshop that "Every step up makes the results look better until there is no similarity between what actually happened in the field and what the people at the top see." Such tendencies may make people feel good, but they also act against making the changes needed for better performance.

Insights into Leadership

- By working together, we can achieve a better society. And we can feel pretty good about it. I have done it, and I believe you can as well.

- Perhaps the most important message of this book is that regardless of your position, you can lead your organization to greater fundraising success.

- You don't have to be the boss to lead, and the challenge to rise as a leader rests in you. There is open opportunity for more leadership in every organization.

- It's this simple: Look for a solution, find a way that others do not see, and just get it done.

- Character is the basis, values are the demonstration, and caring is the result of responsible leadership.

  From *Make a Better World: A practical guide to leadership for fundraising success* by Ken Phillips

Figure 14.2 Some insights into leadership. Infographic by the author.

Key point: Evaluation becomes strategic when it is routinely used to achieve vision and mission, supports personal growth, and includes learning and capacity building to achieve better impact for society (Figure 14.2).

DISCIPLINE 3: A culture of learning – How to assure mentoring and learning (M&L) improve results

An essential purpose of this book is to guide your organization to increase learning and to use learning to build capacity and, therefore, to achieve greater impact. Two interview comments from my research still haunt me. I was told that "NGOs make the same mistakes over and over" and that "NGOs don't seem to care about building the knowledge in their sector and profession."

I know there has been great progress on many issues by many NGOs, but so much remains to be done in most organizations. Most NGO leaders would agree that it is important to use monitoring and evaluation and other assessments to learn and improve, but I have seen that a weak or culture totally undercuts needed changes in behavior. As a fundamental concept, a clear culture of mentoring and learning will overcome resistance to interventions by supervisors and facilitate learning for better performance and personal growth.

The beauty of working in an NGO is that, with a good strategic plan, everyone is committed to working for the vision and mission and following the values and culture. Refer to my book on *Strategic Planning and Culture for Nonprofits*[5] to learn more how to assure your organization has strong values and an energizing culture.

Action steps for a culture of learning and development

1 *Strengthen the organizations' values and culture to support learning and capacity building*. In your regular strategic planning, give serious attention to assure your statements of values and culture create the environment for all staff and volunteers to seriously embrace learning and improving as personal priorities.

2 *Include learning and capacity building as core components of personal responsibility in all operational planning*. Confirm that every department, team,

and individual is expected to contribute to learning and improvement especially by accepting mistakes and failures as opportunities for improvement.

3 *Use all the findings openly and positively.* Use the strengths and weaknesses and the positive and negative findings identified in monitoring and evaluations as the basis to reinforce the energizing culture you want for mentoring, evaluating, learning, and improving.

4 *Lead by example.* Show a willingness to learn from identifying weaknesses and shortcomings that should be corrected. Include an expectation for others to listen and hear about their mistakes and to discuss and correct them. Demonstrate this yourself.

5 *Encourage everyone to focus on "What do we need to do better?" and "What can I do better?"* Acknowledge and reward process and behavior that lead to openness to learning and development in daily action and communication.

6 *Empower everyone to identify learning and improvement opportunities.* Every staff member and every volunteer is an expert in what he or she does. Each person knows the problems from the inside best. Your experts include all staff and board members, partners and volunteers, and beneficiaries in their areas of responsibility. Ask for their assessments, listen openly to them, and put in place actions to overcome their concerns. Let everyone "step up as leaders" to make things go better.

7 *Create learning groups within the organization and with other NGOs.* Use new evaluation findings for learning and development at regular monthly or quarterly meetings to step up to higher levels of learning. Learn from other NGOs what they are doing to identify and correct problems and how they create learning opportunities.

8 *Include learning and capacity building in individual evaluations as well as monitoring and evaluation.* Promote periodic self-assessment in meetings, mentoring, surveys, team assessments, and group discussions as well as in annual performance reviews. Let those learnings flow into actions.

9 *Put it all together in a comprehensive model or plan for learning with specific objectives, activities, and indicators to create a continuous learning system.* Establish systems for management of knowledge and cross-training, so the knowledge stays with the organization.

10 *Smaller organizations can take action as well.* For smaller organizations, abbreviated plans, occasional discussions, and quick reviews may suffice. Collaboration with other organizations may be the best way. It is well worth doing.

Key point: Culture is how people behave. Strong values and energizing culture unify and empower everyone to work together for success. You can see it in well-functioning NGOs! It was the energizing culture I experienced in AIESEC and that I helped develop in other NGOs that facilitated great results.

DISCIPLINE 4: Mentoring (with monitoring) – How to be an effective supervisor for supporting, correcting, learning, and achieving

The discipline of monitoring enables the supervisor to assess what is happening in real time. This means you check regularly (as frequently as necessary) on the progress of activities in your areas of responsibility (program, fundraising, recruitment, finance, or any other function) and make midcourse corrections to achieve or exceed planned objectives. Mentoring also helps to identify lessons and share actions for the future. All of this improves operational implementation, learning, achievement, and accountability.

Action steps for effective monitoring as mentoring

1 ***Conduct monitoring as a form of mentoring.*** Confirm the process and prerogatives of the monitoring and learning function, that is, the ability of the supervisor to come in anytime, as a supporter, to review progress and support changes to achieve agreed objectives, indicators, and timelines. Mentoring, both formal and informal, is an important and ongoing supervisory responsibility. When monitoring is received as a form of mentoring, it encourages more open communication, better identification and correction of any problems, and more personal learning for the individual. All of this makes for a partnership of cooperation and support.

2 ***Remember the connection between monitoring (mentoring) and measurable objectives.*** Draft each operational plan with clear measurable objectives and activities to achieve the objectives, indicators of progress, the individual or teams responsible, and deadlines for progress and completion of important activities. Include in all operational plans a process, timetable, and responsibility for ongoing monitoring/mentoring of progress. This is standard in good operational planning with an emphasis on measurable progress indicators and clear supervisory responsibilities. Monitor program process as you mentor individuals and their work.

3 ***Include monitoring and evaluation from the initial planning stage.*** Involving both managers and implementers in the planning assures that all plans have sufficient clarity, staff commitment, and agreed indicators to assess progress toward expected results. Evaluation at the end includes any monitoring issues and results in its findings and recommendations about what worked and what did not work, the reasons why, and potential solutions. It always works better when the implementers participate in the planning rather than having plans handed down to them. They feel more ownership for the resulting plans as partners in implementation with support from supervisors as mentors for results.

4 ***Always ask "what if?"*** As a standard step in annual operational planning, include "What if ..." steps to raise questions of potential problems or unanticipated developments during implementation and to add contingency planning in the plan itself. The question can also be raised at various points during implementation as part of mentoring. The "What if ..." process helps to avoid serious pitfalls and failures and adds another way to check progress.

5 ***Make early and ongoing adjustments for better results.*** In a well-managed organization, managers, supervisors as mentors, and implementers are in close communication, so emerging conclusions and even early hints of problems are used as an ongoing tool to make early adjustments in plans and implementation for better results. When supervisors and implementers are in partnership (as in a mentoring process), discussions and changes flow more easily.

6 ***Utilize the mentoring function to facilitate monthly updates on progress during the year.*** In a simple *one-page report by exception*, a one-page report from each manager can cover the three essential topics: 1) Are all objectives on track? What specific indicators are not on target? 2) Reasons for any shortfalls and planned actions to get back on track. 3) Other developments of note and questions for needed information or support. With this approach, time is dedicated to recognizing and correcting work rather than creating and reading long reports. The executive director can readily use these one-page monthly updates as the basis to report to the board.

7 ***Assign an independent Monitoring and Evaluation expert, when possible, to support supervisors during implementation and the final evaluation.*** The traditional M&E expert should be available when needed for support during planning and through implementation to completion. It is most effective when the M&E expert or function

has a direct report to the board of directors on substantive findings. Any evaluation findings of lack of compliance with professional standards or ethical behavior are acted on immediately.

8   ***Smaller nonprofits can partner with others for professional M&L.*** For smaller organizations, the M&E function, now M&L, is a good example of the benefits of partnership with other organizations to gain the expertise needed on a shared basis and at a reasonable shared cost.

Key point: To overcome fear of M&E, managers approach the process more as mentoring and less as controlling. That will get better outcomes for both the project and the employee. All the examples of NGO success in this book build on serious implementation of monitoring and learning.

DISCIPLINE 5: Evaluation of program strategy – How to be certain your program strategy is valid

As an essential step, this discipline tests and validates your program concept or core strategy of "how we work" and determines if it is really right to use it. It is essential that you verify that your program strategy is succeeding in its main goal: benefitting participants and helping to achieve the mission you have adopted. Proposed variations of your program strategy should be tested to assure they will be more successful than your existing strategy before continuing or applying them everywhere. When we changed our program strategy at Save the Children from supporting individual children to supporting communities in order to help their own children, we tested it with program participants and with donors as we were implementing it. Implementing the wrong strategy in any of your functions can be disastrous, especially in programs where the wrong strategy can actually do harm to people, in fundraising where it can cause serious losses in income, and in management where it can lead to staff disenchantment.

Remember, strategy is "how" you work to achieve what you want, and it guides everything you do in your objectives, activities, budgets, and staffing. The right strategy will lead to success, but the wrong strategy will lead to failure no matter how hard you try to make it work.

Action steps to validate strategy

1   ***Determine your strategy for program services as well as for information, education, advocacy, fundraising, communications, and other functions.*** Draft and apply each strategy with clear plans, objectives, and indicators as part of your regular operational planning. Use your ongoing monitoring work to assure the best possible progress. Keep your eyes "wide open" as you proceed. Yes, you do monitor program progress all the while you mentor and support staff in their work

2   ***Give priority to strategy for program for testing and analysis.*** Why? Because program defines who you are and what you do. It determines your impact for beneficiaries and value in the world and supports your image, trustworthiness, and fundraising. Marketing strategies in media are more easily tested against each other often with quick conclusions. Strategies for internal efficiency should produce conclusions on a cost-saving basis. Program strategies take longer to bear fruit and therefore to assess, but emerging conclusions at least on outcomes should generally be seen in six to nine months. You have to know you are using the right strategy!

3   ***Include program participants or beneficiaries in the assessment of the effectiveness of the strategy.*** Conduct ongoing research with those involved in your programs in such a way to obtain their truthful impressions of both the process of the

program and its outcomes. Make sure to distinguish appreciation ("Thank you so much. Everything was good.") from honesty ("Thank you so much. Here's where I had problems. Can you help?") by facilitating candid and helpful feedback from participants including suggestions for improvement and ascertaining actual outcomes and potential impacts. In the NGO business model, participants in your program are your priority customers – their feedback is essential to work well.

4   **Compare what happens from a new strategy with what happens from the traditional strategy you have been using.** The initial comparison will be on the immediate outputs of what you are doing, and you can use these to project into possible or probable outcomes and even longer-term impacts based on your traditional outcomes and impacts. Or if you are just beginning, compare your new strategy with organizations that are doing similar work or with the standards established by the profession or by grantmakers.

5   **Include a control group whenever possible.** This way, you can have a clear comparison of the results of one group with a particular strategy applied versus another similar group without that strategy applied. Or use this approach to compare two or more new strategies at the same time. This is sometimes called a "randomized controlled trial", as was used in the highly successful development of vaccinations for COVID-19 in 2020–2021. An example in chapter 15 of the test of "credit with education" versus "credit alone" shows the value of including a control or comparison group.

6   **If the emerging conclusions endorse the new strategy, continue and expand its use. If not, cancel the new approach immediately.** Take time to learn why the new strategy failed. Go back to basics to find a better strategy. Test and test again and then refine your test for further testing to find the program that works best. Getting the strategy right is too important to rely on your own opinion or a few nice examples.

7   **Consider the possibility of diverse characteristics in the population you serve that might influence outcomes.** It was only when medical researchers came to understand cancer was not one disease but included a variety of different cancers that they could focus on one particular form or type and get vastly improved results. (Or that women are different from men!) It was the same when I met four decades ago with the New York City director of drug rehabilitation who told me that all the various interventions for drug addiction had the same high failure rate – but experts later learned that different interventions had greater success with certain populations with specific characteristics.

8   **Assure a "do no harm" approach in all your work.** Be sure to be vigilant for unintended consequences from any new strategy. Outputs and even outcomes may initially look better, but there may be surprising, unintended negative consequences that will turn the impacts upside down and reveal that a strategy that looked good at first is, in fact, counterproductive or even harmful. The examples of strategies gone wrong presented in chapter 12 show how misguided strategies can actually do serious damage to people instead of helping them. Terminate any strategy that is harmful. For technical help, you may need to engage an expert in ethics in research.

9   **Partner with a university department or team of students to provide an external evaluation of what you are doing and what you are achieving.** A university partner can provide such evaluation at reasonable cost to further student learning and would give you the benefit of an impartial external assessment. This can be an important contribution to your own learning and processes and will lend credibility with donors and the public about your work.

10 **Take a fresh look at results.** After sufficient time, analyze the strategy to confirm its longer-term results (the lasting impact) to be sure you are on the right track. Make sure you are on track!

Key point: Save the Children, Plan International, and other leading NGOs have for decades been testing their program strategies. That is the pathway to better programs, and that is the reason they are getting program results, appealing more effectively to donors, and getting bigger and bigger.

DISCIPLINE 6: Evaluation of long-term results – How to know what impact you actually achieve

In financial management, it is routine to have clear procedures, professional standards, and regular reports of actuals versus budgets, plus comprehensive external audits. In fundraising, the real evaluation of effectiveness is clear from the measurable responses, results, and informed projections on a regular basis. A professional approach has been established for effective marketing by companies and nonprofits to get the best possible results. Results in fundraising and finance are relatively easy to measure, because the needed data are readily available in both of the functions.

Program impact is far more difficult to quantify and evaluate, though it is even more important than finance and fundraising in a nonprofit organization. The evaluation part of strategic evaluation proves to your organization and to stakeholders that you have done well with your plans and activities in programs. Evaluation is strategic when findings about long-term results provide lessons and recommendations about what has been achieved and what has not been achieved and the reasons why. Save the Children, for example, is now using "retrospective impact evaluation" to learn by looking back two to ten years after the end of a program to explore long-terms impacts.

Action steps for evaluation of results and lasting impact

1   *The full purpose of evaluation is to measure and assess inputs, outputs, outcomes, and impacts and to produce findings and recommendations to improve future plans and activities.* Evaluation of impact looks closely at long-term, sustainable results, at least to the extent they can be measured or predicted based on actual performance. It considers sustainability and looks for unintended consequences. The findings from evaluations are used in reports to senior management and the board of directors for discussion and action for future plans and action. The very best NGOs are doing this and, as a result, are achieving more, reporting better results, and raising more support to do even more.

2   *In programs, education, advocacy, and other functions, some organizations unfortunately rely on partial, imprecise, superficial evaluations.* A weak evaluation process and unsubstantiated, anecdotal case stories are *not* proof of success. Some nonprofits even declare, "We know that our results are good, and we have many examples to prove it." But what we think we know and examples alone may be completely wrong, leading to false conclusions about impact and value. Note: A most significant finding of impact evaluation is that the strategy is *not* working. This is especially important to determine, so the particular strategy can be terminated. There can be no higher responsibility for a board of directors and managers in an organization to accept such a finding, stop the programs using that approach, and take appropriate action to correct any damage done and make appropriate reparations. Remember: Do no harm. And base your claims for impact on real evaluation rather than what you want to believe.

3   *There are many, I hope a significant majority, of positive impact evaluation findings for NGOs.* This is good news for NGOs and for their beneficiaries and society. When you have clear and positive impact evaluation findings, they should be shared with

donors and others to demonstrate your effective strategy, strong management, and long-term effectiveness, which will boost your reputation and credibility. Such findings should be communicated in the professional literature, with experts in that particular sector, and at meetings with other NGOs. It is important to facilitate learning and improvement by other organizations carrying out similar programs and activities. When ingredients of achieving significant impacts for the benefit of society are clearly documented, they contribute to the professionalization of the civil society sector, just as healthcare breakthroughs are widely announced and implemented. InterAction, for example, has an initiative called the Evaluation & Program Effectiveness Community of Practice to share evaluation findings among its member organizations. You have to prove your program's effectiveness with strategic evaluation – then communicate it.

4   *The greatest challenges in evaluating long-term impact are measurement and attribution.* Accurate measurement is essential to know what has been achieved. Then, the more time that passes after your program work, the less significance it may have; that is, the effect of what you do or the interventions you made may fade and other influences may increase as time passes. Five years later or ten years, how much attribution can you claim for what developed as a result of the services you provided? The caution here is to choose your expected results carefully, be careful with conclusions, and refuse to overstate success – until the impacts are clearly achieved. Retrospective evaluation can demonstrate lasting impacts and guide what to do better in the future.

5   *Your impact may have been very important and even instrumental but skeptics will discount it.* Some people criticize NGOs as "do-good organizations" which discounts their effectiveness and denies their impact. Although this attitude may be motivated more by desire not to donate or by extraneous factors rather than by reasoned analysis, nonprofit leaders should dedicate themselves to producing strong and attributable impacts in their programs, professionally document them, and then communicate them widely. The nonprofit sector is huge globally (equivalent to the gross domestic product of the seventh largest country) but undervalued. Prove how significant your work is with demonstrable results!

6   *Use professional internal or external evaluators.* Evaluation performed by internal M&E experts on staff has the benefit of ongoing involvement and continuity throughout the annual process and year-after-year process. Evaluation performed by external professional experts can also be effective to evaluate the impact of your core program strategy or variations on it. External evaluators will add credibility to the findings, earn respect from the community, and professionalize the sector. Select your external evaluators carefully, as their reputation, experience, and skills are essential to assure acceptance. What you want is a true and accurate conclusion, as only this will provide you with the guidance you need.

7   *Have the evaluators present their findings and recommendations at staff and board meetings and externally as well.* Embrace the findings even if they include some negative conclusions, and use them to take your program to the next level of effectiveness and efficiency. As with the Head Start case study, which demonstrated lasting impact that is measured and meaningful, your strategy could scale up to achieve unprecedented impacts for the benefit of beneficiaries and society. The best NGOs are already doing this, and they are raising more and helping more. When you have a winning strategy, share it. Proclaim it. Gain fame from it. Grow with it!

Key point: Impact is a top concern for donors and, of course, for everyone who cares about people and planet. Comparative tests proved Head Start produced meaningful impact for children, was a good investment for society, and led to dramatic scaling up of its approach. When you think you achieve lasting impacts, prove them and promote them!

DISCIPLINE 7: Organizational self-assessment – How to learn and improve from each other

Organizational self-assessment can improve your workflow and departmental relationships. It is an internal process involving staff to find ways to identify and make improvements throughout the organization. It is not judgmental – it is cooperation to find ways to be better! At Foster Parents Plan, we used personality assessments such as Myers Briggs, facilitated discussions, and staff plans and reviews to improve our work. As a result, we increased productivity and achieved greater results.

Action steps for organizational self-assessment

1   *Recognize that organizational self-assessment offers many benefits.* It can improve workflow, reduce wasted time and effort, develop staff talent, reduce costs, and achieve better performance. In a large organization, self-assessment can be done initially by department and then through inter-departmental connections. In a small organization, it can be done with everyone getting together to talk, share, question, and answer. And laugh!

2   *It is essential to set ground rules including respect for others and communicating with decorum and sensitivity.* This is especially important among different teams, personalities, and backgrounds. Management should establish standards for the process including no disparagement on the basis of race, age, sex, background, or any other personal matter. Strong facilitation is important to maintain process, order, decorum, and time commitments.

3   *When self-assessment is an input into better planning, it is seen as functional rather than judgmental.* The focus is on workflow and how to make improvements. The best use of organizational self-assessment is as a preparation step for strategic and operational planning or separately on its own as a process for staff to take the lead in improving their work. In the planning process, addressing your values and redefining your organization culture is a positive approach to assess and improve your organizational behavior. Done correctly, self-assessment in an organization enables staff to work better and feel better.

4   *Training can be provided through a personality assessment to understand the benefit of different personalities and to see differences in people as assets.* Research indicates that diversity in groups increases innovation and productivity. Today's various personality assessments can spur insight, understanding, and more cooperative cross-departmental teamwork. Tools of various complexity are readily available through an Internet search (search on "personality assessments" and "diversity, equity, and inclusion").

5   *At Foster Parents Plan, we used TQM with inter-departmental working groups focused on reducing unnecessary work.* The working groups were chaired by staff who actually implemented the work rather than having managers lead them. It was effective to involve staff, allowing them to identify bottlenecks and improvements in their work. The total quality management (TQM) process included exploring current workflow and behavior, analyzing potential improvements, and producing plans for change. This concept was key: the person you give your work to is the person who judges its quality. The result was substantial reduction in unnecessary work and improving quality, freeing staff to focus on more productive activities. It led me to adopt the concept of "completed staff work" where each person takes responsibility to complete a quality product or process before passing it on to others.

6   *Organizational self-assessment helps to answer this key question: How can we work better?* Specifically, you can learn how you can reduce wasted time, duplicated efforts, mindless meetings, unnecessary steps, hovering supervisors, and other points of

frustration or inefficiency. The overall objective is learning to make improvements in internal operations and in external relations. In the process, this can also lead to new program approaches, new marketing efforts, and new procedures. Working together, staff can create breakthroughs and make the work exhilarating.

7 **Develop your own self-assessment tool and process**. The first step is to engage the staff in deciding how you will proceed. This is the essence of self-assessment – enabling people to decide how to assess themselves and their work. Sure, they can refer to tools available online, but the value will be in drafting their own approach. Several of my colleagues from those days recently shared with me how important these processes were to them, because those activities enhanced their personal development and the joy they experienced in their work. They are now leading executives in other NGOs.

8 **Use mentoring and learning (M&L) rather than monitoring and evaluation (M&E) with each other.** See earlier sections of this chapter for how M&L is a more effective tool for supervising and supporting staff and therefore in organizational self-assessment as well.

Key point: It is essential for an organization to look inwardly and assess honestly what you are doing well and what you could be doing better. Everyone in an organization can have suggestions for improvements. They should be encouraged, heard, and respected.

DISCIPLINE 8: Mutual accountability – How to know you are working well with partners

With your partners and supported organizations, you need mutual accountability for better collaboration. Similar in some ways to organizational self-assessment, mutual accountability with partners involves addressing relationships and work between completely different organizations with different leadership, different priorities, different world views, and different stakeholders. As in my activity as consultant to NGOs and as mentor to university students, I view such relationships as partnerships with mutual accountability and mutual benefits – and that makes them work well together. See chapter 15 for the processes of World Neighbors with its integrated participatory planning, monitoring, and evaluation for learning and impact and International Youth Foundation with its measurement, evaluation, research, and learning for its partner NGOs.

I experienced a good example of this when I was consulting with a malaria prevention NGO that saw itself in competition with other malaria prevention or cure organizations. They were competing against with each other, even disparaging the others, until the communications person from one of the NGOs brought them all together to identify common goals. By seeing the mutual benefits of cooperating on contain activities such as malaria awareness promotion, they learned how to cooperate with each other.

Action steps for mutual accountability with partners

1 **With partners, there is horizontal accountability, which flows both ways between each other.** This is mutual accountability. Just as with self-assessment, the question is how can we work better together? How can we reduce wasted time, duplicated efforts, unnecessary steps, and other points of frustration or inefficiency? The overall objective is learning to make improvements to achieve more together with external partners.

2 **Mutual accountability is important to improve working relationships and productivity.** This includes mutual accountability between organizations that are collaborating on a project, between headquarters and field offices, between an organization

and its individual beneficiaries, between a supporting organization and its supported partners, between a federation and its members, and in some cases between units within the same office, as between program and fundraising. I also include the relationship between a supervisor and the person reporting to that supervisor and between mentor and mentee. Mutual accountability enables both parties to break out of the pattern of blaming the other and to learn from the other.

3   *The assessment should find ways to accomplish four objectives.* Assess mutual accountability to: 1) improve the relationship, 2) increase efficiency in how you work together, 3) get better results, and 4) make it enjoyable and actually have fun in the process! This is true for all types of partnerships, as listed below. Of course, partners need to keep clear the common interest or goal that brought them together in partnership in the first place.

4   *Partnership means mutual respect and mutual benefit.* Often, partners are perceived to be in a hierarchy with one "partner" having everything to give to the other and the other having nothing or little to give in return – perhaps as with a large grantmaking organization and a small nonprofit that receives a grant or a lead partner and supporting partners. This assumption is not correct, because partners need each other to achieve their own goals and objectives and, therefore, should be accountable to each other in order to meet the other's needs and expectations. An organization whose partner does not produce according to an agreement or who fails to satisfy the other partner cannot succeed.

5   *In all cases, it is imperative to conduct the accountability assessment together in mutual cooperation as equal participants in a relationship.* Each partner is bringing something to the process that the other partner needs. For example, the benefits that member organizations bring to a federation are as indispensable to the federation as the benefits that the federation offers to its member organizations. Similarly, program beneficiaries or partners bring benefits to the funding organization that are as indispensable to that organization as the benefits the organization delivers to its beneficiaries or partners. It is useful to apply this key concept from total quality management: everyone is everyone else's customer, and only your customer can assess the quality of what you do. It is important to pay attention to that.

6   *Assessing mutual accountability offers many benefits.* In all these cases, you will benefit from joint planning about how to proceed with clear agreement on mutual expectations, deliverables, timelines, budgets, and other expectations; understanding that the other partner has other obligations and commitments to meet; commitment to a respectful and supporting relationship; communications that are clear, timely, and complete; periodic assessments together as partners in the relationship; and a process to address and resolve any differences or conflicts.

7   *More mutual accountability is needed among NGOs to make the civil society sector even stronger.* As presented in my book, *25 Proven Strategies for Fundraising Success*,[6] partnership is an essential strategy for all NGOs to share and learn from each other and to find ways to collaborate in expensive systems they could not afford on their own. Partnership is also a responsibility of the big NGOs (the top 5–10 percent) to support other NGOs to strengthen them and to grow civil society.

8   *Use the mentoring and learning (M&L) approach rather than monitoring and evaluation (M&E) with partners.* This will be an effective and appreciated method in mutual accountability as a more respectful and supporting approach with program participants, supported organizations, and other partners.

Key point: By working together, partners are stronger. By collaborating, bigger NGOs and smaller NGOs not only help each other, they also strengthen civil society.

Actions to Improve the Sector
1. Adoption of codes by various NGO groups
2. Compiling and promoting best practices
3. Common approach for enforcement in key areas
4. More standardized measurements for NGOs
5. Measured program effectiveness for results
6. Strategy of trustworthinesssto grow revenues
7. Clear value to donors from all NGOs do
8. Conferences on standards and best practices
9. Concerted attack on abusers

11/22/02   © NGO FUTURES 2002

Figure 14.3 Actions to improve the NGO sector. Infographic by the author.

The eight priority disciplines described in this chapter are all very important for your organization's ability to monitor, understand, learn, and improve – and, ultimately, for your organization's development and success. They are also important to strengthen the entire civil society sector and improve its image. Collectively, we need to get better, and these eight priority disciplines provide a pathway to do that.

Putting these eight disciplines together creates an organization that is more effective, efficient, and accountable as well as a more attractive and enjoyable place to work or volunteer. Employees can know that the board and management are committed to a policy and strategy of learning and improving, that the culture is learning, that supervisors see their role as mentors, that evaluation and assessments are lessons for improvement, and that programs are achieving real and lasting impact. Wow! That is awesome! Read on for actual examples of progress (Figure 14.3 and 14.4).

"A conductor leads the orchestra.
How will you lead in your NGO?"

Figure 14.4 Leadership is like conducting an orchestra. Artwork by Wills Phillips.

Questions for implementation

1 Does your organization have convincing evidence of the effectiveness of your programs – proof of your impact?
2 Which of the eight priority disciplines for strategic evaluation does your nonprofit already have fully in place?
3 What will you do to "raise the bar" in all eight disciplines in the coming year?
4 Who needs to be involved or convinced?

Notes

1 "discipline," *Merriam-Webster Dictionary*, accessed July 4, 2022, https://www.merriam-webster.com/dictionary/discipline.
2 "fiduciary," *Merriam-Webster Dictionary*, accessed July 4, 2022, https://www.merriam-webster.com/dictionary/fiduciary.
3 "trustworthy," *Merriam-Webster Dictionary*, accessed July 4, 2022, https://www.merriam-webster.com/dictionary/trustworthy.
4 "Measuring Effectiveness," BBB Standards for Charity Accountability, BBB Standards for Charity Accountability (give.org)
5 See the author's book on *Strategic Planning and Culture for Nonprofits: Clear and doable steps to create motivating plans and the supporting culture you need for success* (NGO Futures LLC, 2021). Also available in Spanish.
6 See the author's book on *25 Proven Strategies for Fundraising Success: How to win the love and support of donors* (NGO Futures LLC, 2021). Also available in Spanish.

Bibliography

1 "discipline." *Merriam-Webster Dictionary*. Accessed July 4, 2022. https://www.merriam-webster.com/dictionary/discipline
2 "fiduciary." *Merriam-Webster Dictionary*. Accessed July 4, 2022. https://www.merriam-webster.com/dictionary/fiduciary
3 "trustworthy." *Merriam-Webster Dictionary*. Accessed July 4, 2022. https://www.merriam-webster.com/dictionary/trustworthy
4 BBB Standards for Charity Accountability, BBB Standards for Charity Accountability (give.org)

Chapter 15

Eight case studies – Progressing to strategic evaluation with data, research, learning, and accountability

These brief case studies show how various organizations, small and large, value and use evaluation. They provide examples of looking closely at the program, incorporating research, using monitoring and evaluation (M&E), focusing on results, testing strategies, using data, involving participants, incorporating accountability and learning, and establishing a comprehensive approach. As NGOs develop, more strategic evaluation results in significant increases both in program impact and in fundraising. Each case study is unique and each offers insights that may be useful for your nonprofit.

The approaches here are similar to the planning process described in my book on *Strategic Planning and Culture for Nonprofits*[1] in which organizations learn from strategic thinking, external research, evaluation results, and lessons from previous planning. As in other chapters, much of what I write here is based on my personal experience, notes, correspondence, communications, and previous research for clients and Sasakawa Peace Foundation (Figure 15.1).

Case Studies of 5 Small NGOs

How small NGOs developed their evaluation
1. Global Harmony – Embedded evaluation in everything you do, so you always know where you are
2. Civil Society Development Foundations – Action research or action learning as a first step to learn and develop
3. Counterpart Creative Center – More formal monitoring and evaluation as a standard for good management
4. United Way Hungry – Measurable results and quality control to know how you are progressing
5. Freedom From Hunger Foundation – From tracking progress to strategy assessment to getting a better program strategy

Figure 15.1 Five examples of NGOs making progress in evaluation. Sidebar by the author.

Case study: Embedded evaluation in everything you do, so you always know where you are[2]

The chairman Naseeb Dajani of **Global Harmony**, a small NGO working globally, told me years ago: "You can't establish a program without having an initial evaluation. You have to establish benchmarks." He articulated that in this approach the people are responsible, evaluation is part of the program, and improvement is what you do as you work.

DOI: 10.4324/9781003335207-18

Dajani advocated *seven fundamental steps*, each with an evaluation component: "Look, Listen, Learn, Live with them, Lend a hand, Liberate, and Let go."

He cited as a case example their work with a school in India in which no girls were enrolled, because their parents did not want to send them to school in public buses. Global Harmony agreed to provide a driver, gas, maintenance, and $6,000 toward the $16,000 purchase of a private school bus. The result: ninety girls in school! Without evaluation embedded from the beginning, the program might have built a new school. Dajani elaborated:

- Certain results are tangible – you can evaluate them by looking or taking a picture.
- Certain results are semi-tangible – you can still evaluate them by observing behavior.
- Certain results are intangible – you cannot evaluate them.

In the example above, he pointed out that the tangible results were the purchase of the bus and 90 girls attending school. The semi-tangible results were the participation of parents in school activities – 40 parents working in community development after an initial ten became involved through training and education and working with facilitators. The intangible results were certain attitudes we can never measure. Dajani observed, "When you make soup, you don't evaluate it after it is served. As you make it, you add salt or whatever. It's in the making." Dajani valued **embedded evaluation** as a critical component in every stage of program delivery by always asking how you are doing.

In NGOs I have worked for, I have seen or encouraged board members to walk around and experience the programs, much as Dajani advocated.

Case study: Action research or action learning as a first step to learn and develop

Civil Society Development Foundations were created and supported in many countries in Eastern and Central Europe in the 1990s. Their purpose was to support the development of non-governmental organizations and networks through information, training, consultancy, and networking services. I worked with many of them in that decade and later. The best development of this concept is the Civil Society Development Foundation now flourishing in Romania.[3]

Action research is a participatory tool that *combines research and action to help* people identify what is missing and to understand what is needed. A supporting organization and its supported NGOs or informal groups collaborate and use a model of NGO capacities to ask what is missing as an assessment tool and what is needed as a planning process for both the lead organization and its partners. This method has been used by Civil Society Development Foundations in many countries as a key step to promote development of civil society, and it is relevant for many new or small NGOs today.

The challenge is to help the participants move to a higher stage of knowledge and development. The use of action research is based on a model of progressive stages of knowledge: 1) We don't know what we don't know. 2) Then we know what is missing. 3) Then we know what has already been learned. 4) Finally we learn what we need to know and to do.

I prefer to define this as **action learning** with the emphasis on the learning of everyone involved in the cycle of planning, implementing, observing, reflecting, and planning again. The lead organization seeks to achieve four related objectives: 1) to help beneficiaries learn new knowledge, 2) to assess the organization's current services from the beneficiary perspective, 3) to help its own staff grow and develop, and 4) to design future services. By being involved in the research and analysis, staff and volunteers of both supporting and supported organizations think about the data, develop relationships with each other, have a learning experience, and devise better plans.

Please note that most NGOs have programs that involve and rely on partners, as affiliated field offices, independent NGOs, or informal groups. Action learning utilizes evaluation throughout the research and planning process in all three of these structures.

Case study: Training in monitoring and evaluation as a standard for good management[4]

Counterpart Creative Center has been working in Ukraine since 1996 to support the strengthening of pluralistic democratic society in Ukraine and nearby countries. Its mission: "To enhance the development of civic initiatives aimed at strengthening civil society through creative elaboration and implementation of charity programs and active support of civil society organizations, local self-governance bodies, and initiative groups."

Founder and president, Lyubov Palyvoda, told me the organization operates a Monitoring and Evaluation School to provide *training in monitoring and evaluating* projects and organizational development. Training covers the concept and role of M&E, similarities and differences between monitoring and evaluation, their place in management and implementation, determining necessary indicators and sources for data, analysis of collected information, and preparation of monitoring and evaluation reports.

Founded by an experienced American NGO, Counterpart Creative Center strengthened its competence and moved to a higher, more developed state in its own transformation process. Its consultants provide training to aid the national nonprofit sector, combining foreign experience and the realities of local conditions.

Counterpart Creative Center uses the following criteria to assess organizational achievements:

- *Quality of the project* (most important): Relevance to needs of the country and target beneficiaries, methods proposed for execution of projects including cost effectiveness, and likely short-term and long-term impacts for sustainability and replication.
- *Organizational and personnel capacity* (very important): Capacity of the organization and personnel to execute projects plus clear identification of the roles of the partners.
- *Building good relations* (important): Projects relating to national minorities or promoting gender equality, taking place where no or few projects have been supported, and bringing together participants from NGOs to promote cooperation.

The takeaway from this example is that getting to strategic evaluation is a process that begins with monitoring and evaluation and moves on to more comprehensive organizational capacity building. Transformation of an NGO takes time and persistence to move on to higher levels of performance.

Case study: Measurable results and quality control to know how you are progressing[5]

The **United Way in Hungary** raises money from individuals, corporations, and others to support a large variety of NGOs and its own programs. Since its founding in 1998 as a national member of the United Way, it has had two specific targets in its grants: 1) measurable results, which are important for both the NGOs and their donors and 2) continuous quality control, which is required for transparency and accountability to donors. A priority, of course, is to align with the United Way Global Standards for grantmaking, project management, evaluation, and ethical standards.

NGOs applying to the United Way of Hungary for grants must include in their proposal information on *measurable results and quality control* including risks and the strategies to avoid the risks. The grant contract describes the monitoring and reporting requirements including a provision to look into their accounting books. NGOs receiving support prepare for an evaluation visit with a written summary based on a self-evaluation questionnaire. At the end of the project, the final report includes the strategy to respond to issues raised during the monitoring visit.

Zsuzsa Szikszay, community impact leader at the United Way of Hungary, told me that "It is not easy to be sustainable as an NGO in Hungary. These are hard times for NGOs. Philanthropy is still in its infancy. Learning from evaluation is a priority!" For its grantees, ethical processes, financial stability, and monitoring and evaluation with measurable progress indicators are required. In multi-year grants, the United Way of Hungary promotes continuous evaluation and capacity building.

This approach demonstrates, once again, *the value of thinking strategically about the program* you are delivering, how you are evaluating it, what you are measuring, what you are learning, and what you should be changing.

Case study: From progress tracking to strategy assessment to getting a better program strategy[6]

Freedom from Hunger Foundation, founded at the urging of President John F. Kennedy and now merged into the Grameen Foundation, was developing "credit with education" as a strategy for providing small loans and savings services to rural women along with education in health, nutrition, and business. The organization used ***progress tracking*** or monitoring through the collection and use of performance information to better guide and support field agents and their supervisors.

The evaluation challenge was to test the strategy of "credit with education" compared to the strategy of providing "credit alone." The ***strategy assessment*** was about the impact on nutritional status of young children and the empowerment of women when education in income management and health practices was added to loans. Three hundred mother/child pairs were randomly selected for the baseline survey. Field agents measured the children's height and weight and later conducted a follow-up survey with measurements.

The comparative results provided strong evidence that credit plus education was more effective than credit alone to "alleviate poverty, improve health/nutrition knowledge and practice, empower women, and ultimately improve household food security and children's nutritional status."

Progress tracking is something even very small and new NGOs could be doing as a *regular check on progress* in any project or activity. The use of a comparative *test of two program strategies* enabled the organization to know which one was more effective, and this is an excellent model for other small NGOs (Figure 15.2).

Case Studies of 4 Large NGOs

How large NGOs developed their evaluation

1. Children International – Monitoring and evaluation with data for better learning and greater impact

2. World Neighbors – Integrated participatory planning, monitoring, and evaluation for learning and impact

3. Catholic Relief Services – From an M&E beginning to a complete MEAL (M&E with Accountability and Learning)

4. International Youth Foundation – Measurement, evaluation, research, and learning (MERL) for partner NGOs

Figure 15.2 Four examples of larger NGOs making progress in evaluation. Sidebar by the author.

Case study: Monitoring and evaluation with data for better learning and greater impact[7]

For decades, **Children International** has used an annual work plan that emphasizes evaluation. Its mission is to serve people in need, and M&E is an essential component to ensure that programs continually increase their own ability to meet that mission. The organization has a focus on impact: "We own the impact. We are committed to delivering sustainable results, and recognize that clarity, learning and growth are at the heart of the work we do together. When we harness this power collectively, we change the course of history." Its programs "focus on four key outcomes: Health, Education, Empowerment, and Employment."

In 2015, the Children International global program team formulated its *program results framework* with a vision of poverty reduction and identified objectives that would lead to fulfilling that vision and were connected to the United Nations' Sustainable Development Goals. Some of its objectives became more significant at the global level: adopting healthy behaviors, increasing usage of health services, enhancing secondary school graduation rate, and ramping up youth employment, each with five-year program plans and related M&E components.

Its approach in ***monitoring and evaluation with data*** includes: 1) Planning – Each partner agency has specific evaluation plans for each program initiative. 2) Monitoring – Site visits by staff and experts, inventory of supplies, and process statistics. 3) Evaluation – Four key measurements are assessed: rate of malnutrition, parasite infection, school enrollment, and grade promotion.

Children International built its M&E on standards and indicators established by global authorities to assure validity, save time, and enable comparisons to global results. As an example, the organization started with World Health Organization (WHO) scientific standards to determine the parasite infection rate. They then adapted the standards to the local circumstances, piloted studies in four locations, and expanded to 16 locations in the second year. To overcome initial resistance to the stringent WHO standards, they communicated that the evaluation was part of the global initiative.

Erin Morse, senior program officer for monitoring, evaluation, and learning (ME&L), has been with Children International for seven years. Interviewed by my research colleague Aravinda Karunaratne, she said that "There was no dedicated M&E person before I took charge of the function. I made use of the resources that had been developed before me and focused on crafting professional resources that would strengthen the M&E capabilities of the organization. One part of my job is global M&E team development. I work with M&E counterparts in partner agencies [grantees] in other countries, where Children International is the primary donor, to ensure M&E excellence. As the primary funder, we are concerned about accountability as well. While it's not in the title, my job includes accountability, often abbreviated as *MEAL (monitoring, evaluation, accountability, and learning)*."

Morse emphasized that in the nonprofit world, there has been "an exponential shift to using data, ensuring quick access to data, and facilitating technical improvements to work with new trends such as big data." An area of needed improvement is "the balance between collecting data and using them. Constant facilitation and training are required for our staff to reflect on empirical insights that are generated from data-crunching, so they see the big picture beyond a collection of data points and can use the data to drive decisions."

Children International has made *use of data* to improve focus on achieving impact – such as the emphasis on improving secondary school graduation rates – rather than just providing material goods such as school supplies to children. Another example is among grassroots parents and caregivers who collect data by using a special bracelet wrapped around a child's arm to measure nutrition status. Using the arm band, parents and caregivers can see the status and progress of their own child, which must be very reassuring while also leading to a deeper commitment to the program. Better nutrition is the objective, healthy children is the impact.

The story here illustrates how an organization can move from traditional strategic planning with M&E to higher level goals, greater emphasis on the E in M&E, more focus and use of data to achieve results, along with the requisite training for staff in evaluation, learning, and accountability.

Case study: Integrated participatory planning, monitoring, and evaluation for learning and impact[8]

World Neighbors, a medium-size development NGO, defines its approach to M&E as a way to contribute to learning by local staff and partners and to inform decision making and action for program development and impact. Notice those two key words: Learning and impact. Only secondarily is M&E designed to meet the needs of external donors.

World Neighbors' program strategy recognizes that it is the *capacities of local people and their institutions* that build successful and powerful communities. It celebrates community strengths and portrays community members as citizens rather than clients. The role of the outsider in this approach is as a facilitator, rather than the driver of development.

In our recent interviews, Kate Schecter, CEO of World Neighbors, emphasized the importance of knowing what the participants really think and really want – rather than just hearing what they think you want to hear. World Neighbors' strategy is built on the role of leaders in local partners to develop their own plans to enable them to become more effective, viable, and self-sustaining. In this program, investment in action learning and participatory M&E are essential for organizational learning, capacity building, improving program quality, and better performance and impact.

Program participants (villagers) are involved in the collection, analysis, and interpretation of data leading to decision-making. Participatory planning and M&E are an integrated process throughout the program cycle, not just at the midterm and the end of a project. Participants look at trends over time and at comparative analysis between project sites. They focus on whether program objectives are met and analyze underlying reasons for success or failure, particularly in terms of organizational capacity.

Potential constraints to implement this approach include: 1) the capacity of program staff and partner organizations for facilitation, design, and institutionalization of participatory M&E methods; 2) limited understanding that M&E is for organizational learning rather than external control and supervision; 3) weak organizational culture of self-critique and learning with its emphasis on "success stories" rather than "embracing error"; and 4) failure to analyze reasons for poor performance and learn from mistakes.

World Neighbors addresses these constraints throughout the ***integrated participatory planning, monitoring, and evaluation*** process. The villagers themselves set priorities and work toward their own goals, involving community members from the start in generating, analyzing, and owning information about their own situation. The focus is to understand and appreciate traditional knowledge, systems, values, skills, and technologies to help develop a plan of action for development.

The tools they use include:

- ***Appreciative inquiry*** through structured questions about positive changes that have occurred in the past in the absence of external assistance and allowing participants to contemplate, verbalize, and celebrate their successes, and then identify community strengths and abilities to mobilize, overcome difficulties, and create positive change – as initial steps in analysis and planning.
- ***Asset mapping*** of individual and community endowments to identify, define, and delineate the available skills that exist in the community (who has them and how did they acquire them), the formal and informal associations and institutions in the community (what roles they play in development and their relative importance), and the natural and physical resources in the community (to locate on a sketch map).
- ***Community economic analysis*** of the interactions in the local economy, illustrated by using the "leaky bucket" concept to identify sources of money that flow into the community (inflow), sources of money that flow out of the community (outflow), and mechanisms by which money circulates within the community (internal) to formulate intervention strategies that facilitate economic development, identify economic opportunities, and keep money recycling in the community.

The outcomes are visioning and programming. *Visioning* is the determination of the desired change in the community from the current state, considering the internal and external resources required to achieve change through program implementation including government and other development agencies as potential collaborators. Based on the community assessment, participants address *programming* to analyze the assessments, identify key problems and resources, plan what they want to do and how, make agreements and assign responsibilities, and develop a process to manage, monitor, modify, and evaluate the progress. The emphasis on participatory responsibility supports the implementation.

World Neighbors recognizes that change happens slowly, perhaps especially in remote rural communities. In order to ensure the approach addresses all the needs in the community and that all the inputs are sustained for the long-term, they stay in each community for eight to ten years. To know when a community is ready to "graduate" from assistance, World Neighbors has a five-stage model that both the villagers and staff use to assess developmental change: Initiation, Growth, Expansion, Maturity, and Graduation. By moving through the stages over eight to ten years, the community can evaluate its own progression and can be confident and ready to let go of support when it reaches the last stage.

As one program participant told me, "We've never had this kind of training before. Most aid organizations come to give things away or tell us what to do. Instead, World Neighbors asks us what our needs are and trains us to solve our problems. I was elected by my community to be the promoter. I will train the people in my village to what I have learned. This is what we want."

I like World Neighbors' integrated participatory planning, monitoring, and evaluation approach and its recognition of the importance of knowing what participants really think. Its approach facilitates organizational learning, improves program quality, and achieves better performance and lasting impact by rural community participants – it's *a model of strategic evaluation that many small and medium-size NGOs could emulate* (Figure 15.3).

Key Evaluation Terms I

• Embedded Evaluation
• Action Research / Action Learning
• Training in Monitoring and Evaluation
• Measurable Results and Quality Control
• Progress Tracking to Assessment to Strategy
• Monitoring and Evaluation with Data
• Integrated Participatory Planning, Monitoring and Evaluation
• Monitoring, Evaluation, Accountability & Learning (MEAL)
• Measurement, Evaluation, Research & Learning (MERL)
• Learning from Impact

Figure 15.3 Key evaluation terms from these studies. Sidebar by the author.

Case study: From an M&E beginning to a complete MEAL with accountability and learning[9]

Catholic Relief Services (CRS), as an implementing partner of USAID, has carried out projects awarded by USAID since the 1940s. For decades, the Catholic Relief Services approach to M&E in microfinance has focused on assuring consistency with micro-credit lending principles and achieving sustainability for participants.

Catholic Relief Services started using the Grassroots Development Framework developed by the Inter-American Foundation to support the activities of community-level NGOs in Latin America. The framework examines the impacts that occur at three different levels: society, organization, and family/individual. It recognizes that both tangible and intangible impacts occur at all three levels.

A key insight of the framework is that as you go up the chart of impacts from individual to organization to society, over time the impacts become broader, more powerful, and more significant. At the same time, the impacts become less clear, less measurable, and less attributable. For many organizations, this analysis can illustrate the multiple levels of impact and the need to address all three levels – not just to help people directly but also to have an impact on their organizations and society. The framework can influence how an NGO works and what it monitors, measures, and evaluates.

With this framework in mind, Catholic Relief Services created an accreditation system called *Microfinance Alliance for Global Impact Alliance*. The program is aimed directly at building capacity of partner organizations and indirectly at having an impact on individuals and families and on society. It builds on several stages of capacity assessment, capacity building, and accreditation. As soon as an organization or group meets certain minimum standards of being organized, it is accepted at the first stage to work with CRS. When the partner has sufficiently developed, it can progress to the second stage based on a planning assessment with a written mission statement, two years of experience, 3,000 borrowers, and a computerized accounting system.

For the third stage, an accreditation assessment measures if needed systems are in place – leadership and administration capacities, organizational policies and systems, strategic and operational planning, monitoring and evaluation, information systems and internal controls, and financial and other support services. A scoring system sets objectives for each area, and Catholic Relief Services provides support to help partner organizations meet the standards. The benefits include partnership, a higher level of service, improvement in reputation, more referrals, and some funding.

Like many leading NGOs, Catholic Relief Services has made significant progress in its approach to evaluation. In 2015, it published *Our Commitment to Monitoring, Evaluation, Accountability and Learning (MEAL)*, which added accountability and learning to already robust monitoring and evaluation functions in its programs.

The report includes this key statement: "Catholic Relief Services' commitment to operational and programmatic excellence demands continuous improvement in our ability to document, analyze, and apply learning at the project, sector, and agency levels and to share our reflections with stakeholders, practitioners, and policymakers." The significance here is the organization's emphasis on learning and improving program quality while ensuring accountability and transparency with the people served and with donors.

According to Heather Dolphin, deputy director of MEAL at Catholic Relief Services, "We partner closely with Caritas (the international Catholic network of assistance organizations) in practically all countries where we work. CRS focuses our 2030 Strategy on social justice and peacebuilding, emergency response, agriculture and livelihoods, health, human services, education, and youth training and employment. MEAL has a role to assess progress toward this strategy by aggregating results across twenty-one global agency sector-specific indicators and capturing and sharing lessons learned related to CRS influence on others. The MEAL process is driven by ten policies and procedures, and is subjected to quality control by internal auditors who work internationally."

Responding to a question about how Catholic Relief Services developed its approach to evaluation, she replied, "CRS developed MEAL standards and policies starting in 2010. I have contributed to developing a more robust MEAL framework that is followed up by a systematic audit procedure conducted internally. The auditors are independent and are not under my supervision."

Important aspects of improvements in MEAL at Catholic Relief Services include: encouraging staff to become critical thinkers about their roles rather than being reactionary, empowering them to activate their *adaptive management* and always think about what is actually going on in their program, taking technology closer to participants through participant-driven data collection to gather real-time data where the participants' voices and narratives are taken into consideration directly, and being responsive and agile.

She added: "In addition to CRS' years of experience [in monitoring and evaluation], the size of the organization presents a number of opportunities in terms of number of quality resources available to inform quality programming across many sectors. Donors rely on CRS based on our capacity demonstrated by past performance in multiple sectors as well as our capacity to implement complex, multi-sectoral, multi-year programs."

This case study highlights a number of key developments, in particular, making significant *progress from early M&E to more comprehensive MEAL*, which continues to focus on the important processes of monitoring and evaluation while greatly increasing attention to accountability and learning.

Case study: Measurement, evaluation, research, and learning (MERL) for partner NGOs[10]

International Youth Foundation (IYF) is an intermediary organization working to improve the conditions and prospects for young people where they live, learn, work, and play. They work with partner organizations focused on youth. Monitoring and evaluation play a major role with an increased focus on learning and sharing.

For the 2000 International Youth Foundation publication, *Growing Your Organization: A Sustainability Resource Book for NGOs*,[11] I wrote chapters on "Thinking Strategically about Sustainability" and "Building a Sustainability Team and Culture" based on my work with IYF and other NGOs. I had provided training to IYF youth affiliates in Slovakia and Mexico and facilitated a workshop in London on strategic planning and development with all its partners. The top conclusion from the workshop was the importance of learning! In the follow-up to all the partners, I stressed the importance of "sharing the learning from the workshop with your colleagues and carrying out your role as a change agent."

In the 1990s, International Youth Foundation created a *department dedicated to learning and evaluation* with an evaluation plan and an *Evaluation Grapple Group* of staff from various departments that met monthly to discuss issues related to evaluation. Through mini-grants and training, the organization encouraged its partners to conduct evaluations on outcomes. Because evaluation goes hand-in-hand with learning, IYF published publications on "what works" based on the learnings from its partner organizations. It also developed *Youth Net International*, a database of effective programs describing best practices in child and youth development.

The organization considered its efforts in evaluation and learning successful if it contributed to tangible improvement in the lives of children and youth around the world. According to a staff evaluator:

- IYF used evaluation and learning tools to identify what works in the field.
- The NGO analyzed that information and looked for trends and patterns across all partners.
- The next step was dissemination, but dissemination was not enough.
- Partners must make use of the information and then tailor it to local conditions.
- The process is only complete once those new approaches can be implemented and shown to produce tangible improvements.
- And this information can once again be analyzed through the use of evaluation and learning tools.

For IYF, ***Learning for Impact*** is a cycle that moves from learning through identification to analysis, dissemination, tailoring, and application, measurement of outcomes, and back to learning again.

This organization's tool for measuring effectiveness of programs was based on assessing 300 programs worldwide, 160 of which were effective according to 17 criteria. The goal was to show what works, so others can learn from the findings. The real benefits of NGOs participating in the IYF Network are sharing and learning from each other.

The evaluation plan has *five levels*: Basic documentation of program activities, outputs, and outcomes; IYF and the partners' self-assessments; case studies that examine the impact of IYF strategies; youth outcomes evaluations through local independent evaluators; and capacity building of partners through training and technical assistance in evaluation design and implementation.

The following update was provided by Linda Fogarty, head of International Youth Foundation's MERL team: "Since 2000, IYF renamed the unit to ***Measurement, Evaluation, Research, and Learning (MERL)***. The new name continues to emphasize learning but elevates our obligation to be active thought leaders within the positive youth development technical community – to both contribute to and be informed by the growing body of evidence. This reflects *IYF's commitment as a learning organization*, always growing and open to new ideas."

She added: "We use participatory measurement methods, engaging young people and partners throughout the process, ensuring our projects address youth-defined problems within the local context. Collaborating, Learning and Adapting [CLA] principles and processes are woven into our work from project outset to close. We added agency-level measurement, using a set of outcome-level strategic indicators tracked at project and country level, compiled at institution level, and reflecting progress against our strategic plan targets. We developed an ambitious learning agenda reflecting priority global positive youth development questions. We prioritize rigorous external evaluations."

Many NGOs could not support such a comprehensive approach to measuring, evaluation, research, and learning (MERL), but all can learn from the work of others. International Youth Foundation presents an inspiring model for both larger and smaller NGOs.

Key point: Using the comprehensive MEAL or MERL approach, an NGO can achieve lasting impact for individuals and families, organizations, and society. Adopting MEAL/MERL is a complex and expensive process that can be managed well by larger organizations where costs are spread over many partners and projects. Smaller NGOs can implement MEAL/MERL by partnering with others to use all the lessons above.

The cases shared above provide a view on how NGOs have developed and can now have excellent systems to measure more, evaluate more, learn more, and build more capacity to become more effective in programs, more accountable to stakeholders, and more successful with donors. By utilizing strategic evaluation for greater impact and codes of ethics for greater trust, NGOs can achieve so much more in their services, information, education, advocacy, and independence. All this is important, because we are all part of a broader civil society and, together, we can make a better world (Figure 15.4).

"Those evaluations were tough to finish, but the results will really help us do better in the future."

Figure 15.4 NGO workers celebrating after achieving a breakthrough in strategic evaluation. Artwork by Sawyer Phillips.

Questions for implementation

1   Which of the case studies presented in this chapter will help your NGO the most? Explain why.
2   Have you gone to that organization's website to get more information? What have you learned?
3   What is your plan to scale up your M&E process to ensure your organization is conducting strategic evaluation that results in participant involvement, continuous learning, greater results, and improved accountability?

Notes

1   Ken Phillips, *Strategic Planning and Culture for Nonprofits: Clear and doable steps to create motivating plans and the supporting culture you need for success* (NGO Futures LLC, 2021).
2   "Global Harmony Foundation [Facebook page]," accessed July 4, 2022, https://www.facebook.com/globalharmonyfoundation.
3   "Fundatia Pentru Dezvoltarea Societatii Civile ['Foundation for the Development of Civil Society' website homepage]," accessed July 4, 2022, https://www.fdsc.ro.
4   "Mission of CCC Creative Center," *CCC Creative Center*, accessed July 4, 2022, http://ccc-tck.org.ua/eng/.
5   "United Way of Hungary [website homepage]," *United Way*, accessed July 4, 2022, https://www.unitedway.org/local/hungary/.
6   "Freedom From Hunger [website homepage]," *Freedom From Hunger*, accessed July 4, 2022, https://grameenfoundation.org/about-us/the-grameen-family/freedom-from-hunger.
7   "Children International [website homepage]," *Children International*, accessed July 4, 2022, https://www.children.org/learn-more/mission-vision-values.
8   "World Neighbors [website homepage]," *World Neighbors*, accessed July 4, 2022, https://www.wn.org.
9   "Catholic Relief Services [website homepage]," *Catholic Relief Services*, accessed July 4, 2022, https://www.crs.org.
10   "International Youth Foundation [website homepage]," *International Youth Foundation*, accessed July 4, 2022, https://iyfglobal.org.
11   Susan Pezzullo, Angela Venza (contributor), and Ken Phillips (contributor), *Growing Your Organization: A Sustainability Resource Book for NGO's* (International Youth Foundation, 2000).

Bibliography

1   "Catholic Relief Services [website homepage]." *Catholic Relief Services*. Accessed July 4, 2022. https://www.crs.org.
2   "Mission of CCC Creative Center." *CCC Creative Center*. Accessed July 4, 2022. http://ccc-tck.org.ua/eng/.
3   "Children International [website homepage]." *Children International*. Accessed July 4, 2022. https://www.children.org/learn-more/mission-vision-values.
4   "Freedom From Hunger [website homepage]." *Freedom From Hunger*. Accessed July 4, 2022. https://grameenfoundation.org/about-us/the-grameen-family/freedom-from-hunger.
5   "Fundația Pentru Dezvoltarea Societății Civile ['Foundation for the Development of Civil Society' website homepage]." Accessed July 4, 2022. https://www.fdsc.ro.
6   "Global Harmony Foundation [Facebook page]." Accessed July 4, 2022. https://www.facebook.com/globalharmonyfoundation.
7   "International Youth Foundation [website homepage]." *International Youth Foundation*. Accessed July 4, 2022. https://iyfglobal.org.

8 Pezzullo, Susan, Angela Venza (contributor), and Ken Phillips (contributor). *Growing Your Organization: A Sustainability Resource Book for NGO's.* International Youth Foundation, 2000.

9 Phillips, Ken. *Strategic Planning and Culture for Nonprofits: Clear and doable steps to create motivating plans and the supporting culture you need for success.* NGO Futures LLC, 2021.

10 "United Way of Hungary [website homepage]." *United Way.* Accessed July 4, 2022. https://www.unitedway.org/local/hungary/.

11 "World Neighbors [website homepage]." *World Neighbors.* Accessed July 4, 2022. https://www.wn.org.

Chapter 16

Three case studies – Developing strategic evaluation in practice

My interest in evaluation started early in my career. What makes things work well? I thought everyone in the general public believed in the mission and goals of nonprofit organizations, but then I actually heard people laugh with stories about them! People were *not* convinced of their honesty, efficiency, and effectiveness. So I concluded that if NGOs performed better, they would raise the level of trust and support by the public, governments, corporations, media, educators, and professional associations.

Key point: Strategic evaluation is using monitoring and evaluation and other inputs *strategically* as steps to learn and develop the organization to improve its honesty, efficiency, and effectiveness, and raise more funding to achieve even more.

The development of my thinking about evaluation as a critical, strategic effort is based on my lifelong work in civil society. This began with my learning as student president responsible for everything at AIESEC-U.S., as coordinator and creator of new projects and fundraising at the Institute of International Education, as vice president of development and public affairs at Save the Children US, and as president and executive director at Foster Parents Plan (now Plan International USA). As a volunteer, I served on a variety of committees and commissions including charity evaluation reviews for the Better Business Bureau Wise Giving Alliance and Maryland Association of Nonprofit Organizations, drafted new ethics requirements in Rhode Island's Constitutional Convention, and led the creation of the NGO Standards for InterAction and its NGO members.

I have also supported new NGO leaders in Lithuania, Poland, Romania, Slovakia, Ukraine, and other newly independent countries, conducted research for the Sasakawa Peace Foundation on how major NGOs evaluate their work, and crafted a clear approach for organizational development for the International Federation of Red Cross and Red Crescent Societies.

All these activities involved a long-term exploration of what organizations do well and what they don't. These experiences led to the obvious realization that monitoring and evaluation provide the insights to know what to improve. Here are three examples illustrating how various nonprofit organizations developed – and used – strategic evaluation. I want you to learn from these examples and find ideas and inspiration to develop or improve strategic evaluation at your nonprofit organization or volunteer group.

The material this chapter is based on my own personal involvement with the three organizations, interviews with their representatives, and my notes and papers (Figure 16.1).

DOI: 10.4324/9781003335207-19

3 Detailed Case Studies

1. Save the Children U.S. – Progress in evaluation for program development and learning

2. Plan International – Development of evaluation as a comprehensive approach to learning and improving

3. INTERTEAM – A model for smaller organizations that cannot afford sophisticated evaluation processes

Figure 16.1 Three detailed cases of developing evaluation. Sidebar by the author.

EXAMPLE 1. Save the Children US – Evaluation for program development and learning[1]

This case study explores how Save the Children US used grants not just to do good programs but, even more important, to learn and build its capacity. Subsequent paragraphs describe the organization's more recent commitment to monitoring, evaluation, research, and evaluation (MERL). Save the Children International is now one of the leading international development NGOs with 30 national members and activities in 118 countries. This case study is about its American member where I worked for ten years.

In the 1970s and 1980s, Save the Children US benefited from its many grant evaluations to make substantial improvements in planning, evaluating, and learning. During those years, evaluations for various grant programs enabled Save the Children to get so much better, and we used that to raise more funds. The organization developed a broader context for its planning and evaluation by developing program indicators tied to global and regional goals and priorities established through broad consensus at major international conferences. Over the years, its evaluations became better, increasingly involved local participants and governments, and improved project results. "Eyes wide open to learn" was the approach.

I joined the organization in 1972 as corporate and foundation fundraiser and was soon named vice president for development and public affairs. At that time, the organization was small, unknown, and, if I can say so, surprisingly amateurish in its work. Within ten years almost everything had changed – program strategy, professionalism, scope and scale of its work, funding, reputation, and leadership in the sector. The executive director, David Guyer, was an inspiring and demanding boss with a strong vision of making the organization a leader in the field. He expected outstanding performance by staff, especially the top managers and, as an indication of the mentoring he provided and the leadership he required, 20 years later, a total of eight (yes, eight!) of us who had worked for him had become executive directors of other major NGOs. One aspect of his leadership was to embrace both program and personnel evaluations as a good thing, a way to learn and improve.

Developing new program strategy at Save the Children US

One of the first things we did after I arrived was to develop an entirely new program strategy. Working closely with the executive director, I drafted the new strategy, which we called Community-Based Integrated Rural Development (C-BIRD). The new strategy switched funding from cash subsidies to individual children to funding for families and communities. The program goals switched from education, healthcare, and development for an individual child to broad community progress in education, healthcare, and economic development for an entire community and all its children.

The correlated fundraising strategy to attract sponsors changed from "You can save a child by supporting her education, healthcare, and other steps to a career" to "You can save a child by supporting her family and community to develop education, healthcare, housing, and incomes in her community." We explained that by combining the funds from a number of sponsors in the same community, we could help all the children and families achieve greater development. In both cases, the individual sponsor could have a personal relationship with a specific child through an exchange of letters, photographs, and progress reports.

We called the former strategy "check to child" – and because we were convinced the new strategy was better, we called it "a better way to help kids through community development." We also strengthened the message and positioning of Save the Children and expanded its marketing and public outreach to generate substantially increased public funding.

How did we know the strategy was better? Although we did not conduct formal evaluations in the beginning, we knew it was an improvement based on advice from development experts, the professional literature about successful development, and extensive feedback from families that the old approach was not fair to other children in the same community or even in the same family who were not helped. The initial program strategy failed to address the real issue of a seriously insufficient supply of education, healthcare, and economic development in the community. So our decision to adopt the new strategy was based on values, professional literature, community research, and conviction that it was the right thing to do. As the new program got underway, our field staff was in close contact with families and community leaders and regularly reported back that the new approach was achieving higher goals and was appreciated by participants. It also led to increased community involvement and self-help in program.

A significant and intended consequence was that the new strategy would open up substantial new funding opportunities through grants for development that would not have been available for the individual-child approach. I recall vividly the occasion when our nutrition specialist returned from a trip to Washington, D.C. to meet with USAID (the U.S. Agency for International Development). She ran into the building with the news of a confirmed new grant for child survival and exclaimed, "But they require that we have a doctor, an actual doctor, on staff to make sure we are approaching healthcare in a professional manner. Imagine that! We'll have to pay a doctor more than the executive director gets." That was the beginning of the professionalization of the program.

As I look back, I realized I was already being guided by five essentials and six key attributes for nonprofits, which I subsequently articulated in my recent books (Figure 16.2 and 16.3).

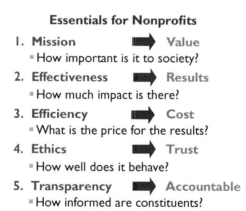

Essentials for Nonprofits

1. **Mission** ➡ Value
   * How important is it to society?

2. **Effectiveness** ➡ Results
   * How much impact is there?

3. **Efficiency** ➡ Cost
   * What is the price for the results?

4. **Ethics** ➡ Trust
   * How well does it behave?

5. **Transparency** ➡ Accountable
   * How informed are constituents?

Figure 16.2 The five essentials for nonprofits. Infographic by the author.

Key Attributes of Nonprofits

1. Providing services **important to society**

2. Promoting **a socially worthwhile vision**

3. Educating **the public about this vision**

4. Advocating **to all sectors of society**

5. Independent **status and voice**

6. Private voluntary **not-for-profit**

To succeed, earn trust and achieve impact.

Figure 16.3 The six key attributes for nonprofits. Infographic by the author.

Using ongoing evaluations to learn and grow

Many factors contributed to our progress, but grant evaluations especially were welcomed and played an indispensable role in enabling the organization to become professional in its program. In the 1970s alone, grants and their evaluations in health, education, child-survival, and micro-credit enabled Save the Children to learn from what it does, expand technical skills, enhance management support, develop overall capacity, and raise more funds.

Lessons from the experience of Save the Children with grants and evaluations include how an NGO can learn from donor-required evaluations, how it can develop skills and capacities, and how it can secure additional resources as a result. When a consultant assessed the evaluations of grants by USAID, he concluded that "The capacity of an organization to look constructively on its own strengths and weaknesses and respond effectively to dynamic change yet retain its core values, as these evaluations suggest Save the Children has done, are a good indicator of institutional strength and vitality."

Some years later, Charles MacCormack, who was then CEO of Save the Children US, told me: "USAID has certainly strengthened our sectoral and project management skills. We have lots of examples at the project level of evaluation recommending changes that have led to improved program delivery."

Save the Children actually began to implement community development programs in the late 1960s with a few grants from foundations and USAID. Most of these early grants were focused on community training, and evaluation was primarily seen as a method of assessing compliance with the terms of the grants. Back then, the thinking among most American NGOs was that donors were too demanding in their reporting and evaluation requirements. However, they accepted such requirements as necessary conditions to obtain and, ideally, renew funding. Thus, the initial motivation for evaluation was the fact that it was required by grants, and the organizations wanted to raise more funds for their programs. This was important but not (yet) relevant for learning.

By the 1980s, these grants had progressed in their level of complexity so that an organization needed to have technical skills in education, microfinance, health, child survival, and other specialized sectors. Evaluation became as important for lessons learned as for grant compliance. The requirements by the external funding sources now required more discipline and rigor and a higher level of professionalism in order to implement and evaluate programs.

An independent consultant at that time concluded that: "Consistently, Save the Children gets strong marks for the skill, creativity, and motivation of its field staff, technical home office support, and coordination with local institutions and government agencies, other program implementers, and other donors." This progress was possible, because the organization regularly used its evaluations to learn and build capacity.

How evaluation has changed for the best NGOs

In 1993, Save the Children started developing ten-year goals for global impact in quality and access in education, gender equity for girls, meeting the needs of children in war and crisis, improving family planning and reproductive health services, and saving newborn lives. They reassessed plans every three years and each year dedicated an entire board meeting to review the accomplishments toward these goals. The reviews addressed long-term sectoral goals, learning group conclusions, IT impact, management indicators, institutional strength indicators, needed policy changes, realigning the organization, and allocating resources toward the goals.

In those years, their ongoing evaluations included qualitative and quantitative measures, lessons learned, applications for the future, and sharing of best practices. To support dissemination of what's working and build it into future applications, they brought staff together in program learning groups in major areas such as health, education, economic opportunities, and children in crisis.

With top staff members participating from headquarters and field offices, the learning groups met at least once a year to share project results and best practices and develop learning agendas. Each year the focus shifted to look at what has been learned in the various components of work. The meetings were supplemented through further questionnaires, focus groups, interviews with clients, numerical indicators, rapid rural appraisal, external evaluations, and random samples of children to evaluate both systems and the impact throughout the life of a program. Learning group conclusions were then applied in multiple locations.

In the early days of its community development programs, the organization would go into a community and build a school. While this activity looked good to program managers and donors, in truth, it usually did not improve education in a meaningful way. Simple school construction alone does not work. Through the learning process, the education learning group developed a more sophisticated strategy for educational support, including community involvement in deciding what to do and how to do it, contributing their own labor in any building projects, securing government support for teachers, curriculum development, and other important practices in education. The education learning group would focus one year on improving access to primary schools and the next on building the capacity of school management committees.

Key point: M&E brought learning from different projects into a structure that facilitates co-ordinated planning and better implementation of programs around long-term strategic objectives.

How evaluation contributed to a poverty alleviation and nutrition program in Vietnam

At the request of the Government of Vietnam in 1990, Save the Children developed a prototype community development program with a focus on malnourished children. The goal was an affordable, measurable, sustainable nutrition model that could be widely replicated. Measurable results were essential in order to convince parents, government officials, donors, and staff that the program was effective and should be replicated. Program managers selected enhancement of nutritional status of children under the age of three as the key indicator to measure the impact of the program – certainly a measurement that would appeal to parents and officials.

The program enabled communities to achieve the following overall results: an 80% reduction in malnutrition among zero-to-six-month-old infants, a sustainable 75% reduction in second-degree malnutrition, and a sustainable 95% reduction in third-degree malnutrition in children. How did it achieve such impact?

The program and its monitoring and evaluation were designed with priority consideration on the issues of measurability, sustainability, and replicability. An initial intensive baseline survey was conducted by the Vietnamese Institute of Sociology on "such issues as access to food, access to clean water and latrines, income, household size, and of health clinics. The findings made it clear that, as expected, there were a wide variety of highly intractable factors contributing to malnutrition."

In the pilot stage, several communes were selected to be a "social laboratory" for the model. Initial results were impressive: after two years, the number of children under three suffering from second- or third-degree malnutrition fell from 36% to 4%, according to data compiled by commune health volunteers. Two years after the program ended, the National Institute of Nutrition studied one of the original pilot communes and found second- and third-degree malnutrition to be only 5%.

Along with other inputs, a key ingredient for success was the concept that staff involved called "positive deviance." This refers to the common observation that even in harsh environments, a few families almost always succeed in raising healthy, well-nourished children against the odds. In this case, positive deviance refers to the child, the caregiver, the family, and specifically to their behaviors, which likely account for the child's nutritional success. Identifying the "positive deviants" that some families were taking advantage of could reveal hidden resources already present in the environment, from which it is possible to devise solutions that are cost-effective, sustainable, culturally acceptable, and internally owned and managed. In the Vietnamese paddy ecology, "positive deviant" foods such as small shrimps, crabs, and greens, which were not generally given to toddlers, seemed to promote better growth.

Phase two expanded to four communes with a total population 24,000, and phase three expanded to 250 communes. In both phases, the expansion was based on lessons learned. The program had the following components:

1 A growth-monitoring promotion program to weigh all children under three years of age every two months;
2 A nutrition education/rehabilitation program to rehabilitate malnourished children and enable parents to sustain their child's enhanced nutritional status;
3 A nutrition revolving loan program to provide poor families with malnourished children with supplementary food through a laying hen program, which would be gradually paid back when some of the eggs were sold;
4 A healthy pregnancy/new mother program to address the problem of malnutrition before birth through improved health centers and antenatal care; and
5 A variety of other interventions such as scholarships, irrigation, and agriculture loans requested by villagers.

Following the initial evaluations, the programs expanded to cover more children but only provided the first two program components. The local health volunteers and community leaders implemented, monitored, and evaluated the program. They collected the data and kept their own scoreboard in the commune from the beginning with periodic progress as a result of their work.

The program has been evaluated a couple of times and in a couple of ways including a rigorous qualitative and quantitative evaluation by American and Vietnamese public health physicians. The program implementers had been collecting data on 1,800 kids, and it was all on a computer. The evaluation team reviewed the data and concluded that the program was successful.

Three years later, in partnership with Emory University in Atlanta, Georgia, a graduate student revisited the area and looked at pairs of siblings. Older children who had been in the program were still better nourished then non-exposed children from a comparison commune, and the younger siblings were even better nourished even though the program had ended before their birth. This is logical as the mother applied her knowledge from the project to the younger sibling from birth.

In addition to the dramatic reduction in the incidence of malnourished children and development of the program, some other results of the project are:

- Demonstration of the impact of "positive deviance" research applied to the broader population;
- Identification of readily available shrimps, crabs, and greens as the "positive deviant" foods to promote better growth;
- Endorsement by the Vietnamese government of the project as a National Community Development Model;
- Replication and expansion of the same model in more than a dozen countries; and
- Demonstration of the value of professional M&E, testing strategy, monitoring results, and involving participants for learning and capacity building.

To these positive program results, I would add the significant increase in the program's attractiveness to donors. Success breeds success, as they say, and this program's evaluations showed ongoing "healthy" progress in improving children's nutrition. Stories and pictures from the field coupled with real data made for compelling fundraising promotions that earned significant new support.

Data-driven evaluations help to win a $50 million grant for newborn children

The award of a $50 million grant by the Gates Foundation to Save the Children US is an example of the long-term impact of good programs, good evaluations, and good learning. Save the Children's long-term use of M&E to learn and build capacity was the critical factor. Without this newly developed organizational capacity, Save the Children would not have received such a substantial grant.

The grant was the first phase of a ten-year Saving Newborn Lives global initiative to reduce dramatically the estimated 5.4 million annual deaths of newborns (infants in their first month of life). Ninety-eight percent of all newborn deaths were in the developing world, and more than 90% of these deaths occurred in the home generally in the absence of a trained healthcare provider.

Save the Children led this initiative with prominent technical and academic institutions, non-governmental organizations, and government agencies in selected developing countries. Partnership was the organizational strategy for the project to test new technologies and approaches, refine and confirm programs that show promise, expand the scale and reach of successful programs, and launch a global information and advocacy campaign.

According to Save the Children, the following factors contributed to its success in securing this grant:

1   The quality of the proposal itself;
2   The organization's global presence;
3   The ability to create and sustain partnerships;
4   The community focus of the organization's work;
5   Credibility as an organization and of key health staff;

6   The nonprofit's experience in child survival programs;
7   The initiative addressed a key component of the donor's global health strategy;
8   And especially its reputation for careful documentation of programs.

Development of retrospective impact evaluation (RIE) and research evidence and learning (REL)

In a recent conversation with Dr. Lauren Pisani, who was then Advisor of Research, Evidence, and Learning at Save the Children US, I heard that major donors have driven organizations to utilize more advanced evaluation systems and accountability systems for more innovation and sustainability. There is also more focus on looking at communities to become sustainable on their own, rather than relying on outsiders.

Dr. Pisani added: "We use retrospective impact evaluations of what happened ten years after the program and find lots of positives. The global Save Alliance has been really helpful in providing different perspectives on different outcomes with the resulting soul-searching of how best to approach the whole field. Learning from competitors is more robust than in the past. New alliances address different topic areas. Especially notable is the impact of lobbying together. Such networks can use evaluation results to affect policy changes at the government level."

Save the Children utilizes *Retrospective Impact Evaluation* (RIE) to learn by looking back two to ten years after the end of a program with a set of high-quality *Key Evaluation Questions* (KEQs). The questions explore core programming implemented and current status; outcomes and impacts influenced by the organization; side impacts and ripple effects; value for investment, sustainability, and ownership transition; and exit. An RIE truly assesses the longer-term impacts of a program and how to make improvements with questions such as:

•   "Is this working? Does it last? How could we make a more lasting impact?"
•   "What helped solutions, outcomes, and impacts to last and be built upon?"
•   "What were the gaps or challenges that limited sustainability?"
•   "What can we tell donors about the difference we are making?"

Capturing and documenting data in the programs is essential in a retrospective evaluation. Save the Children emphasizes that it is "important to engage MEAL [Monitoring, Evaluation, Accountability, and Learning] specialists in thinking through the evaluative monitoring data to start capturing, from the initial needs and strengths assessment to ongoing data capture for adaptive management."

Following the completion of a retrospective impact evaluation, staff compile "a list of findings and learnings to facilitate a conversation with our sponsorship program and MEAL leadership groups. Through our collective thinking, we will be better placed to incorporate learning into our programs." Research is used to learn to make a better program and to confirm value to donors as the results are shared with the organization's marketing and retention team.

Dr. Pisani praised the proliferation of electronic data collection systems as a significant benefit in the humanitarian and development sector in the past five years – open-source data, the qualitative nature of data, and connectivity in communities. However, the digital divide is huge and smaller organizations need to partner up and develop with technology companies. Biomarkers and scans are needed to be sure eligible families get the services they need. She added that, unfortunately, there is not a lot of pressure on corporations to become responsible for the effects of their products on children, and that's an area of need in advocacy. She looks forward to more sharing at the global level. She added that "folks are seeing the power of people coming together in the NGO sector by sharing what works."

I especially like the implications of Dr. Pisani's position as advisor for research, evidence, and learning. This is what a true professional does – conduct research, gather evidence, and learn to perform ever better. She concluded optimistically that: "Altogether, NGOs are getting smarter." I agree, many are!

The takeaway from Save the Children's experience is that an NGO will improve and grow significantly if it takes advantage of major grant requirements and turns evaluations into learning and capacity building opportunities. Globally, Save the Children has grown significantly as a result and, therefore, has made a tremendous impact in many countries.

Key point: All NGOs around the world who have not developed their own research, evidence, and learning capacities can partner up with others for collaboration, cost-sharing, learning, and developing.

EXAMPLE 2. Plan International – A comprehensive approach to evaluation and learning[2]

Plan International, formerly Foster Parents Plan, is a major international child-focused development organization active in 75 countries, supported by 20 national member organizations, and working through 50 unified field programs.

This case study explores the following simple but essential questions, which we asked when I was executive director (now called CEO) of the American national member:

- How can we assure donors of our results?
- How can we develop new monitoring and evaluation?
- How can we incorporate accountability in our work?
- How can we use assessment and evaluation results?
- How can we develop continuous learning – and use what we learn?

The story here is an example of progression to increasingly effective yet feasible M&E systems, development of important strategic tools, and efforts to become a learning organization. Although we made mistakes along the way, this case study may provide guidance for your organization.

Early efforts at evaluation

Foster Parents Plan (as it was called when I was there, with Plan also used) has long evaluated its programs. Like most organizations in the 1980s, it measured its effectiveness by budget expenditures, overhead ratios, and immediate outputs of its expenditures.

In the early 1980s, the organization began looking seriously at what more was needed. Thinking on behalf of our individual and group donors and in a global planning process, we formalized organizational priorities into eight goals (access to clean water, vaccination coverage, nutritional status, sanitation and waste disposal, housing, formal education, literacy, and income). These goals focused our approach to helping children and their families and were also appealing to our donors.

The global evaluation unit was then tasked to develop a standardized evaluation system to measure the beginning situation for planning purposes, progress toward program goals, and results for participating families. This served to focus previously diverse activities on priorities and to be able to measure achievement. So far so good.

Standardization was necessary, because management needs data that can be compared to assess progress and performance, and an organization in many locations cannot afford different systems for each (with significant cultural conditions considered). Accordingly, we wanted a field office evaluation system that would provide "meaningful and useful objective information" for communities and local program managers to design and implement programs and to monitor their effectiveness. Board members, international managers, and fundraisers could also use this evaluation system to meet policy, budgetary, and accountability needs. The system was intended to be the standardized approach for Plan throughout the world. Still good.

The process appropriately identified key factors to establish an evaluation system including:

1   Organizational commitment from the board, management, and staff;
2   Structure to support evaluation within the organization;
3   The need to measure performance over time;
4   The value of specific data to measure and compare;
5   Communication to overcome misunderstanding and resistance;
6   Use of evaluation for planning, assessing, comparing impacts, and reporting.

The steps used to develop the system were also good:

1   An initial conference to present, discuss, and develop the system;
2   Trips to involve and discuss the system with implementing staff;
3   Drafting a concept paper outlining operations and defining indicators;
4   A second conference to present and review instructions and the questionnaire;
5   Circulation of the revised plans and instrument;
6   A pre-test of the system in selected locations;
7   Technical review of the results and process;
8   Training of local staff and community volunteers;
9   Implementation, analysis, and interpretation.

There was broad agreement that a comprehensive evaluation system should provide accurate measures of performance in relation to goals, allow for planning and budget adjustment, permit targeting of particular projects for specific populations, and inform key managers if the organization is actually doing what it says it is doing. Excellent! We needed that information to know we were doing well in our programs and for effective fundraising.

However, the questionnaire used in this process ended up with 137 questions. After actual field testing of the questionnaire, it was agreed that it was far too complex and detailed to be used. Back to the drawing board – and a new planning process. Lesson: Keep it manageable.

Next steps included new grants, more meaningful evaluations, and an emphasis on quality

New grants from USAID secured by our U.S. staff for international programs in health, education, and microcredit led to higher commitment for more meaningful field evaluations. These evaluations were to be conducted according to the standard USAID evaluation approaches at that time, requiring more systematic setting of objectives and measurement of progress along the way. Largely based on the Logical Framework, this approach to evaluation was useful for its clarity in identifying assumptions and measuring objectives. Assessments were required at the beginning of each grant, at the mid-term, and at the conclusion.

All this was good, but it did not apply to the rest of the organization's work funded by individuals, school and business groups, and a few family foundations. Several of us had been agitating for more organization-wide evaluation. We felt increasing pressure on behalf of donors to demonstrate the effectiveness of the programs they were funding.

As the executive director of Foster Parents Plan USA, I was a member of a small international planning group that led a comprehensive global strategic planning process. I brought with me my fundraising perspectives of what donors wanted from us. We decided to improve evaluation from three perspectives – results for participants, accountability for donors, and feasibility for staff. A new international executive director from the business world brought with him a commitment to quality.

In a careful process, we developed an updated mission statement and included for the first time commitments to quality and continuous improvement as well as a realistic and feasible field-based M&E system. The updated vision, mission, identity statement, and commitment to quality were approved in an organization-wide participatory process and were applicable in all programs.

We also had established seven key principles: Child centeredness, empowerment and sustainability in communities, gender equity, environmental sustainability, cooperation, integration, and institutional learning. Together, these statements guided the planning, activities, and evaluation throughout the Plan world. The commitment to quality and continuous improvement of the organization's programs, processes, and services led to a major emphasis on assessment, monitoring, and evaluation – and on learning!

The purposes of evaluation were to serve several audiences:

1   Organizational learning for our internal audience to get better at what we do;
2   Capacities in communities to support their own projects and development;
3   Accountability to donors who were increasingly interested in their impact on families;
4   Demonstration to grant providers who want to see their partners be more professional.

We defined evaluation as the "systematic collection of information related to the design, implementation, and impact of programs in order to assess the logic and quality of that design, progress of the implementation, and final results of the work." This definition integrated evaluation fully into program planning and implementation to "measure the situation before the intervention, determine quantitative and time-bound objectives, monitor the program and its environment, and measure the situation after the program."

Implementing a new corporate planning, monitoring, and evaluation system (CPME)

Based on the new strategic framework, technical experts then created a comprehensive corporate planning, monitoring, and evaluation system including a baseline of the program, relevant indicators, periodic assessments, and progress base on the indicators.

The director for the system described it to me: "The system provides the framework within which we measure our performance based on outputs, outcomes, and impacts. Generally speaking, *outputs* such as the number of health centers built are the easiest to measure but do not tell you if anyone used the center, what the quality of care was, or how it improved people's lives. *Outcomes* such as children using the new health center are relatively easy to measure and provide an indication of Plan's progress toward an impact. *Impacts* such as healthier children are the most relevant but are the hardest to measure. To measure outputs, outcomes, and impacts – and to improve our overall performance – indicators have been developed."

The system was intended to enable field staff to plan, implement, monitor, complete, and evaluate within overall organizational policy. The new system was built on the work of the 1980s and provided a more cohesive and feasible set of instruments, supported by training and manuals.

The steps in the system were:

1   Extensive surveys to collect country and project-level baseline data with quantitative data on the status of children and the broader population;
2   Strategic planning at the country level for the next three to five years from highest level strategies right down to project activities, linking the strategic level and operational level in the implementation;
3   Monitoring as an ongoing process to support implementation, looking at what is happening and the progress on the indicators month by month;
4   Evaluation including a collection of the baseline and progress indicators and looking at the higher level targets and bigger issues and supporting those with quality studies and strategic thinking.

Compared to the organization's earlier work in evaluation as an occasional process and then in an overly complex process, this was a management system that has evaluation baked into it. The director for the system noted, "We collect baseline data to provide a picture of where each country's program unit or community is for each of the indicators."

Once programs and projects were in place, monitoring of the outputs, outcomes, and impacts began. The system provided tools, guidance, and software to monitor programs, projects, outputs, outcomes, and impacts. The director for the system added, "After a period of time (usually three to five years), we re-collect the information from the baseline to assess whether we have contributed to the impacts we intended and whether our choice and implementation of programs and projects can be improved."

The next step: Adding a program audit (PA)

Plan also initiated a program audit system, which audits the program and checks whether the rules have been followed. This is comparable to the approach, processes, and tests used in financial audits. Program auditors look from the outside at the planning, implementing, and evaluating process in a country by sampling the whole, as in a financial audit. The program audit has dual objectives: organizational learning and accountability.

Auditing is a formal process to collect evidence and draw conclusions, a discipline that can be applied to program as well as finance. A program audit team of professional auditors and development experts reviews program reports, evaluations, workshop outputs, and other documents with particular attention on planning, implementation, monitoring, and evaluation with reference to output and impact objectives for a particular period. During a week-long field visit, the team examines projects and interviews field staff, parents, community leaders, local associations, and authorities.

The result is a document written on site, discussed, and agreed with local management. The final report is an executive summary of two pages with about ten pages of bulleted highlights that is given to the field staff, regional management, headquarters program department, and the international executive director. The executive summary is given to the global executive and program staff and to the program audit committee of the board. The program audit function is independent with a direct report to the board.

Strategic thinking is informed by evaluation data

For Plan, strategic thinking is setting the most important goals, identifying the highest level strategies, and crafting the best long-term plans – all based on assessing the internal and external situation, considering all key stakeholder needs, and using relevant evaluation data to reach planning decisions to achieve the organization's mission.

The country plans are a translation of global mission, vision, and goals into the local context. Thinking is now more strategic, plans are informed by baseline data, and objectives are more refined and more precise. It was a big cultural shift to move from what was operational planning to strategic planning, informed by strategic thinking. When the local operational plan is done within the context of the global strategic plan, it gets its focus, priority, and coordination from global strategy. It supports established goals within the short-term with activities to achieve objectives and responsibilities to carry out the activities.

Ongoing, in-depth evaluation is key to becoming a learning organization (LO)

A guiding principle for Plan is institutional learning, which it states as: "Drawing upon internal and external sources, Plan will promote learning for itself, its partners, and the development community in order to achieve its mission." In a message to all staff, the international executive director wrote, "It is necessary that our collective behavior adapts to a learning culture, where successes and failures are shared, where internal competition disappears, and where learning is managed systematically and professionally at every level."

This approach to evaluation for learning was described as (lightly edited): "*Our approach to evaluation* includes monitoring, evaluation, lessons learned, and recommendations to the evaluation's users. *Program/project plans* describe country issues and objectives; project details; baseline versus actuals for inputs, outputs, outcomes, and impacts; how did the implementation proceed; did the implementation have the desired result; why or why not. *Evaluation reports* include: who requested the evaluation and why; who will use or be affected by it; how will those people be involved in the evaluation's design, implementation, and dissemination; what are the key questions the evaluation will address; what programs and planning will be affected by the results; who is doing the evaluation and when; how will the lessons be used; where will the findings be stored for reference; and the costs."

Key point: The conclusion of the evaluation process is detailed lessons learned and recommendations to the evaluation's users for changes to be implemented.

Improving habitat: An example of evaluation, learning, and development (ELD)

Let's look at an example of how Plan worked to improve habitat for children. The impetus for developing a habitat focus in the program was increasing interest by communities and the resulting increased spending in this area.

The organization convened a conference of staff, community representatives, and outside experts to explore what it should do regarding housing and related fields. The workshop confirmed habitat as a domain or major area of interest. For Plan, habitat links housing to a much broader spectrum of community physical and social components and includes: housing quality, security of tenure, community use of space, accessible and affordable resources, access to essential institutions and facilities, management of shared natural resources, and protection from hazards, pollutants, and disasters. Plan's goal in this domain became "to ensure that children live in secure, safe, and healthy habitats."

As the next step, Plan published an initial program guideline on habitat, which was a compilation of twenty-seven case lessons from Plan and other NGOs. These case studies were, in fact, evaluation assessments of good (and not so good) examples as learning tools. Based on these studies, Plan identified four roles for its work in and with communities:

- **Information** – Provides options in how to address the problem, offers technical input and assistance, consults through research, develops new designs and innovations, and provides technical training.
- **Assistance** – Addresses the immediate problem, provides direct assistance in the form of grants and subsidies including credit, and implements projects for the direct benefit of the target population.
- **Organization** – Supports long-term capacity to solve the problem and build sustainable local organizational strength and capacity.
- **Negotiation** – Addresses the larger context of the problem, advocates changes in laws and informal systems, and brokers agreements with government, larger institutions, other NGOs, and community organizations.

The organization then identified learning sites in seven countries in which to design, test, and evaluate approaches to improve habitat. In the process, the nonprofit secured input from outside experts, its own staff, and the communities where Plan was working. Note that they were called learning sites rather than testing sites.

Detailed assessments of habitat needs were carried out in the learning sites. The assessments were designed to identify methodologies to collect habitat needs, determine how to establish priorities, and identify needed resources and capacities at the community level. The assessments tested the validity of the strategic framework, the usefulness of proposed objectives, new methodologies, and related issues. Experts with experience in participatory assessments and skills in habitat issues from Plan staff and external sources conducted the assessments through a variety of approaches.

One of the most useful research technique turned out to be focus groups formed with adults, women, adolescents, school non-attenders, community and NGO leaders, traditional leaders, and children. Supporting techniques were household surveys, data from local and national sources, key informant interviews with local leaders, semi-structured interviews with parents, participatory rural assessment through mapping and community transects, visioning exercises and discussions with pictures, and bar graph rankings.

After review by a special team, the assessments were presented to a workshop with program managers from the learning sites who had prepared preliminary program designs. Plan documented what was learned at these habitat learning sites and follow-up meetings. The resulting guidelines for program managers included priority objectives, steps to determine program design, and comprehensive guidelines based on experience in the learning sites.

Out of this process, the organization identified key steps to assess and evaluate habitat projects including to:

- Conduct a comprehensive habitat assessment;
- Define the most urgent problems;
- Make strategic choices on what to do;
- Decide the program scale and needed inputs;
- Define standards and identify technology options;
- Define program monitoring and evaluation;
- Build sustainability into the program design.

Because sustainability of the community's habitat (housing and surrounding conditions) is the real impact of a program, Plan believes it is essential to involve community people in all stages of the program planning, designing, implementing, monitoring, and evaluating. Increased skills and commitments by community participants are probably more important than physical improvements. Their learning and their use of that learning are two essential steps to sustainability. The extensive process to understand habitat needs and develop appropriate responses was valuable in planning the organization's activities in this domain for years to come.

Plan's current approach: Monitoring, evaluation, research, and learning (MERL)

Lorie Broomhall is the senior MERL advisor at Plan USA and has been with the organization for five years. Plan's early work in the field office evaluation system, the corporate planning monitoring and evaluation system, the program audit, and focus on quality and learning have merged into its current approach of Monitoring, Evaluation, Research, and Learning (MERL).

Broomhall stated that, previously, M&E was done as good management practice and as donor-mandated evaluation. Now all Plan projects have baseline and online data and a best approach in addressing longer-term impacts evaluation looking back ten years, known as retrospective impact evaluation. The Logical Framework and Results Monitoring approaches promulgated by USAID decades ago helped lead to better planning and better results through better monitoring and evaluation.

Another significant development for Plan is a practice that Broomhall called "***reflecting using data***," which takes place every quarter. In this process, program people meet to focus on progress for the quarter, make adjustments to targets, refine indicators, and improve implementation. Plan now presents data visually in ways that make mathematical analysis clear and understandable. The organization uses a dashboard on mobile phones with monthly data and resulting improvements, which Broomhall called "***fixing it on the way***" for all involved.

These initiatives are intended to counter the traditional management approach that too many organizations have of doing things as they have been done in the past – taking direction from the top leadership with a checklist mandating certain action items – into the far more effective approach of empowering local managers and participants to help design their programs, establish the objectives, and monitor and manage the process during implementation.

Plan International prioritizes accountability to both program participants and donors, and it broadcasts its commitments through its "accountability policies and commitments" statements. Here is an excerpt: "Plan International recognizes its duty to be as effective and efficient as possible and to be accountable to all our stakeholders. Our aim is to take full responsibility for the way we work, the decisions we make, and the impact we have." The accountability section of its website has subsections on accountability, finance, keeping children and young people safe, and workplace culture. It includes global policies on "values, conduct, and whistleblowing" and "global anti-fraud, anti-bribery, and corruption" which apply to all staff, volunteers, partners, and other stakeholders.

Plan International subjects itself to a variety of external evaluations and assessments. It has received external confirmation of its compliance with the standards of the International Committee on Fundraising Organizations, is externally verified by the Humanitarian Quality Assurance Initiative, and has been assessed affirmatively by One World Trust (see chapter 6).

As I talked with Broomhall about Plan's decades-long progress toward strategic evaluation, we discussed the importance of communication to donors. She asked me about the issue of story-based outcomes versus hard-evidence outcomes. My reply was that you clearly need both. On one hand, stories all by themselves can be inspiring, but they run the risk of being misleading if they are not validated by real evidence. On the other hand, evidence without human interest can be boring and uninspiring. For both internal learning and external accountability, both story-based outcomes and longer-term, evidence-based reporting are essential.

Key Evaluation Terms II
* Corporate Planning, Monitoring & Evaluation (CPME)
* Data Driven Evaluations (DDE)
* Evaluation, Learning & Development (ELD)
* Fixing it on the way
* Key Evaluation Questions (KEQs)
* Mentoring and Learning (M&L) – replacing M&E
* Monitoring, Evaluation, Accountability & Learning (MEAL)
* Monitoring, Evaluation, Research & Learning (MERL)
* Program Audit (PA)
* Reflecting using data
* Retrospective Impact Evaluation (RIE)

Figure 16.4 Key evaluation terms from these studies. Sidebar by the author.

Key point: The takeaway from the Plan story is that strategic monitoring and evaluation is a continuous process of learning to become a more effective, responsible, and accountable organization which enables it to achieve significantly greater results.

The case studies from Save the Children and Plan International as well as other studies in this book show how NGOs can benefit from major external developments:

1   With the expansion of global needs identification and priority setting as in the Sustainable Development Goals, NGOs can tie their plans, strategies, and evaluations into established priorities at the global, national, and local levels.
2   With modern IT capabilities, nonprofits can have access to much more data including detailed feedback from clients and beneficiaries.
3   With awareness of the skepticism of many people about the trustworthiness and effectiveness of NGOs, smart NGO leaders are stepping up their commitment to codes of ethics and accountability.
4   The process to develop strategic evaluation may not be short and simple for a given NGO, but it enables the organization to rise to a professional level and attain more learning, increased program effectiveness, more appeal to donors, and expanded programs to make a better world (Figure 16.4).

EXAMPLE 3. InterTeam – A model for smaller organizations that cannot afford sophisticated evaluation processes[3]

Very few organizations have the resources that Save the Children or Plan International have, so here is a story of collaboration that solves that problem. This case study indicates how small organizations can work with others to develop sophisticated and effective monitoring and evaluation systems, which none of them could have developed or afforded on their own.

The Swiss NGO InterTeam had a program to place well-qualified volunteers in other countries who functioned like staff or Peace Corps volunteers to support project implementation. InterTeam joined together with other NGO partners in a consortium to develop and provide effective monitoring and evaluation for small NGOs that could not have done this with their own limited budgets. (In 2020, InterTeam merged with Comundo,[4] a leading Swiss organization in the field of personnel development cooperation.)

The main task of the InterTeam volunteers was to teach groups in developing countries how to organize, plan, and manage projects whether in business, nonprofits, or government. As a small organization, InterTeam did not have the resources or expertise to develop a model of competency in new, sophisticated monitoring and evaluation methods. The projects were large, such as regional road construction with a thousand workers, and the evaluation was not for the whole project but for how the individual volunteer fit into and supported the project.

In this approach, the volunteer needed to be competent both as a professional expert and as a community worker. Professional competencies are those expected in the particular profession of the worker such as mechanical engineering, farm production, or marketing systems. Competencies in community work are planning, group process, conflict resolution, interpersonal relations, cultural understanding, and communication.

Under pressure from its government donors, InterTeam needed to upgrade its evaluation system for program work and for volunteer (staff) competency. Its reality had become more complex, for example, teaching community organizing and long-term planning, negotiating with government, dealing with change, cooperation within the sector, sustainable development, and working with the local partner and the Swiss coordinator. The organization lacked the resources to do this.

However, the new consortium of 27 Swiss development NGOs called Unité collectively had sufficient resources to develop the needed monitoring and evaluation instrument.

Developing a new evaluation method in a consortium

The process began with Unité gathering a large group of staff from all twenty-seven organizations to share their experiences and identify possible shortcomings in what they were doing. Because Unité was a facilitating organization rather than a controlling one, people saw they could be open in both the smaller groups and the larger sessions. The open discussion helped overcome resistance to measurement of personal performance. With this process, participants could see that learning from measurement would benefit their own organizations.

Luc Bigler, InterTeam's director at the time, told me: "This would not have been possible for us as a small organization. The umbrella organization developed the system, but it is really the people from the member NGOs that developed it by working together. We developed an instrument and process for twenty-seven organizations." As a result, InterTeam and the other participating organizations could integrate evaluation into all stages of their work. The system was adopted by all the Swiss organizations working in development, so findings were comparable and could be shared for further learning.

The overall approach included the following steps:

1   Set objectives for a specific project;
2   Monitor progress as the project develops;
3   Make changes in the assignment and project;
4   Learn from the experience;
5   Change the next approach;
6   Report to donors.

The monitoring and evaluation instrument addresses issues such as the institutional framework, teamwork, coordination, participation, conflict, handing over responsibility, impact, and personal growth for volunteers. It includes a set of competencies for selection of the volunteers. It also provides a way to measure the living situation, supervision, support, security, needs, and personal growth for the volunteer.

Soft indicators versus measurable verification

Another result of the collaboration was development of a process to measure progress with soft indicators when measurements are not possible.

Once on the ground, the volunteer drafts or updates the plans with the partner representative and the staff coordinator including objectives, activities, and monitoring. Every six months, the same three people meet to review what has been done and what needs to be done. Using the same questionnaire, all three prepare written reports and then sit together to discuss their conclusions. If they have differences, they have to work together to resolve them. The co-ordinator plays the role of moderator, but all three are equal in the process.

The question of impact is the most difficult in a program like this where the program activities fit into a bigger project. It is not always possible to have quantifiable measure-ments, for example, in the process of community development. Accordingly, the agreed methodology introduced soft indicators, not just measuring what happened but providing descriptive information, not just showing figures but explaining processes. For example, the number of meetings with women or how often the community meets are measurable in-dicators, but they are not particularly valid. Do participants meet because they always have, or does the impetus come from the volunteer? What is really going on in terms of changing behaviors and patterns of thought? Is the program moving in the right direction, or is it stuck?

This approach encompasses both self-assessment for the volunteer and evaluation for the local organization. It measures processes and impact – processes such as learning in the project, conflict within the group, the success of the volunteer, and the significance and potential for impact. It asks about the extent of learning and continuation of the work after the volunteer leaves.

Soft indicators can address:

- Does it look as if the program will have significance or impact?
- How much confidence has the local organization in expressing itself to government?
- How easy is it for them to reply to government, to fight a government decision, or to propose its own recommendations to government?

In the final analysis, the important thing is not to get people to measure; it is to get them to sit together to decide what they want to achieve and evaluate their progress and then their achievements.

The evaluation process needs to include information on what is really happening, on the team, on strengthening the local partner organization, and on unexpected effects. For this, it is impossible to measure in numbers. Instead, categories such as *totally*, *strong*, *weak*, or *not at all* are used. By having three people look at the same situation from different angles, the subjective views of three people gain more objectivity. It is the triangulation of the views of volunteer, partner, and coordinator that produces clarity and understanding. When the three observers agree, their soft evaluation of what is going on is probably valid. If the volunteer, partner, and coordinator agree, for example, that the team is functioning more effectively, this is probably a valid finding.

Conclusions from the shared evaluation process

1   Many NGOs are too small to develop a sophisticated and effective monitoring and evaluation system or a comprehensive code of ethics on their own. They cannot afford to do what the larger NGOs can do.

2   What Unité did for evaluation demonstrates that collaboration can work very well. The collaboration was based on true partnership with great benefits at relatively small cost for each participating NGO.
3   It is necessary to have a process to create cohesion and trust among the participants before engaging in substantive dialogue about the evaluation you want to develop, just as it is among different functions and offices in a single larger NGO.
4   Through collaboration and partnership, the results were far more significant than if each organization had pursued the same issue on its own. The benefit of learning from the collective knowledge of all the participants improved outcomes.
5   What initially began in response to donors became valuable tools for organizational learning, capacity building, and greater achievement of goals. It also led to closer relationships and increased sharing among NGOs that are important for further development in the civil society sector.

Key point: This example indicates how a small NGO can partner with other NGOs to develop sophisticated and effective monitoring and evaluation systems which they could not have developed on their own.

How can YOU implement strategic evaluation to improve your impact?

The approach I am advocating presents evaluation as a *strategy for learning and building capacity* to attain higher levels of performance. To review, PART II (chapter 10) presents the problem of insufficient impact by many NGOs. Chapter 11 presents two common problems with evaluation, chapters 12, 13, and 14 present strategic evaluation as the solution, chapters 15 and 16 share eleven case studies of NGOs making evaluation more strategic, and chapters 17, 18, and 19 provide lessons and the roadmap for its implementation.

The key for me, as I have shared before, is for everyone who wants to make a difference to follow six simple steps to lead when needed: *Network* so you have allies, *See* what needs to be done, *Seize* the opportunity when you see a problem, *Step up* to find a solution, *Persist* when you encounter resistance, and *Run meeting* well so you get agreement and action forward.

Here is the rationale: A nonprofit that embraces strategic evaluation, an open culture of learning, and a commitment to improve will achieve better performance, more impact in programs, increased fundraising appeal, more funding, bigger and better programs, and greater job satisfaction by all. The biggest and best organizations already do this; those that don't must!

➡ You can do it in your own NGO or in partnership with other NGOs if yours is too small to do it on your own.

Key point: Performance flows from capacity. Capacity flows from learning. Learning flows from evaluation. Evaluation flows from monitoring. Monitoring flows from planning.

Organization leaders often recognize the need for more learning and developing within their own organizations but may lack a clear and simple model to do it. This book presents a straightforward and comprehensive strategic approach to evaluation as a process for developing and shows the busy leader (executive, fundraiser, or implementer) how to start using evaluation as an effective path to continuous learning and development. It shows how to assure evaluation is planned and managed, and then used strategically to learn and build capacity. In this strategic model of evaluation, separate disciplines used in evaluation are combined into a single approach for learning and developing to enable your organization to achieve its mission more effectively and more efficiently.

Improved performance starts with a planning process with good indicators and proceeds from there through effective monitoring and evaluation to lessons learned and active learning to improve your organization's capacity to deliver great results. When indicators are Meaningful (important and relevant), Measurable (accessible and timely), Manageable (available and sufficient), and Motivational (directional and achievable), they will dramatically improve ongoing performance. Remember 4MPIs for indicators.

Because donors are interested in how NGOs learn, build capacity, and achieve better results, the approach shown in this book should contribute to better relationships with your donors and improved public confidence in your organization. You can tell them how you are doing all this. Donors do want to receive more than just fundraising letters. By placing evaluation in a strategic framework, this approach transforms required, tactical M&E reports into ongoing, strategic organizational learning and development. Strategic evaluation enables executives and board members to see evaluation in the correct light of learning with strategic benefits, not just as a tactical activity that meets grant requirements.

Key point: YOU can help your NGO to be trusted (code of ethics) and respected (strategic evaluation) and accountable (communicating (about all you do, rather than just asking for money, you can make your donors' experience with your organization truly awesome!

Small trees collaborate together. Big trees help other trees.
A healthy forest comes from mutual support.

Figure 16.5 Trees help each other and that makes a healthier forest. Artwork by Wills Phillips.

In closing this chapter, I want to emphasize that developing strategic evaluation and meaningful ethics and providing engaging communications are urgently needed throughout the NGO sector to gain trust, respect, and commitment from the public.

It is important to remember that the nonprofit business model is based on the power of the vision, mission, and values and that the effectiveness of nonprofits depends on culture, goals, and strategies. Public support depends on these and the trust and impact you achieve and your communications for accountability. I encourage you to step up in your organization to spearhead the development (or strengthening) of meaningful ethics, strategic evaluation, and communications.

All NGOs have a responsibility to the whole sector to improve the trust (meaningful ethics), respect (strategic evaluation), and accountability (communications) for civil society to make a better world. By helping the sector improve, you will be helping you own organization (Figure 16.5).

Questions for implementation

1   How can you move your organization to better M&E for learning?
2   How can you integrate research, planning, monitoring, evaluating, and learning?
3   How will you partner with other organizations to have better evaluations?

Notes

1 "Save the Children [website homepage]," *Save the Children*, accessed July 4, 2022, https://www.savethechildren.org
2 "Plan International [website homepage]," *Plan International*, accessed July 4, 2022, https://www.planusa.org
3 "Interteam [website homepage]," *Interteam*, accessed July 4, 2022, https://www.interteam.ch
4 "Comundo [website homepage]," *Comundo*, accessed July 4, 2022, https://www.comundo.org

Bibliography

1 "Comundo [website homepage]." *Comundo*. Accessed July 4, 2022. https://www.comundo.org
2 "Interteam [website homepage]." *Interteam*. Accessed July 4, 2022. https://www.interteam.ch
3 "Plan International [website homepage]." *Plan International*. Accessed July 4, 2022. https://www.planusa.org
4 "Save the Children [website homepage]." *Save the Children*. Accessed July 4, 2022. https://www.savethechildren.org

Lessons for leaders, managers, fundraisers, and grantmakers for trust and impact

Creating a strong code of ethics and following best practices in evaluation directly affect trust and impact. These activities stimulate improved organizational performance, increase public trust and confidence in individual NGOs and the entire NGO sector, assist beneficiaries through improved and expanded program performance, and reinforce professionalization of the sector. Recall the example I shared earlier in chapter 5: The 120 executive directors I surveyed assessed their own organizations as beyond reproach in their ethics and effectiveness; simultaneously, they suspected that most other NGOs were woefully at risk in their ethics and effectiveness. The truth is that no organization is beyond reproach, and every nonprofit must regularly conduct honest and thorough evaluations and self-assessments.

The lessons presented in this chapter are recommendations to build capacity in an organization through *meaningful ethics* and *strategic evaluation* to learn and develop in order to achieve better performance, higher trust, and greater impact. When meaningful ethics and strategic evaluation are priority for the organization, behavior and results will be better, because focus will be on learning from experience and improving everything as they go along.

As you know from the NGO business model I presented in the Introduction, the two priority external stakeholders for nonprofits are beneficiaries and donors. The organization can be successful over the longer term *only if* the long-term needs of both groups are met with increasing competence. Moreover, every nonprofit has responsibility to further the development of the civil society sector, because we are all in this together, everyone's actions affect the others, and everyone will benefit from higher trust resulting from impeccable ethics and higher respect resulting from demonstrated impact (Figure 17.1).

➡ *Good strategic planning now includes vision, mission, values, culture, goals, strategies, trust, and impact with communications and accountability.*

Based on my many discussions and experiences over the decades, here are my conclusions and lessons for moving forward.

To have better results and raise more money, address ethics for trust and evaluation for impact

1 Organization leaders need to recognize that public trust in NGO behavior and respect for their results are dangerously low – and that curtails both fundraising and program.
2 Trust requires impeccable ethical behavior and respect requires top-notch program results that are demonstrated, verified, and communicated.
3 The board of directors is responsible to make meaningful ethics and strategic evaluation are formal policy and standard practice.

DOI: 10.4324/9781003335207-20

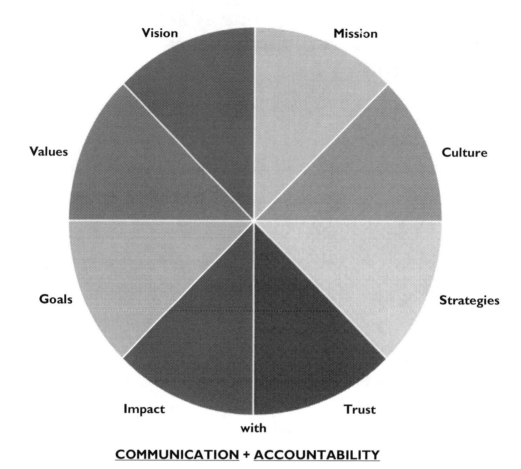

Figure 17.1 Strategic planning circle image with vision, mission, values, culture, strategies, goals, trust, and impact plus communications and accountability. Image by the author.

4 Management is responsible to make meaningful ethics and strategic evaluation are priority strategies that are followed in all organization plans, activities, and behaviors.

5 The behaviors that matter for trust by donors must be demonstrated as truthful and accountable in all you do and all you say.

6 The results that matter for respect by donors must be demonstrated in measured long-term impacts to benefit beneficiaries.

7 Inclusion of strong commitment to ethics, evaluation, and accountability in your vision, mission, values, culture, and strategies will lead to improved trust, respect, and involvement.

8 Supervisors should transform monitoring into mentoring as the better way to make corrections, foster staff development, and improve work outcomes.

9 Staff will thrive when they participate in planning, work in a learning culture, receive mentoring, see assessments with each other and with partners as further learning and development, and know the program is achieving impact.

10 Donors want to get more from you than fundraising letters. How are you accountable? Trustworthy? Effective? Sharing all you are doing in services, information, education, advocacy, and maintaining your independent voice?

11 Participation in professional associations and NGO networks is valuable to facilitate sharing, learning, and improving to upgrade the performance and image of the entire NGO sector.

A simple evaluation framework for smaller NGOs

1 **Step up** – Update plans with a new commitment to ethics, evaluation, and accountability.
2 **Do it** – Implement these plans, monitor progress, and get useful lessons learned.
3 **Learn** – Apply lessons learned to improve your ethics, impact, and communications.
4 **Achieve** – Identify what you have done in trust, impact, and accountability.
5 **Share** – Communicate to donors your accountability, effectiveness, and all you do.
6 **Partner** – Connect with other NGOs to have affordable and effective systems.

Lessons about earning trust by behaving well and achieving impact

1 *The results that matter to participants and to donors are ethical and trustworthy behavior and measured long-term impacts.* To earn trust, it's not just words. It is planning, achieving, assessing, and verifying (proving) integrity in all your do – not just having a code – that assures good behavior that will satisfy donors. The results must be measured and validated, not assumed from anecdotal evidence or one's own opinion. The results of the organization's programs flow from its activities (outputs) to short-term changes (outcomes) to measured long-term changes (impacts) in the conditions of program participants. It is the long-term program results (impacts) – not the outputs or short-term outcomes – that really benefit participants (change their lives) and will satisfy donors (continue their contributions).

2 *Organizations that make unsubstantiated claims are untrustworthy.* Claims about behavior or results with no measurement and only colorful anecdotes that may not be representative are not reliable. Exaggerated claims are false advertising, and false advertising is destructive for the entire civil society sector, because prospective donors and non-donors may well decide to distrust everyone in the sector. Contributing and grantmaking are based on trust – and verification. Unsubstantiated claims, inept implementation, unintended consequences, and just wishing to do good things (but not doing them well) are hazards of the unsubstantiated strategy. Trust betrayed is trust destroyed.

3 *Having a code of ethics and conducting impact assessment are as important in a nonprofit as anything else.* Both good conduct and program effectiveness are essential. Just as a person cannot claim to be of good character (others determine that), so an organization on its own cannot claim its integrity and effectiveness (others need to do that based on what you actually do). Periodic assessments and ongoing efforts to improve performance should address organizational integrity, transparency, public accountability, fundraising honesty, financial probity, administrative efficiency, and governance responsibility as well as all the components of program effectiveness. Verification by external experts is the proof you need.

4 *The board of directors is responsible to assure their nonprofit conducts valid integrity assessments and program evaluations.* In an annual report on its website, a nonprofit should share publicly what it considers success, how it assures its code of ethics is followed, how it evaluates its program results, what methods for beneficiary participation

it follows, and how it utilizes assessments and evaluations for learning. It requires responsibility, accountability, and communication by the board to be trusted.

5   ***NGOs should work to innovate new approaches (strategies) to solve problems.*** It is a breakthrough when an NGO develops a new strategy to provide improved care and help. As the original social entrepreneurs and caring agents in society (now formalized as legally recognized nonprofit organizations), NGOs need to test and evaluate every program strategy through a professional evaluation of results. Outside experts and academic involvement are most effective to verify the hypothesis of a new strategy and confirm its effectiveness. Effectiveness confirmed is trust redeemed, and verified new approaches will be expanded.

6   ***What more can you do to earn more trust and achieve more respect?*** How could nonprofits possibly survive and thrive if they don't commit to understand donors and to earn their trust and respect? Ask your donors and non-donors! Absolute commitment to transparency and accountability for both ethics and impact are imperative. It requires everyone to step up and help to make certain their organization is trustworthy, effective, and accountable.

Lessons about demonstrating excellence in management

1   ***The first task of managers (especially executive directors/CEOs) is to demonstrate their commitment and ability to lead a trustworthy organization and achieve meaningful results for their program beneficiaries.*** Is there anything else that even comes close? A trustworthy organization with meaningful results is built on the best leadership and management practices, and it produces more successful fundraising and expanded program outreach.

2   ***It is no excuse if an NGO does not know how to do integrity assessments, support mentoring and learning, or implement effective evaluation.*** Your nonprofit should be using the best tools available to assess the situation, set objectives and indicators, determine appropriate activities, monitor and correct the progress, evaluate results, identify lessons learned, and build capacity to do better – for both trust and impact. By doing this, NGO leaders will also be strengthening the profession. Leadership to assure excellence in the planning and implementing process for trust and impact is a leader's top job and supporting learning, organizational development, and growth are next.

3   ***Good strategic planning is the beginning and ending of assuring trust and impact.*** The first step is review of the organization's vision, mission, values, culture, goals, strategies, and learning processes to assure excellent implementation for both trust and impact. All plans need to be designed with clear and measurable indicators to know the beginning (baseline data), the middle (mentoring/monitoring), and the end (evaluation). When participating in planning and when mentoring, evaluation, and learning are seen by staff as a way forward for organizational achievement and personal development, they will embrace supervision and evaluations as further learning and improving opportunities. Clear and thorough evaluation findings are both the end of the planning process and the beginning of the next one.

4   ***What can you do to demonstrate or promote excellence in management?*** How could an NGO possibly survive and thrive if it doesn't have and demonstrate excellence in all it does, starting with trust and impact? I firmly believe based on 60 years of experience that every person in an organization has the right – and the obligation – to help further the organization's mission and, therefore, help to make a better world. This includes leading by example, involving staff in strategic and operational planning, supporting staff development through a mentoring and learning process, and letting leadership flourish at all levels. As my father always said to me: "Whatever you do, do it well!"

Lessons about involving participants in sustainability and impact

1   *For nonprofits working in social services, community development, and humanitarian support, full and meaningful involvement of participants demonstrates the organizations' respect for their clients.* It is the program participants, beneficiaries, or clients who best know their needs and the problems facing them. They know the short- and long-term barriers, potential benefits in their lives, and often what is needed from programs and services provided. The nonprofit brings technical expertise, facilitation skills, encouragement, and financial support to enable the participants to progress. For success, participants need to be respected, involved, and influential. I recognize there are limitations or exceptions to this principle in some programs, but as a general rule: Let your client help lead the process.

2   *For participant involvement, NGOs should utilize proven methods.* You can use any of the following proven approaches to involve your participants: facilitated meetings; candid interviews; action research/action learning; appreciative inquiry; analysis of strengths, weaknesses, opportunities, and threats; participatory planning, mentoring/ monitoring and evaluation/learning; full-scale strategic and operational planning; mutual accountability; and community or group planning processes. Also, of course, apply the professional methods available in your particular sector of services.

3   *For participants, the only path to long-term sustainability is to assume responsibility to sustain their progress and development from the program.* It is the participants who will sustain and expand important results from a program. Organizations will move on to other programs or other regions, but participants continue with their lives. You should develop and support program components that enable participants to acquire skills and knowledge to assume responsibility for sustaining successful programs. They can "graduate" from being program beneficiaries to partners and even to leaders with responsibility for program success. What you leave behind is most important.

4   *What can you do to promote more participant involvement and sustainability?* How could nonprofits possibly survive and thrive if they don't commit to sustainability for participants? With the right support, participants will determine and support the sustainable impacts. Empowered program participants can continue a program and ensure lasting impacts well into the future. This builds on the famous sayings "Teach a person to fish, and you won't need to provide the fish" and then "Support development of their own local business."

Lessons to strengthen the NGO sector

1   *NGOs need to put in more effort to protect and advance their profession.* "We keep making the same mistakes," said one evaluator. "We don't cooperate enough," said another. NGOs individually and collectively need to foster a culture of openness, sharing, and learning from each other. Just as competitors in business come together and cooperate to protect and strengthen their specific industry, so NGOs need to come together and cooperate to protect and strengthen the civil society sector. This means supporting development of best practices, clear performance standards, meaningful ethics, peer review, model programs, unified advocacy, and other practices for professional progress.

2   *NGO associations and networks are useful for organizational development, sector learning, personal growth, and advancement of the profession.* In many

areas, nonprofits are setting up their own consortiums and networks to promote cooperation, sharing, and learning. These consortiums receive funding from their members or foundations (especially for startups) and government agencies. Small nonprofits are especially in need of consortium sharing and learning opportunities to keep up with bigger and better-funded NGOs. Informal gatherings (brown bag meetings) of representatives from different organizations can be easily organized and highly effective. Sharing is learning!

3　***NGOs should incorporate expert outreach and support in their work.*** NGOs behave selfishly if they "do their own thing" without regard for the work of others who may have relevant experience, proven strategies, and model standards. NGO leaders should support staff to become more professional through university courses and degrees in nonprofit leadership, management, and fundraising. There is a growing body of knowledge to guide nonprofits working in education, healthcare, child support, community development, housing, microfinance, preventing violence and discrimination, and many other program sectors. NGOs do not work in a vacuum but are part of a global effort to make a better world. Active support of the United Nations' Sustainable Development Goals and national and global priorities and plans is now expected of nonprofits. Board members, advisors, consultants, and external auditors and evaluators should be selected for their expertise and credibility in these areas.

4　***Leading NGOs are putting in place systems for learning and knowledge management.*** Professional M&E staff and directors of ethics and compliance are now found at a growing number of the larger NGOs. More nonprofits are creating sector learning groups composed of staff and consultants for specific areas of operations. An important position is the knowledge manager who leads the organizational process to collect, retain, use, and share knowledge located in staff, files, and databases. Bigger organizations can play a role to share technical expertise with related smaller organizations. International NGOs with national affiliates in many countries and national nonprofits with local affiliates have the capacity to contribute to developing the effectiveness and prestige of civil society by convening others for sharing, learning, and joint advocacy action.

5　***What can you do to promote civil society?*** How could nonprofits possibly survive and thrive if they don't commit to strengthening their sector? We are all in this together. The world needs a trusted, effective, and efficient civil society – and all NGOs should actively support cooperation, sharing, and professional development (Figure 17.2).

Using strategic evaluation to...

1. Achieve greater results and raise more funding
2. Earn respect by achieving and demonstrating impact
3. Earn trust by demonstrating meaningful ethics
4. Improve excellence in management and planning
5. Progress from monitoring to mentoring
6. Progress to learning, innovation, and collaboration
7. Involve participants in sustainability and impact
8. Strengthen civil society and the overall NGO sector
9. Show donors how grants improve your performance
10. Get donors to support learning and capacity building

Figure 17.2 Using strategic evaluation to achieve important outcomes. Infographic by the author.

Lessons from grantmakers

The history of support of NGOs by the U.S. Agency for International Development (USAID) is revealing in its expanding commitment to evaluation and learning by NGOs. The following paragraphs present a short case study on USAID's shift over the decades from providing general support to NGOs to evolving into an important grantmaker that now requires learning, innovation, and collaboration.[1]

I recall the work of USAID in the 1960s that was mainly delivering food and services through its own staff in response to emergencies. Support in the 1970s became more focused on building NGO capacities as well as delivering services. Its priority then shifted to enabling the NGO community, universities, and other contractors to carry out increasingly sophisticated and professional development programs. As its reliance on NGOs grew, USAID increased its support of these organizations and identified its use for monitoring and evaluation with three objectives: to assess the work of its grantees, to build their capacity, and to report progress to the U.S. Congress.

In the early 1970s, USAID developed the Logical Framework (known as logframe). USAID provided training workshops and training materials to NGOs on how to use the logframe and required its use in grant applications and implementation. The Logical Framework approach to project planning has been widely used, adapted, and simplified by NGOs around the world.

From my perspective, the logframe is useful, because it is built on logic and requires you to answer the most essential questions of "Why, What, How, When, and What if?" It requires you to show why you are doing what you propose to do and to have objective, measurable indicators as well as a means of verification. It requires you to state your assumptions about outside influences that may affect the objective, lay out causes and effects, and identify necessary and sufficient action of what you will do to achieve stated objectives. This is a logical approach to good planning.

What was next? In the 1990s, USAID went through a reengineering process with a focus on results. Good planning, logic, and evaluation were not enough; it's results that really matter. True! Accordingly, it adopted a new results-based management approach with an emphasis on monitoring as the key tool. In the results orientation, the emphasis is on outcomes and longer-term results or impacts. The transition from Logical Framework to Results Monitoring combines elements from both the logframe and the results matrix. Using a logframe forces you to focus on purpose, assumptions, and measurement. Results forces you to focus on measurements and ultimate impact.

Although the Logical Framework and Results Monitoring approaches to project planning and evaluation appear complex and burdensome, they provided a valuable discipline to NGOs in their professionalization. USAID has also supported a number of collaborative groups to support NGO planning, implementation, monitoring, and evaluation. Among the support networks were: CORE working in child survival and other health issues; MEASURE Evaluation working to improve data collection, data quality, and the global capacity for research; and SEEP working to empower its member NGOs to be effective agents of change and enhance their collective ability to accelerate learning and scale impact.

USAID's next approach is called Monitoring, Evaluation, Research, and Learning Innovations (MERLIN)[2] and a focus on Collaborating, Learning, and Adapting (CLA)[3] to plan and implement the program cycle. I continue, of course, to endorse using logic and results in strategic planning and evaluation for any project or program, and I applaud the new emphasis on research, learning, collaborating, innovating, and adapting. NGO practitioners can find a wealth of easily accessible information about monitoring and evaluation tools from USAID, the World Bank, and other major funders from those organizations' websites.

Key point: Take care about what you measure and base it on solid research. Indicators will drive organizations in certain directions, so make sure your indicators drive you to the results you want, step by step. And never stop learning.

In addition to the work of USAID, leading foundations have long had comprehensive approaches to evaluation and excellent guidance for their grantees. A few common themes run through most of their guidance: planning ahead and setting indicators for success are generally expected; the project cycle is generally accepted as a basis of project management; the logical framework or its basic components are often required, especially for larger grants; results are important; and monitoring and evaluation are expected.

Here are just a few examples of leading grantmakers' expectations for grantees:

- The Bertelsmann Stiftung in Germany reports that "impact and the evaluations we carry out of our own projects serve as the basis for ensuring our activities are successful and seen as valuable by others. They also help us as we further develop our work."[4]
- The Mott Foundation supports communities in many locations. "Local communities are where people most directly relate to the social, economic and political processes taking place in their countries, and where they can be most active in shaping them. That's why our Civil Society grantmaking focuses on building vibrant communities where all people can engage in decision-making that affects their day-to-day lives. We work with grantees to strengthen the space for civic engagement, enhance local philanthropy and increase access to justice so all communities can address challenges and seize opportunities that lie ahead. When people get involved in their communities, things change for the better."[5]
- The Rockefeller Brothers Fund is as concerned with the long-term development of recipient organizations as with the immediate project results. Bill Moody, former executive at the Fund, says, "We believe in finding good people and betting on them! If an organization is to survive on its own and continue its activities, then institutional development is as important as the end impacts. So strengthening the organization is even more important than the immediate impacts."[6]
- The W.K. Kellogg Foundation opens its excellent 2017 guide to evaluation with the statement that project evaluations must "improve the way projects deliver services, improve project management, and help project directors see problems more clearly and discover new avenues for growth."[7]
- Working with 6,000 grantmakers from around the world, Grantmakers for Effective Organizations is "a community of funders committed to transforming philanthropic culture and practice by connecting members to the resources and relationships needed to support thriving nonprofits and communities." I am particularly impressed with their emphasis on supporting capacity building, learning, and evaluation along with smarter grantmaking that strengthens grantees. "Grantmakers who put the work in to provide effective capacity-building support help to ensure that nonprofits have what they need to deliver on their missions over the long term."[8]

Lessons for grantmakers to further the development of society

A 2015 report by the Center for Effective Philanthropy found that only one-third of U.S. nonprofits responding reported receiving help from foundations about evaluation, while the two-thirds claimed they received no guidance "about how to use data to measure their performance."[9] Successful grant implementation is based on knowledge, skills, and incentives to use effective monitoring and evaluation. You would think all grants would provide standards or guidance for how to evaluate their programs.

I want to believe that government, corporate, foundation, and other grantmakers would want to facilitate the development of their grantees, so their grants can be used in ever-more effective and productive ways. Based on my experience with the grantmaking process for NGOs around the world, here are my specific recommendations for grantmakers:

1   ***Support proposals by NGOs that include learning and development activities to enable them to carry out their programs better***. Grants should include support for strategic planning, design with indicators, monitoring and evaluation, and learning and developing (MERLs and MEALs and M&Ls). Only in this way can grant support lead to lasting impacts and not just short-term grant outcomes.

2   ***Support NGO-initiated consortiums to facilitate cooperation, learning, and development.*** I prioritize such consortiums in health, education, poverty reduction, equality, relief, international development, and other sectors in support of the United Nations' Sustainable Development Goals. Grantmakers should provide increased incentives to large NGOs and small ones to work together as partners. As noted previously in this book, small NGOs can share M&E costs in a partnership to ensure evaluation is affordable and feasible, especially if they receive grant support.

3   ***Transform your evaluation requirement.*** Grantmakers should shift the requirement from what they, as donors, want to know into a requirement to demonstrate effective use of M&E strategically for learning and capacity building in the grantee organization and sharing in the sector. Grants should include the expectation to contribute to the knowledge base by sharing in print and on the Internet the lessons learned from the implementation of their grant programs.

4   ***Improve your partnership with NGOs.*** I strongly encourage all grantmakers to improve their relationships with NGOs through ongoing dialogue, shared membership in advisory committees, joint review of grant processes, participation in NGO-sponsored meetings, development of training opportunities, advocacy to increase the charitable deduction and support for fair taxation, and other efforts to increase the important and needed public support for charities/NGOs.

5   ***Promote to the public the important role NGOs play in their programs to help people and planet.*** In presentations and on their websites, grant leaders can highlight the development of professional capacities in grantees and in the civil society sector. They can publicly recognize the unique advantages of NGOs and civil society compared to efforts by the government and business sectors while highlighting the results and lasting impacts revealed from evaluation of grants and grantee accomplishments.

6   ***As a grantmaker, what other steps can you take?*** How could NGOs thrive if grantmakers fail to support grantees in their learning and development as well as supporting the important role they play in society? What will you do, right now, to further the development of trust and ethics as well as impact and evaluation in NGOs? They are your partners.

Lessons about stepping up to lead inside your NGO

Smart program managers, fundraisers, financial managers, and others are those who step up to assure all systems in their organization are working, so the organization is Trustworthy, Effective, Responsible, and Accountable, and donors can be confident in their giving. This necessarily stretches traditional responsibility for a manager or fundraiser to make sure the NGO is attractive to donors.

1   ***The CEO/executive director is responsible to assure the organization is Trustworthy, Effective, Responsible, and Accountable*** (**TERA**). This leader must put systems in place to ensure the organization is trustworthy through meaningful ethics,

effective through strategic evaluation, responsible through good management, and accountable through good communication to the public, donors, beneficiaries, partners, authorities, and others. A confident leader and manager also recognizes that others in the organization will have insights that lead to improvements.

2   ***Stepping up for change – To support your NGO to do the best possible work in the most effective way.*** Wherever you are in the organization, **you** will see things that could be better, that should be better – things that no one else notices. In the best performing organizations, staff are encouraged to step up to identify things that need to change, bring them to the attention of supervisors, and take suitable actions to get them fixed.

3   ***Stepping up for planning – To be able to assure stakeholders of the state-of-the-art practices of your planning.*** Wherever **you** are in the organization, you should be able to communicate: "We use our vision, mission, values, strategies, plans, and evaluations to assure stakeholder satisfaction. We have a strong code of ethics and regular assessments to assure it is followed. We design projects with indicators for baseline, progress monitoring, and evaluation. We measure outcomes and long-term impacts as our most important results."

4   ***Stepping up for fundraising – To be able to assure donors your NGO is trustworthy, effective, and accountable.*** Wherever **you** are in the organization, you should step up as needed to identify ways to improve trustworthiness, effectiveness, and accountability to support fundraising and make your organization attractive to donors. When everyone does this, an organization will be more trusted, more respected, more appealing, and more involving and will therefore attract and renew more funding and be able to provide more services.

5   ***Stepping up for assessment and evaluation – To be able to assure donors of good results for beneficiaries.*** Wherever **you** are in the organization, you need to be able to say: "We develop program approaches with expert opinions from board members, advisors, and consultants. We budget monitoring and evaluation, so we can always develop and improve our work. We verify any new strategy through careful evaluation of our results. We involve our beneficiaries meaningfully, or their representatives, in all aspects of our program."

6   ***Stepping up for staff – To be able to assure donors of your internal systems.*** Wherever **you** are in the organization, you should be ready to say: "We recruit, train, and support staff to get excellent results. We follow best practices, performance standards, and good staff management. We budget carefully and keep overhead costs to a minimum and have good management. We join NGO networks for learning, developing, and advancing the profession. We treat staff with respect, recognize their dedication and hard work, and have no tolerance for abuse or discrimination."

7   ***What can you do to lead from inside your NGO?*** How could nonprofits possibly survive and thrive if people on staff don't step up to make sure their organization is trustworthy, effective, responsible, and accountable to donors? **You** must step up to help lead your organization to higher levels of efficiency, professionalism, and success.

Conclusion

Meaningful ethics and strategic evaluation are internally driven – often promoted by one person or a small team within the organization who seek to do better, to learn what to continue and what to change, and to know what to share with others. Organizations that give priority to implementing meaningful ethics, strategic evaluation, and involving communications become

"Hey guys, here's what you need to do!"
YOU must learn from what you are doing wrong to get
the results you want!
It is not that hard to do. You have the tools.

Figure 17.3 You must learn from what you are doing wrong to get the results you want! Artwork by Sawyer Phillips.

better organizations. They are more trusted and more respected by donors and other stakeholders – and with greater funding, they become bigger, even better organizations.

Smart executives and smart fundraisers know their organizations must be attractive to donors in order to have fundraising success, and they use all the strategies in this chapter to gain the trust, respect, and support of donors. Follow these steps for the benefit of your organization:

1   Accept that trust and respect for NGOs are not as high as you need.
2   Prioritize putting in place meaningful ethics and strategic evaluation.
3   Include mentoring and learning (M&L) and improving in all you are doing.
4   Make everyone responsible for learning and building capacity.
5   Encourage everyone involved to step up to correct problems.
6   Take time to reflect at "lessons learned" retreats to get better.

➡️ *Step up to be Trustworthy, Effective, Responsible, and Accountable (TERA).*

In this book, I share many stories from my work with multiple NGOs and the progress and development they achieved. For sure, I can take a small part of the credit for success, but credit for success in its full measure belongs to so many others. What I did was just part of the long continuum of many people stepping up to build trust and build capacity to achieve better results. This is how organizations develop and improve.

Key point: My message is that you can play a major role in your organization to produce needed change. Just do it. Step up now (Figure 17.3).

Questions for implementation

1   What more do you need to move ahead for better trust and more impact?
2   How will you get what you need? Who will support you?
3   How will you convey to donors and the public what you do and learn in evaluations?

Notes

1 "How to Work With USAID," *USAID*, November 8, 2020, accessed July 4, 2022, https://www.usaid.gov/work-usaid/how-to-work-with-usaid.
2 "Monitoring, Evaluation, Research and Learning Innovations Program (MERLIN)," U.S. Agency for International Development, https://www.usaid.gov/PPL/MERLIN
3 "Collaborating, Learning, and Adapting (CLA)," U.S. Agency for International Development, https://usaidlearninglab.org/cla
4 "Die Bertelsmann Stiftung," accessed July 4, 2022, https://www.bertelsmann-stiftung.de/de/ueber-uns/auf-einen-blick.
5 "Civil Society," *Charles Steward Mott Foundation*, accessed July 4, 2022, https://www.mott.org/work/civil-society/.
6 "Program Impact and Learning," *Rockefeller Brothers Fund*, accessed July 4, 2022, https://www.rbf.org/programs/program-impact-and-learning.
7 "Resource Directory," *W.K. Kellogg Foundation*, accessed July 4, 2022, https://www.wkkf.org/resource-directory.
8 "What We Care About: Capacity Building," *GEO*, accessed July 4, 2022, https://www.geofunders.org/what-we-care-about/capacity-building.
9 Alex Daniels, "Foundations Fall Short in Giving Grantees Advice on Evaluations, Says Report," *The Chronicle of Philanthropy*, April 13, 2015, accessed July 4, 2022, https://www.philanthropy.com/article/foundations-fall-short-in-giving-grantees-advice-on-evaluations-says-report/.

Bibliography

1 "Civil Society." *Charles Steward Mott Foundation*. Accessed July 4, 2022. https://www.mott.org/work/civil-society/.
2 Daniels, Alex. "Foundations Fall Short in Giving Grantees Advice on Evaluations, Says Report." *The Chronicle of Philanthropy*, April 13, 2015. Accessed July 4, 2022. https://www.philanthropy.com/article/foundations-fall-short-in-giving-grantees-advice-on-evaluations-says-report/.
3 "Die Bertelsmann Stiftung." Accessed July 4, 2022. https://www.bertelsmann-stiftung.de/de/ueber-uns/auf-einen-blick.
4 "How to Work With USAID." *USAID*, November 8, 2020. Accessed July 4, 2022. https://www.usaid.gov/work-usaid/how-to-work-with-usaid. https://www.usaid.gov/work-usaid.
5 "Program Impact and Learning." *Rockefeller Brothers Fund*. Accessed July 4, 2022. https://www.rbf.org/programs/program-impact-and-learning.
6 "Resource Directory." *W.K. Kellogg Foundation*. Accessed July 4, 2022. https://www.wkkf.org/resource-directory.
7 United States Agency for International Development. https://www.usaid.gov/ and https://usaidlearninglab.org/evaluation/evaluation-toolkit.
8 "What We Care About: Capacity Building." *GEO*. Accessed July 4, 2022. https://www.geofunders.org/what-we-care-about/capacity-building.

Chapter 18

Worksheets for evaluation, learning, and impact

Strategic evaluation is essential for your organization to earn the respect of donors (Figure 18.1).

Strategic Evaluation
1. Establish the Policy
2. Implement the Strategy
3. Create a Learning Culture
4. Mentor and Improve Progress
5. Test and Prove Program Strategy
6. Verify Long-Term Program Impacts
7. Conduct Self-Assessments Internally
8. Assess Accountability with Partners
These eight disciplines make evaluation strategic.
NGO Futures LLC © 2021

Figure 18.1 The eight disciplines for strategic evaluation. Infographic by the author.

Here are four worksheets to guide readers in implementing strategic evaluation and engaging communications with their donors and other stakeholders. They lay out the steps any NGO can take to achieve and communicate real impact through strategic evaluation to secure increased donor support and better programs (Figure 18.1 and 18.2).

Worksheet I: Assessment of the evaluation process by an evaluation specialist

1 Name of this meta-evaluation (evaluation of multiple evaluations), the evaluator, and date
2 Description of the programs, projects, or activities evaluated

(Continued)

DOI: 10.4324/9781003335207-21

3 Evaluation objectives, processes, context, users, questions, people, and other issues

4 Learning objectives of the evaluations

5 Conclusions from the review of evaluations

6 Recommended actions based on the lessons learned (for whom and to do what)

7 Date evaluation was completed and actual cost

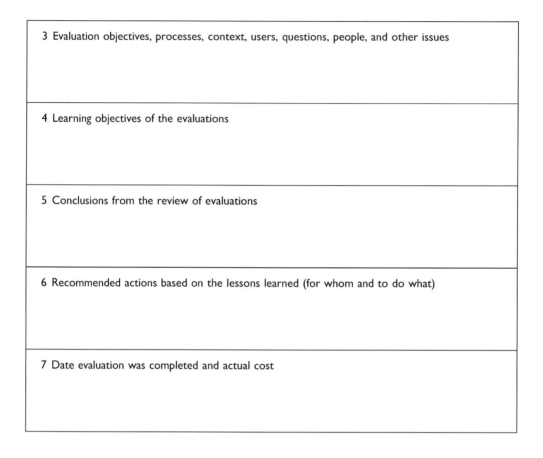

Figure 18.2 The strategic evaluation model. Image by the author.

Worksheet II: Review – How we used the different evaluation disciplines

Completed by: Date:	Person responsible	What happened	What worked	What didn't	Lessons learned	Lessons applied	Results
Policy and priority	Board chair						
Strategy and practice	Executive director						
Culture of learning	Every manager						
Progress monitoring	Every supervisor						
Program strategy	Program director						
Program results	Program director						
Self-assessment	Every unit leader						
Mutual accountability	Executive director						

Worksheet III: Report by each department director

Completed by: Date:	Person responsible	What happened	What worked	What didn't	Lessons learned	Lessons applied	Results
Policy and priority							
Strategy and practice							
Culture of learning							
Department monitoring							
Department strategy							
Department's key results							
Our self-assessment							
Our mutual accountability							

Worksheet IV: Report by the person responsible for monitoring and evaluation

Recommendations based on monitoring and evaluation to improve our impact:
Evaluator:

Fiscal year:

For each department or function, describe the M&E tools used, lessons learned, how the lessons were applied, and the resulting improvement and development.

1.

2.

3.

4.

5.

6.

7.

8.

9.

10.

About the author
Get involved! Step up! It is easy to do.

Since this is the fourth book in my *Civil Society Series*, I want to take a new approach to this section. It is all about my learning and developing over the decades. In addition to learning values from my family and learning about people from extensive reading of literature, philosophy, and economics, my greatest learning came from experience. My hope is that, by sharing this information, you will be inspired on your path to continuous learning and developing – and doing. The goal, of course, is for everyone to step up as leaders in your work and as volunteers to help make this a better world. This chapter is based on my personal experience, notes, and records (Figure 19.1).

Here are highlights of my learning and development over the years:

- As a college student, I got involved with AIESEC, the international student-run organization now with 70,000 youth members in 2,500 university committees in 114 countries and territories, and more than one million alumni. Its traditional program of youth-led local committees in universities, international internships in business and nonprofits, and its leadership development model taught me so much. After serving as local committee president for AIESEC at both Princeton and University of Michigan, I was elected national president of AIESEC-United States at the age of 24 in 1964. My focus for two years was on strategies to increase international exchanges and expand international business education and leadership development. I learned that strategy and motivating others were essential to success.
- My next job in 1966–1972 was at the Institute of International Education in New York City, which now has 600 staff worldwide, 2,900 program participants, 1,600 higher-education partners, a budget of $250,000,000, and a major Carnegie African Diaspora Fellowship Program. I planned and coordinated its 50th anniversary campaign that funded its new building on United Nations Plaza and created new programs which I called Project City Streets to provide international travel and academic for African Americans and anti-poverty work assignments for international students in the U.S. I learned that I could innovate new programs to generate new funding and that the whole organization – president, board members, staff, and volunteers – are all needed to make fundraising successful.
- In 1969, after my wife delivered our third child, we decided it was time for me to "step up and do my part" by taking (what was in those days) a highly unusual step. I got a vasectomy. Responding to a follow-up survey from the Association for Voluntary Sterilization, I reported how simple the procedure was and added that they needed more publicity because male sterilization was misunderstood, rare, and unpopular. Following an interview, a few months later my story was front-page news in the *Wall Street Journal*. As a result, I was invited to appear on national TV on the *David Frost Show* advocating what has now become a very common procedure. A year later, I wrote a piece called "One Couple's Decision" for

DOI: 10.4324/9781003335207-22

Figure 19.1 The author with his books on leadership, planning, and strategy. Photograph by Rebecca Phillips.

Foolproof Birth Control: Male and Famine Sterilization published in 1972. I learned it is important to share your convictions and inspire others to action. Close friends and relatives have followed.

- A few years later when needing to move to a larger home just out of New York City, we insisted on finding a house in an integrated neighborhood. Settled in New Rochelle, NY, and with an extra bedroom, we were able to welcome students, one each year, from Gambia, Iran, Nigeria, Trinidad, and Vietnam to live and eat with us, as the nearby college had too few dormitories. Later, we also hosted a regional promotor for the United Farm Workers grape boycott. Our kids grew up with African-American friends and living with people from other countries. In this way, we brought the world into our own home and learned it was not hard to reach out to new friends.

- In 1972–82 as head of fundraising for Save the Children US, I drafted new core program and funding strategies, initiated strategic planning for fundraising, professionalized fundraising and marketing, put in place new branding and new advertising, increased public awareness, and laid the groundwork for future growth. I learned that participatory strategic planning and understanding management are essential to achieve needed internal changes and greater fundraising results. Now, Save the Children International Alliance with 30 national members and program activities in 117 countries raised more than $2.2 billion in 2020.

- In 1982–93, as executive director and president of Foster Parents Plan (now Plan International USA), I led the process to draft a new growth-oriented strategic plan, transformed the board of directors, created a prestigious honorary board, experimented with new marketing channels, coached staff to grow and develop, and worked together with other national directors to increase accountability to donors. Plan International now has its International Hub in London, 20 national members, activities in 75 countries, and global revenues of $1.1 billion in 2020. I learned about stepping up and leading our staff and board and our affiliates and partners around the world.

- In 1995, I established NGO Futures Sàrl in Geneva, Switzerland, and later recreated it as NGO Futures LLC in the United States. This launched me on twenty-five years of training and consulting with NGOs in numerous countries. Throughout the years, my consulting, training, and mentoring focused on helping NGOs and their staff achieve financial sustainability and growth through organizational development based on strategic and operational planning, encouraging fundraisers to step up, new strategies for fundraising, and mentoring senior executives and board members in leadership and governance.

- In 2004, I was recruited for a two year contract as head of organization development for the International Federation of Red Cross and Red Crescent Societies (IFRC). This followed extensive editing and writing key documents for the Federation, in-depth consulting with National Societies in Belarus and Uganda, and leading courses for National Society board members and executives on fundraising, organizational development, leadership, and governance. In two years, we created a theory of how the National Societies develop, outlined the stages of their development, identified how to know they are making progress in multiple functions, and drafted guidance on several dozen organization issues. We brought IFRC and ICRC (the International Committee of the Red Cross) closer together in a "Common Approach" for unified support for National Societies around the world. This laid the groundwork for subsequent progress of more rigorous self-assessments, external reviews, and sanctions when warranted.

- This brings me to my third career as author of everything I have learned in my first career as executive, fundraiser, and board member in NGOs and their associations and my second career as teacher, trainer, and consultant for NGOs and their associations in many countries. I have been so fortunate to have been a frequent presenter and 'student' at meetings and conferences in cities around the world and to have had interviews with many thousands of NGO staff, board members, volunteers, and donors to learn what they thought made a great NGO and what made them fail. A key theme throughout my entire career – and in my volunteer work – is a commitment to guiding and inspiring others to step up to make this a better world by creating a more trusted, respected, and supported civil society.

Standards for organizations have always been high in my priorities to help professionalize the sector. I think this flows from my sense of what is right and what is needed to strengthen civil society. Remember? My mom said "do something good" and my dad said "do it well." My consulting, training, and writing always include key sections on standards. (Figure 19.2)

Figure 19.2 The author with a sign urging people to get involved in their community. Photograph by Rebecca Phillips.

As initiator and supporter of codes of ethics and evaluation

In the 1970s, my first major effort in standards occurred when I was head of fundraising at Save the Children US. The *New York Times* wrote a lead story about questionable fundraising practices of what were then called child-sponsorship agencies. I called a meeting of the fundraisers from five other agencies (our competitors), and in one day we hammered out a code of ethics, which required changes in advertising practice for all of us. We all went back to our agencies and said we have to approve this code, as all the others would certainly approve them. All six agencies quickly approved the new code of advertising ethics, and we went back to the media with a good story: "We heard you, and we changed. We have new standards." The media coverage shifted from criticism to praise!

In the 1980s, Rhode Island was known to be one of the most corrupt states in the nation. When voters approved the 1988 Constitutional Convention, I decided to seek election as a candidate to be one of the 100 delegates. Following my election, I chose to be on the Ethics Committee and was selected to be its secretary. I advocated and helped to draft an amendment on ethics for the state Constitution, which the voters approved by a significant margin. The Rhode Island Constitutional

Convention created a new independent ethics commission with the responsibility and authority to assure good behavior by elected and appointed officials at state and local levels. As a result, Rhode Island eventually became one of the best-rated states for its open and ethical government. In this process, I experienced that citizens can, in fact, step up to make big changes in how their governments operate and behave. The ethics commission has been called the most effective state ethics commission in the country.

InterAction, the largest alliance of international NGOs in the United States, supports its members in collective action to serve the world's poor and vulnerable based on a shared belief that we can make the world a more peaceful, just, and prosperous place. InterAction is a voice for NGOs working globally, and its members raised an estimated $15 billion in private funding. Working for a member NGO, I helped to draft the original strategic documents (1983), raised fundraising as a priority for its member organizations (1986), initiated strategic planning for the members to work together (1988), led the creation of its NGO ethical standards (1989–1992), and served as board chair (1990–1992). I learned that, yes, you can step up when you see a problem, turn it into an opportunity, and get something done.

Other highlights:

- Appearance on the PBS MacNeil/Lehrer Report New Year's Eve interview on "Charities," December 31, 1977
- Member, Committee on Standards, Council of Better Business Bureaus' Philanthropic Advisory Service on strengthening standards on governance, management, and fundraising, 1978–1982
- Witness at U.S. Congressional Committee hearings and U.S. Agency for International Development meetings on NGOs, standards, and international assistance, Washington, DC, 1980s
- Member, Board of Directors, Common Cause Rhode Island, the leading American NGO demanding government integrity and openness, Providence, RI, 1987–1991
- Initiator and Chair, Ethics Task Force for EUConsult, a membership organization for consultants in the European Union drafting a new code of behavior for consultants, 1997–1999
- Member, Standards Review Panel, Better Business Bureau Wise Giving Alliance strengthening existing standards and adding a requirement on program evaluation, 1999–2003
- Board member, Alliance for Nonprofit Governance, an important American NGO promoting good governance standards, New York, NY, 2001–2004
- Member, National Advisory Committee on Standards for Excellence Program, Maryland Association of Nonprofit Organizations, Baltimore, MD, 2002–2004

As author on NGO ethics and evaluation

- Author, "Point of Solicitation Disclosure: A Case Study of Voluntary Regulation," KRC Letter, 1977
- Author, *Illustrative Standards for Not-For-Profit Organizations*, World Learning, English and Russian, 1994
- Editor and author, *Resource Development Handbook*, International Federation of Red Cross and Red Crescent Societies (IFRC), Geneva, 1994
- Author, "The Importance of Self-Regulation of Nongovernmental Organizations" in the *Handbook on Good Practices for Laws Relating to Non-Governmental Organizations*, the World Bank, 1997
- Editor and author, *National Society Governance Guidelines*, IFRC, Geneva, 1997

- Author, "Strategic and Operational Planning Workbook" in English, French, Polish, Romanian, Russian, Spanish, and Ukrainian, NGO Futures LLC, 1997–98
- Author, "Capacity Building - Building Blocks: What are the essential elements in building capacity in your organization?" *Professional Fundraising Magazine*, London, 1999
- Editor and author, *Framework for National Society Capacity Building*, IFRC, Geneva, 2000
- Author on strategic positioning and capacity building in *Growing Your Organization: A Sustainability Resource Book for NGOs*, International Youth Foundation, Baltimore, MD, 2000
- Author, *Considering International NGO's Evaluation*, published in Japanese by the Sasakawa Peace Foundation, Tokyo, 2001
- Author, "NGO Standards: Self-Regulation and Beyond," *Alliance Magazine*, London, December 2001
- Editor and author, *The Framework for National Society Development*, IFRC, Geneva, 2006
- Author, *Make a Better World: A practical guide to leadership for fundraising success*, NGO Futures LLC, 2020
- Author, *Strategic Planning and Culture for Nonprofits: Clear and doable steps to create motivating plans and the supporting culture you need for success*, NGO Futures LLC, 2021
- Author, *25 Proven Strategies for Fundraising Success: How to win the love and support of donors*, NGO Futures LLC, 2021 (Figure 19.3)

Figure 19.3 Newspaper article written by the author urging people to help green their community. Photograph of news clipping by Rebecca Phillips.

As a presenter on ethics and evaluation at workshops and classes

- Consultant and trainer for new NGOs helping children in Estonia, Latvia, Lithuania, Poland, Romania and Ukraine, Child Fund International, 1994
- Keynote speaker and expert advisor at the "NGO Trustworthiness and the Role of Self-Regulation - International Conference on the Legal and Regulatory Environment," Sinaia, Romania, published by the World Bank – facilitated the development of model laws and codes of ethics for Eastern and Central European NGOs, Sinaia, Romania, 1994

- Presenter, "In The Public Trust: The Experience of Non-Profit Organizations with Codes of Ethics," 10th AIESEC Alumni International Congress on Business Ethics in a Multinational Environment, Prague, Czech Republic, 1996
- Presenter, "The New Fundamentals of Fundraising – Total Organization Fundraising™," Federation of International INGOs in Geneva, Switzerland, 1996
- Organizer and lead speaker at three day workshops for NGOs from Central and Eastern Europe, HelpAge International, AARP, Ukrainian Centre for Philanthropy and Institute for Professional Fundraising, and others, 1996–2022
- Presenter, "NGO Standards and NGO Associations: Essential Steps for NGOs," CIVICUS General Assembly, Budapest, Hungary, 1997
- Organizer and lead speaker at three day workshops for staff of individual NGOs including Alzheimer's Societies, CARE, Caritas/Catholic Relief Services, Romanian Civil Society Development Foundation, International Step by Step Association, International Youth Foundation, National Center for Healthy Housing, NGO Black Sea Forum, Mexican NGOs (virtually), Red Cross, Romanian NGOs working with children, Ukrainian Newspaper Publishers Association, World Wildlife Federation, and others, 1999–2022
- Presenter, "Sustainability in Eastern and Central Europe," Civil Society Development Foundation Conference, Budapest, Hungary, 2000
- Presenter, "How to Increase the Prestige of Charity," International Fund Raising Group Workshop, Moscow, Russia, 2000
- Presenter, "Why Should the Public Trust You? Sustainability of the Third Sector in Central and Eastern Europe," Civil Society Development Foundation Conference, Budapest, Hungary, 2000
- Presenter, "Ethics and Standards for Civil Society: Key Steps to Trustworthiness," CIVICUS General Assembly, Vancouver, Canada, 2001
- Presenter, "So Much Money – So little for Charity: Why Charities in Affluent America Aren't Generating More Support," Connecticut Philanthropy Day, Hartford, CT, 2001
- Moderator and presenter, "Evaluation Tools Workshop," InterAction Forum, Washington, D.C., 2001
- Presenter, "Holding Ourselves Accountable," InterAction Forum, Washington, DC, 2001
- Organizer and lead speaker, "Master Classes: Critical Strategic Fundamentals for Nonprofit Executives," for the Connecticut Association of Nonprofits, Hartford, CT, 2002–2003
- Speaker, "Strategic Evaluation: What Fundraisers Can Do," Association of Fundraisers Professional Forum, Meriden, CT, 2002
- Presenter, "Strategic Evaluation: Powerful New Tool for Capacity Learning and Building," Center for Women and Families, Bridgeport, CT, 2002
- Organizer and lead speaker, "All the Components of Fundraising and Capacity Building," East African National Societies of the International Federation of Red Cross and Red Crescent Societies, Nairobi, 2002
- Featured speaker, "Strategic Thinking about Local Sponsoring and Fundraising," at the Final Regional Conference for NGO Grantees in North Eastern Europe, Swedish International Development Agency, Vilnius, 2002
- Featured speaker at International Fundraising Conferences by the Polish Fundraising Association in 2007, 2008, 2009, and 2022
- Lead presenter, "Leadership Roles in Fundraising: Who leads and when do you lead?" at the Fall Conference, Massachusetts Nonprofit Network and Association of Grantmakers, Boston, 2009

- Keynote, "Fundraising on the Titanic: What's it mean to you?" at the 20th Austrian Fundraisers Conference, Vienna, 2013
- Keynote speaker at Better Business Bureau Wise Giving Alliance and the International Committee on Fundraising Organizations on "Advancing Trust in the Charitable Sector: Communicating Charity Value and Inspiring Trust," Washington, DC, 2015
- Co-Presenter, "How to lead your organization to get the internal support you need for fundraising success," virtually, AFP ICON 2021
- Presenter, "Wednesday Night Workshops," virtually, six sessions on steps to NGO success, YZ Proyectos and La Red de Asociaciones de Grupo México (Network of Associations), 2021
- Speaker on ethics and evaluation at conferences and meetings in cities around the word including Bangkok, Belgrade, Bogota, Boston, Bratislava, Bucharest, Budapest, Cape Town, Chisinau, Geneva, Istanbul, Krakow, Kyiv, Lviv, Ljubljana, Madrid, Nairobi, Minsk, Moscow, New York, Paris, Prague, Riga, Sofia, Tallinn, Tokyo, Vienna, Vilnius, Warsaw, Washington, Yerevan, and others

As a researcher

Effective strategic planning and NGO development must always be based on the reality that comes from external research. Market research, competitor analysis, stakeholder assessments, assessments of external opportunities and threats, informed board discussions, and research about society are the basis of my work, consulting, and lectures on organizational development and capacity building.

- My studies and writing in literature at Princeton University (BA) and the University of Michigan (MA) and work as a Teaching Fellow at Michigan
- My studies and writing in economics and work as Research Fellow in economics at New York University (MA)
- The hundreds of market research projects I conducted for my employers and clients over 60 years
- The thousands of interviews I conducted with NGO leaders, staff, volunteers, and donors about what makes an NGO succeed and what make it fail
- The research findings from consulting and mentoring in depth on repeated assignments with major clients
- The research for the publications that I have authored or edited
- My research for Sasakawa Peace Foundation on international NGO evaluation methodologies
- Research on potential countries for CARE International to enter for fundraising expansion

Honored with many awards and recognition

- Honored by the Ford Foundation with a travel grant to the "Education for International Business," 1966
- Save the Children Korea Field Office staff for "your hard work and guidance for the future progress of our program in Korea," 1978
- "Portraits in Philanthropy. Ken Phillips: Hard head, big heart" in *Management Review*, American Management Association, February 1987
- Common Cause Rhode Island Governing Board for "his commitment to open and honest government," 1991
- Father Flanagan's Boys Town of New England Spirit of Youth award for "keeping hope alive in the hearts of the world's needy children and youth," 1992

- InterAction Board of Directors for "your leadership, commitment and vision as chairman," 1992
- Mayor of Providence, Vincent Cianci, Proclamation for "invaluable service to the West Broadway Neighborhood Association and the City of Providence through his leadership and guidance," 1993
- Foster Parents Plan Board of Directors and staff for "outstanding leadership, commitment, and success as president," 1993
- InterAction in its historic *PVO Standards* publication for "his vision and the skillful way in which he guided the open process to assure full involvement of InterAction's membership," 1993
- Mayor of Boston, Thomas M. Menino, recognized GreeningRozzie, the community NGO I help found and led, with the city's Green Residential Award as Climate Action Leader, 2011
- AIESEC International and AIESEC Alumni's prestigious AIESEC Peacebuilder Award for his "contribution to AIESEC's vision of peace and fulfillment of humankind potential," 2019
- Morristown Beard School for outstanding leadership of the Morristown School Class of 1958 campaign. "You were the one who took charge and made sure that this idea became a reality. You and your classmates exceeded your goal and have positively impacted the future of the School," 2020
- West Broadway Neighborhood Association's "most prestigious award for leadership and dedication," 2021

As an activist where I lived or worked – I did it and you can, too

Throughout my career, I regularly served as a board or committee member, for example, at the AIESEC Alumni Association, Alliance for Nonprofit Governance, Association for Voluntary Sterilization, Bryant College Non-Profit Curricula, Common Cause Rhode Island, the Institute of Professional Fundraising in Ukraine, the NGO/UNICEF Committee for Children in Eastern Europe, and the Rhode Island Constitutional Convention, and as chairperson for the Brown University Hunger Briefing, GreeningRozzie, the Needs Assessment Committee for Affordable Housing in Washington, CT, InterAction, and International Service Agencies.

As a volunteer and then as its board chair in 1992–1993, I led a significant development for the West Broadway Neighborhood Association in Providence, Rhode Island. We put in place new strategic and operational planning, created a "can-do" culture, and expended community involvement and fundraising. I now see it as a model for community organizations with outstanding leadership, committed board members, extensive volunteer involvement, comprehensive programs, great results, and close cooperation with local government, business, religious, and community partners. It was here that I learned a lot about leading and transforming a volunteer-based association.

In 2020, several friends and I established a new community nonprofit in Roslindale where we lived called GreeningRozzie, which I chaired in its first year. In just a few community meetings, we developed the strategic plan with its vision for a green community; its identity as a community that cares about the people who live here, the space we live in, and the future we create; its mission to make Roslindale a greener, cleaner and more cohesive community by working together to promote and implement grassroots projects and activities; and its activities focused on eight issues (green spaces, local food, energy efficiency, water conservation, waste reduction, efficient transportation, healthy homes and gardens, and information and advocacy).

Figure 19.4 The award ceremony with the Mayor and other Boston dignitaries honoring GreeningRozzie which was led by the author. Photograph by Rebecca Phillips.

Working with a very small budget, we organized many educational events, signed up hundreds of volunteers at local farmers markets, and generated educational media coverage. I authored news articles like "What's it mean to be green?" and "He makes it easy to be green." After just one year, we were honored with the city's Green Residential Award as Climate Action Leader.

It is not difficult to volunteer for a local nonprofit, to initiate an advocacy activity with your friends and family, or to step up to initiate a fundraising effort where you work or study. Society needs more leaders and helpers to make a better world. With the knowledge from my books, you can do that. You will do something important and feel good about that (Figure 19.4).

For further information, detailed worksheets, and updates – and to receive notification of newly published books in the *Civil Society Series* as well as translations and other documents – go to www.NGOFutures.com (Figure 19.5).

Figure 19.5 The author's logo prioritizing strategy, teamwork, and leadership.

Index

Note: Page references in *italics* denote figures, in **bold** tables and with "n" endnotes.

Entries in bold are especially important.

Printed in the United States
by Baker & Taylor Publisher Services